Bloom's Modern Critical Views

Bloom's Modern Critical Views

ALDOUS HUXLEY
New Edition

Edited and with an introduction by
Harold Bloom
Sterling Professor of the Humanities
Yale University

BLOOM'S
LITERARY CRITICISM
An imprint of Infobase Publishing

Bloom's Literary Criticism
An imprint of Infobase Publishing
132 West 31st Street
New York NY 10001

Library of Congress Cataloging-in-Publication Data

Aldous Huxley / edited and with an introduction by Harold Bloom. — New ed.
    p. cm. — (Blooms's modern critical views)
    Includes bibliographical references and index.
    ISBN 978-1-60413-866-5 (hardcover : alk. paper) 1. Huxley, Aldous, 1894-1963
—Criticism and interpretation. I. Bloom, Harold.
    PR6015.U9Z5645 2010
    823'.912—dc22

                                        2010006251

Bloom's Literary Criticism books are available at special discounts when purchased in bulk quantities for businesses, associations, institutions, or sales promotions. Please call our Special Sales Department in New York at (212) 967-8800 or (800) 322-8755.

You can find Bloom's Literary Criticism on the World Wide Web at
http://www.chelseahouse.com

Cover design by Alicia Post
Composition by Bruccoli Clark Layman
Cover printed by IBT Global, Troy NY
Book printed and bound by IBT Global, Troy NY
Date printed: May 2010
Printed in the United States of America

10 9 8 7 6 5 4 3 2 1

This book is printed on acid-free paper.

All links and Web addresses were checked and verified to be correct at the time of publication. Because of the dynamic nature of the Web, some addresses and links may have changed since publication and may no longer be valid.

Contents

Introduction

ALDOUS HUXLEY (1894–1963)

Aldous Huxley cannot be judged to have achieved lasting eminence either as a novelist or as a spiritual guide. The best of his novels were *Antic Hay* and *Point Counter Point,* which I enjoyed in my youth, but now regard as very literate Period Pieces. His most famous fiction, *Brave New World,* scarcely sustains rereading: its basic metaphor, in which Henry Ford replaces Jesus Christ, now seems strained and even silly. Huxley's one great book is his *Collected Essays,* which includes such superb performances as "Wordsworth in the Tropics," "Tragedy and the Whole Truth," and "Music at Night." In this Introduction, I turn mostly aside from Huxley-as-essayist in order to center upon his anthology-with-comments, *The Perennial Philosophy,* and two curious little books, *The Doors of Perception* and *Heaven and Hell,* both concerned with his visionary experiences induced by taking drugs.

Huxley defines the Perennial Philosophy as: "the metaphysic that recognizes a divine Reality substantial to the world of things and lives and minds; the psychology that finds in the soul something similar to, or even identical with, divine Reality; the ethic that places man's final end in the knowledge of the immanent and transcendent Ground of all being." The figures and texts testifying to this metaphysic, psychology, and ethic are very various: St. Augustine, St. Bernard, the Bhaghvad-Gita, the Buddha, St. Catherine of Siena, Chuang Tzu, *The Cloud of Unknowing,* Meister Eckhart, Fenelon, St. Francis de Sales, St. John of the Cross, Lao Tzu, Jalal-uddin Rumi, *Theologica Germanica,* Thomas Traherne. It will be noted that my list of these fifteen spiritual authorities is alphabetical, they being so diverse that no other ordering seems possible. But, to Aldous Huxley, they are all One Big Thing: The Perennial Philosophy. This Californian eclecticism helped make

1

Huxley one of the gurus of the New Age, but it renders me uneasy, despite my own spiritual convictions, which are not wholly antithetical to Huxley's.

Huxley's second wife, Laura, wrote a poignant memoir of her husband, *This Timeless Moment,* in which she reveals that she aided him in his dying moments with a substantial shot of LSD, as he desired. One hesitates to call the death of any distinguished author a Period Piece, but 1963 (the year of Huxley's death) cultivated very different fashions than 2003, when the dying are likelier to prefer morphine to mescalin or lysergic acid. I recall reading *The Doors of Perception,* and its sequel, *Heaven and Hell,* when they were published in the mid-fifties, with a certain skepticism, as to whether aesthetic or spiritual experiences ought to be so palpably ascribed or reduced to a chemical base. Almost half a century later, rereading these treatises, my skepticism increases. Is there a difference, *in kind,* between the strawberry ice-cream *soma* of *Brave New World* and swallowing mescalin dissolved in water, as Huxley does at the onset of *The Doors of Perception.*

Huxley would have pointed out, with exquisite courtesy, that his mescalin-induced visions increased his awareness of Art and of God, while the Brave New Worlders, stuffed with *soma,* merely danced a sort of conga, spanking one another to the beat of:

> Orgy-porgy, Ford and fun
> Kiss the girls and make them One. Boys
> at one with girls at peace; Orgy-porgy
> gives release.

It is rather a distance from that to the Perennial Philosophy, but in each instance a chemical substance gives release. New Ages are always destined to become Old Ages, and Huxleyan spirituality alas now seems antique. Aldous Huxley was a superb essayist, but not quite either a novelist or a sage.

ROBERT CECIL BALD

Aldous Huxley as a Borrower

At the beginning of *Left Hand Right Hand,* the first volume of his autobiography, Sir Osbert Sitwell introduces some reflections on the significance of heredity for the creative artist. "It is important," he maintains,

> for the creator to have sources of energy that have not been tapped, to come of blood, at any rate in part, that has not been obliged to endure too great a strain upon it; an artist—not a cultivated lover of the arts—flowers best when the blood flows most freely in the veins, from stock that has not, intellectually, been overworked.

Then, by way of elucidation, follows this sentence:

> To generalize, governesses are the friends of culture, but the foes of the artist; and, to particularize, were Mrs. Humphry Ward *my* aunt, as she is my friend Mr. Aldous Huxley's, and Matthew Arnold *my* great-uncle, and Thomas Huxley *my* grandfather, I should find the joys of artistic creation attenuated and not easy to capture; but I should be more cultivated.

College English, Volume 11, Number 4 (January 1950): pp. 183–187. Copyright © 1950 National Council of Teachers of English.

One does not need to assent to Sir Osbert's theorizing to perceive that the very left-handed compliment to Aldous Huxley masks an astute piece of criticism. No definition of the cultivated man is attempted, but it will probably not be far wrong to regard him as one marked by an eclectic and critical awareness—awareness not only of the arts, and of the arts in particular, but of science and philosophy as well. Such an awareness makes difficult the creative concentration of the artist because it dissipates his energies and comes between him and the object of his creation. This is the reason for Sir Osbert Sitwell's sharp distinction between culture and creation.

To what extent the blood streams which flowed through Matthew Arnold and Mrs. Humphry Ward and T. H. Huxley are wholly responsible for Aldous Huxley is at best matter for amusing speculation. Their influence, however, must have helped to create the family environment in which he grew up, and one can at least see in his description of himself as "by nature a natural historian" of human society the influence of his scientific grandfather. Furthermore, there is no doubt that Huxley, to a degree unusual even among modern writers, "sees life through the spectacles of books," so much so that he constantly reveals his awareness of the way in which this situation or that technical problem has been handled by some other writer. But that is not all; constantly at the back of his mind are the very words and rhythms in which his predecessors have expressed the feelings which he is trying to express. This is why Huxley never succeeded in becoming a poet. He has published no verse since *The Cicadas* (1931), and that volume contains so many imitations of Eliot as to read like a collection of parodies.

Huxley's too acute literary awareness, with its consequent attenuation of creative power, betrays itself in all sorts of ways. A symptom, comparatively slight but highly significant, is the fact that on occasion Huxley can become so caught in the toils of an effective phrase that he is not above borrowing from himself. The early poem *Frascati's* concludes:

> when the wearied Band
> Swoons to a waltz, I take her hand,
> And there we sit in blissful calm
> Quietly sweating palm to palm.

And in the story *Cynthia* there is a conversation in which one of the characters tells of the beginning of a love affair with a girl who had happened to be sitting next to him at the theater:

"... In the course of the act, entirely accidentally, I knocked my programme on to the floor, and reaching down to get it I touched her hand. Well, there was obviously nothing to do but to take hold of it."

"And what did she do?"

"Nothing. We sat like that the whole of the rest of the act, rapturously happy and—"

"And quietly perspiring palm to palm. I know exactly, so we can pass over that. Proceed."

Here the author seems to have felt that so neat a phrase was wasted on the comparatively small audience that would read the poem and so incorporated it into the story to secure for it a wider circulation. Real creative fecundity never needs to descend to such shifts.

Each reader, according to the degree in which he approximates Huxley's standard of "cultivation," will be able to make his own list of the more striking indebtednesses in the novels. Here are some of them. Huxley was deeply influenced by the appearance early in the twenties of *Ulysses* and *Les Faux-monnaieurs,* and these two works have affected the structure of all his subsequent novels. The influence of Gide is strongest in *Point Counter Point* and in *Eyeless in Gaza;* that of Joyce is most obvious in *Time Must Have a Stop* (which is Huxley's *A Portrait of the Artist as a Young Man*) and in the third chapter of *Brave New World.* Again, characters and episodes with literary origins are not uncommon. The early story *The Farcical History of Richard Greenow* was suggested by the literary dualism of William Sharp; Lypiatt, the painter in *Antic Hay,* is really a study of the character of the artist Benjamin Robert Haydon, for whose *Autobiography* Huxley later wrote an introduction. Gumbril senior's plan for a harmonious and symmetrical London is, of course, based on Sir Christopher Wren's, and in *Crome Yellow* Sir Ferdinando Lapith, builder of Crome, pioneer of sanitation, and author of *Certaine Priuy Counsels by One of Her Maiesties Most Honorable Priuy Counsel* (1573) is obviously Sir John Harrington. In descriptive passages and in briefer episodes one can also catch literary echoes. In *Point Counter Point,* for instance, the description of the performance of Bach's *Suite in B Minor* at Lady Edward Tantamount's reception recalls Browning's *Master Hugues of Saxe-Gotha,* and, in a lesser degree, Forster's description of Beethoven's *Fifth Symphony* in *Howard's End,* while Walter Bidlake's application to Burlap for a higher salary is a variation on the Spenlow and Jorkins episodes in *David Copperfield.* Even words and phrases, too, have their origins in the writings of others. For example, the term "pneumatic," used so frequently to describe the physical characteristics of the doxies in *Brave New World,* is taken, of course, from Eliot's *Whispers of Immortality:*

Grishkin is nice: her Russian eye
    Is underlined for emphasis;

> Uncorseted, her friendly bust
> Gives promise of pneumatic bliss.

Indebtedness such as has just been catalogued can scarcely be classed as literary allusion, although that too is uncommonly frequent in Huxley's novels. It is true that Gumbril senior introduces Wren's name into the discussion of his model, that there is a discreet reference to Fiona McCleod in *The Farcical History of Richard Greenow*, and that such references may not unfairly be compared to the footnotes in which a scholar cites his authorities. But there are no similar references to Haydon and Harrington in *Antic Hay* and *Crome Yellow*, and one can easily believe that many a reader has given Huxley full credit for having invented the characters of Lypiatt and Sir Ferdinando Lapith. Not everyone is familiar with the life and character of Haydon, while acquaintance with Harrington's *Metamorphosis of Ajax* from the very nature of its subject demands a mild, if perverse, sort of erudition.

The problem of Huxley's attitude to his borrowings comes up most sharply when one considers individual phrases and sentences. A significant example occurs in the antepenultimate paragraph of *Point Counter Point:*

> The afternoon was fine. Burlap walked home. He was feeling pleased with himself and the world at large. "I accept the Universe," was how, only an hour before, he had concluded his next week's leader. "I accept the Universe." He had every reason for accepting it.

There is no question that the reader who knows the anecdote about Carlyle and Margaret Fuller will find this passage more richly amusing than the one who does not. Accordingly, one might be perfectly justified in citing this passage not as an example of borrowing but merely of literary allusion. Yet it is not in the least necessary to have heard about Carlyle's explosive guffaw and his chuckling "Gad, she'd better!" to get from Huxley's passage all of what might be called its essential meaning. The fact is, Huxley has used the freedom of an Elizabethan dramatist in appropriating whatever suited his purpose.

As for "pneumatic" in *Brave New World*, it is perhaps better to be ignorant of its source. There was, indeed, a real danger shortly after the book was published that the term would pass into popular currency, and, had that happened, the credit—or blame—would have been entirely Huxley's. Yet, if he had intended a mere literary allusion, he was in a position where he could, with perfect justice, have disclaimed all responsibility for the actions of half-educated readers, who cannot even recognize a literary allusion when it is set before them. But, after all, the important thing for critic and author alike is not how often a writer borrows, or whether he expects his readers to recognize his sources, but what he does with his borrowings.

One of Huxley's involuntary collaborators has stated, with a satisfying finality, a set of criteria applicable to literary borrowings:

> One of the surest tests is the way in which a poet borrows. Immature poets imitate; mature poets steal; bad poets deface what they take, and good poets make it into something better, or at least something different. The good poet welds his theft into a whole of feeling which is unique, utterly different from that from which it was torn; the bad poet throws it into something which has no cohesion. A good poet will usually borrow from authors remote in time, or alien in language, or diverse in interest.

This statement of Eliot's, so illuminating with regard to his own practice, helps to explain why Huxley realized that it was no use to go on and try to be a poet. But the defect of creative capacity his poems reveal is not quite so fatal to a novelist. Obviously it prevents him from reaching the highest ranks, but it can leave unimpaired his capacity for wit and satire. Yet to compensate for his lack of real creativeness, Huxley has been forced to use various shifts. Not only does he frequently introduce into his novels easily recognizable caricatures of his contemporaries, but, as has been seen, when the creative impulse flags, he seizes upon the invention of other writers. It is, in fact, one sign of Huxley's essential secondrateness as an artist that, for all his sharpness and "cultivation," he should fail almost completely to meet the tests suggested by Eliot. It is his misfortune to have a positive talent for "defacing what he takes," and, if he succeeds in making it into "something different," it is into something shoddier, more vulgar, than the original.

Even in matters of technique is this so. The structure of *Eyeless in Gaza*, for instance, lacks justification; there is no inner necessity why the events should be narrated in the particular order chosen, and in that alone; they might just as well have been narrated in the conventional temporal and consecutive order. Joyce's still more significant experiments in the management of time and contemporaneity fare even worse in Huxley's hands; in chapter iii of *Brave New World* they are reduced to the level of a showman's trick.

It would be instructive to undertake a detailed comparison between the first chapter of *Time Must Have a Stop* and the secton of chapter v of *A Portrait of the Artist as a Young Man*, which describes the composition of Stephen Daedalus' poem; but it must suffice here to illustrate Huxley's failures in handling borrowed material from two of the briefer episodes in *Point Counter Point*. There it will be found that he weakens his originals by his inability to concentrate. The setting of *Master Hugues of Saxe-Gotha* is skilfully and briefly suggested at the beginning and end of the poem; for the rest, Browning's ill-paid and choleric organist grapples with the intricacies of a Bach fugue in such a way that every detail of his environment on which his mind seizes becomes relevant to his problem. Huxley's mind, on the other hand, likes to dwell on the irrelevant. In his description of the concert he does not even seem to want to separate the music from the conductor's "swan-like undulations from the loins," and he finds it amusing to record that the sounds which seem so significant are merely "vibrations in a cylindrical air column" blending with the noises produced as "the fiddlers draw resined horse-hair across the stretched intestines of lambs." There is no attempt to relate these impressions to any of the characters or their thoughts; it is Huxley's own mind which is too aware of too many things.

The episode in which Walter Bidlake asks to have his salary raised is longer than the account of David Copperfield's first interview with Mr. Spenlow, but detailed comparison of the two leaves the impression that Huxley is unnecessarily diffuse:

> "The premium, stamp included, is a thousand pounds," said Mr. Spenlow. "As I have mentioned to Miss Trotwood, I am actuated by no mercenary considerations—few men less so, I believe—but Mr. Jorkins has his opinions on these subjects, and I am bound to respect Mr. Jorkins's opinions. Mr. Jorkins thinks a thousand pounds too little, in short."

Compare this with Huxley:

> "I wish for your sake," Burlap continued, "for mine too," he added, putting himself with a rueful little laugh in the same financial boat with Walter, "that the paper did make more money. If you wrote worse, it might." The compliment was graceful. Burlap emphasized it with another friendly pat and smile. But the eyes expressed nothing. Meeting them for an instant, Walter had the strange impression that they were not looking at him at all, that they were not looking at anything. "The paper's too good. It's largely your fault. One cannot serve God and mammon."

Dickens needs neither a gesture nor a reference to the feelings of Mr. Spenlow's auditors; Mr. Spenlow's idiom and intonation are so characteristic that further comment is unnecessary. Even when due allowance is made for the difference of period and method, it is noteworthy that Huxley cannot rely on Burlap's rather colorless words; his comment and analysis are essential to the scene. Here is Dickens again:

If a clerk wanted his salary raised, Mr. Jorkins wouldn't listen to such a proposition. If a client were slow to settle his bill of costs, Mr. Jorkins was resolved to have it paid; and however painful these things might be (and always were) to Mr. Spenlow, Mr. Jorkins would have his bond. The heart and hand of the good angel Spenlow would have been always open, but for the restraining demon Jorkins.

And here is Huxley:

"I'll go and talk to Mr. Chivers," said Burlap. Mr. Chivers was the business manager. Burlap made use of him, as the Roman statesman made use of oracles and augurs, to promote his own policy. His unpopular decisions could always be attributed to Mr. Chivers; and when he made a popular one, it was invariably in the teeth of the business manager's soulless tyranny. Mr. Chivers was a most convenient fiction. "I'll go this morning."

Huxley's sense of style gives neatness and point to his writing, and the apt classical allusion comes naturally from him; but the passage is pale beside the fecundity of Dickens' invention.

Huxley is at his worst, however, when he sniggers over Sir John Harrington or turns Eliot's sardonic wit into a piece of salacious slang. One recalls that he once wrote: "The fact that many people should be shocked by what he writes practically imposes it as a duty upon the writer to go on shocking them." There is something of the adolescent in the Huxley of the novels; it is as though he had never completely grown up. What one resents in the transmutation of his literary material is the tarnishing it undergoes at his hands, and in that resentment one thinks of a passage—a passage much to Huxley's taste—in Virgil. He is like one of those harpies who afflicted Aeneas and his companions in their wanderings:

at subitae horrifico lapsu de montibus adsunt Harpyiae et magnis quatiunt clangoribus alas, diripiuntque dapes contactuque omnia foedant immundo; tum vox taetrum dira inter odorem.

Yet this is too strong; it is better to recover one's sense of proportion and be grateful for the pleasure and entertainment Huxley's novels have given—so long as one does not take him too seriously as a novelist. And it is evidence of a real measure of artistic integrity that of recent years Huxley has been turning more and more from pure fiction to other forms in an effort to find the means of expression best suited to his needs.

CLYDE ENROTH

Mysticism in Two of Aldous Huxley's Early Novels

That Aldous Huxley, who was once thought the spokesman for a skeptical generation, is now the writer of novels in which mysticism is much in evidence, is well known and deplored on every side. The received opinion is that Huxley was a brilliant and promising novelist—in 1927 T. S. Eliot called him one of the four chief contemporary English novelists—who fell among mystics and was converted, to our sorrow. Huxley's career, according to this view, can be neatly divided into the regulation three periods: the first, including *Crome Yellow, Antic Hay,* and *Those Barren Leaves,* in which Huxley was a skeptic, a materialist, and a satirist; the second, including *Point Counter Point* and *Brave New World,* in which he was converted to the doctrines of D. H. Lawrence, who fortunately showed Huxley how absurd his tentative inquiries into mysticism at the end of *Those Barren Leaves* had been; and the third, or later Wordsworthian, in which Huxley, under the regrettable influence of Gerald Heard, was converted to mysticism and wrote generally inferior novels, including *Eyeless in Gaza, After Many a Summer Dies the Swan, Time Must Have a Stop, Ape and Essence,* and *The Genius and the Goddess.*

But the received opinion concerning Huxley's two so-called conversions is mistaken. The argument against the prevailing view has two parts: that the mystical tendencies in Huxley's novels appeared earlier than has

---

Twentieth Century Literature, Volume 6, Number 3 (October 1960): pp. 123–132. Copyright © 1960 Hofstra University.

generally been supposed, and that even when the mysticism was supposedly suppressed, in *Point Counter Point* and in *Brave New World,* it can nevertheless be found. A more accurate description of Huxley's career is that
it displays the consistent development of tendencies discoverable even in
the earliest novels. Though consistency is not always a virtue, and Huxley
himself does not much admire it, it is important in considering Huxley's
reputation, for one of the staples of criticism is that his great promise has
come to nothing because, though he is surely one of the most intelligent
men of his generation, he has irresolutely followed one leader after another
in increasing confusion until he has become lost in the swamps of mysticism.
One sample of this line of criticism is William York Tindall's "But after
composing their manifestoes, master and disciple [i.e., Heard and Huxley]
retired to California where, when they are not walking with Greta Garbo or
writing for the cinema, they eat nuts and lettuce perhaps and inoffensively
meditate, Huxley in Hollywood and Heard on a convenient mountainside."[1]
Whether mysticism is a swamp is not the issue here; the problem is to show
that Huxley, contrary to the view usually taken by his critics, set his course
toward mysticism early and did not undergo the two so-called conversions
that have so damaged his reputation as a responsible thinker.

This paper, then, will be concerned only with the early novels, those in
which Huxley was supposedly not a mystic; it will not be concerned with those
novels beginning with *Eyeless in Gaza,* in which Huxley is avowedly a mystic,
nor with the single early novel, *Those Barren Leaves* (1925), in which, all of the
critics agree, Huxley first flirted with mysticism. Let us examine two novels,
one from the period before Huxley had supposedly first concerned himself
with mysticism, and one from the period in which Huxley supposedly had
been converted to D. H. Lawrence's doctrine of life-worship. Showing that in
both of these novels, *Antic Hay* (1923) and *Brave New World* (1932), Huxley
clearly displays an active interest in mysticism will support the two divisions
of the argument, i.e., that Huxley was concerned with mysticism earlier than
has been supposed and that he continued to be concerned with mysticism
even at a time when he supposedly was a Laurentian life-worshipper.

The last remaining preliminary operation is to define mysticism. In the
standard work on the subject, Evelyn Underhill defines mysticism as "the
expression of the innate tendency of the human spirit towards complete harmony with the transcendental order; whatever be the theological formula under which that order is understood."[2] Any definition of mysticism involves
us in as many difficulties as it gets us out of, but we can agree upon two
characteristics of mysticism: the mystic presupposes two entities that the materialist does not, i.e., something called the soul or the spirit or, the Eternal
Self, and something called God or the World Spirit or the oversoul or the
transcendental order or the Divine Ground; and the mystic declares that his

awareness of the second of these two entities, the Divine Ground as Huxley calls it, is acquired not by means of the senses or the intellect but by means of immediate intuitive union with the Divine Ground. Human beings presumably have achieved such union, and the means for attaining such union are known and can be taught. Often various occult phenomena such as telepathy, extrasensory perception, prevision, and psychokinesis are associated with mysticism, but they should not be confused with mysticism itself.

In *Time Must Have a Stop* (1944), Huxley set down a Minimum Working Hypothesis for "research by means of pure intellectual intuition into non-sensuous, non-psychic, purely spiritual reality":

> That there is a Godhead or Ground, which is the unmanifested principle of all manifestation.
>
> That the Ground is transcendent and immanent.
>
> That it possible for human beings to love, know and, from virtually, to become actually identified with the Ground.
>
> That to achieve this unitive knowledge, to realize this supreme identity, is the final end and purpose of human existence.
>
> That there is a Law or Dharma, which must be obeyed, a Tao or Way, which must be followed, if men are to achieve their final end.
>
> That the more there is of I, me, mine, the less there is of the Ground; and that consequently the Tao is a Way of humility and compassion, the Dharma a Law of mortification and self-transcending awareness.[3]

With this brief definition of mysticism in mind, let us turn to an examination of the mysticism ill two of Huxley's supposedly non-mystical novels.

Huxley published *Antic Hay* in 1923. Earlier he had published three volumes of verse, many periodical articles including a number of reviews of books about religion, mysticism, and the occult, and a first novel, *Crome Yellow* (1921), in which mysticism was seemingly an object of Huxley's amused contempt. In that novel, Mrs. Wimbush says "I have the Infinite to keep in tune with. And then there's the next world and all the spirits, and one's Aura, and Mrs. Eddy and saying you're not ill, and the Christian Mysteries and Mrs. Besant. It's all splendid. One's never dull for a moment." Another character, Mr. Barbecue-Smith, a popular journalist, the author of *Pipe-Lines to the Infinite* and other uplifting works on positive thinking, says that the trick for producing 1500 saleable words in an hour is to establish "the connection of the Subconscious with the Infinite. Get into touch with the Subconscious and you are in touch with the Universe." He brings down the Infinite, he says, through pipes to work the turbines of his mind. Thus Huxley apparently scoffs at mysticism by putting parodies of its principles into the mouths of these two ridiculous characters. But Mr. Scogan, a character whose counterpart appears in several of Huxley's novels, takes mysticism seriously enough to say that though he finds the writings of mystics deplorable claptrap, still he wishes that he could enlarge his experience through mystical communion. We might observe that Huxley frequently sets forth his own ideas in the speeches of comic characters.

By 1923, then, when *Antic Hay* appeared, Huxley had ridiculed mysticism but had done so in such a way as to permit us, with the wisdom of hindsight, to see that the issue was not altogether closed. In *Antic Hay*, too, the mystical theme is stated so cautiously that the critics have ignored or overlooked it; but it is nevertheless unmistakably there.

The novel, whose main theme is that human life is an antic hay, a mad dance, opens in 1922 (the book appeared in 1923) as Theodore Gumbril, who was born about 1891 (Huxley was born in 1894) and who is an usher in a boys' school (as Huxley was, briefly, a teacher), sits in the hard oaken stalls of the school's chapel and speculates "in his rapid and rambling way about the existence and nature of God." The lesson, from the sixth chapter of Deuteronomy, enjoins him to love God with all his heart, and with all his soul, and with all his might. Gumbril muses upon this text. "No, but seriously, Gumbril reminded himself, the problem was very troublesome indeed. God as a sense of warmth about the heart, God as exultation, God as tears in the eyes, God as a rush of power or thought—that was all right. But God as truth, God as 2 plus 2 equals 4—that wasn't so clearly all right. Was there any chance of their being the same? Were there bridges to join the two worlds?"(4)[4]

Here Gumbril states a problem that Huxley turns to again and again, until it becomes central in his work: how can one reconcile his religious intuitions and his skeptical intellect? Is it possible that a source of knowledge exists that cannot be apprehended by the senses (i.e., is it possible that the God apprehended by intuition "really" exists, is "true" in the sense in which "2 plus 2 equals 4" is true)?

Gumbril cannot construct a bridge between the two worlds, especially since the more distant one seems to be in the possession of the foghorning Reverend Mr. Pelvey. Upon the second lesson, "Father, forgive them, for they know not what they do," Gumbril says "Ah, but suppose one did know what one was doing? Suppose one knew only too well? And of course one always did know. One was not a fool. But this was all nonsense, all nonsense. One must think of something better than this." (7) And so Gumbril thinks of air cushions, of English Gothic architecture, of Gumbril's Patent Small-Clothes.

Having thus vigorously stated a theme, that one knows what one is doing but prefers to think about something else, that one sees a possible goal but prefers to wander aimlessly, Huxley proceeds to illustrate that theme in the ineffectual life of Theodore Gumbril, particularly in the part of the novel that deals with Gumbril's affair with Emily, the only person with whom Gumbril is able to establish what he feels is a meaningful relationship. "Unreal, eternal in the secret darkness," Gumbril says of their night together. "A night that was an eternal parenthesis among the other nights and days." (236) Note the repeated word "eternal," which Huxley means quite literally here. The rest of the novel is Huxley's monument to life's meaninglessness.

Life is utterly pointless in this novel, a hay danced by human beings whose motivation is chiefly the goaty urge. Marlowe's lines "My men like satyrs grazing on the lawns / Shall with their goat-feet dance the antic hay" are the epigraph. Conventional religion is a tiresome succession of words droned out by dull-witted Pelveys. Love is mere itch and ennui. Patriotism is absurd. Progress means hideous suburban "little sham half-timbered houses near the station." Science is a technique for developing strains of rabbits with defective eyesight. Mass education has simply increased the number of semi-literate gullible people who delight in whatever inanity the advertisers provide for them. One lives as Mrs. Viveash (does her name mean "a living death"?) does, desperately trying to find some diversion to make the hours bearable until one is tired enough to sleep, but one has long ago given up any idea that what one does is of any significance, except perhaps to amuse the gods, if there are any. Morality is a meaningless concept, because one cannot accept any absolute standards against which to measure conduct. "Good; good? It was a word people only used nowadays with a kind of deprecating humourousness. Good. Beyond good and evil? We are all that nowadays. Or merely below them, like earwigs? I glory in the name of earwig." (5) In a world devoid of absolute values, a world in which human beings are beyond, or below, good and evil, an earwig is no more and no less important than a painter or a physiologist. One accepts the world, empty as it is; one flaunts his realization of life's pointlessness—one glories in the name of earwig.

In such a world, only pleasure can stir human beings or keep them from ending their pointless lives. Gumbril therefore sets out to find pleasure, in the arts, in sex, in living comfortably, in science, in politics. Huxley gives us a picture of each of these activities, but each is a picture of futility. His artist is a self-deceived mediocrity. His amorists, Mercaptan and Coleman, find pleasure only when the circumstances are witless and sordid. "The real charm about debauchery," says Coleman, "is its total pointlessness, futility, and above all its incredible tediousness." (236) The amateur politician, Mr. Bojanus, wants a revolution not because it would accomplish anything but because it would provide a change and a little excitement. The scientist, Shearwater, grafts ovaries into roosters and produces beetles that cannot crawl straight because their heads have been cut off and replaced by heads from other beetles. His bored wife passes through the beds of several of the characters while the scientist himself pedals a bicycle desperately on a treadmill so as to lose himself in experiments and thus not think about his passion for Mrs. Viveash. The novel ends in an aimless circling taxi ride during which Gumbril and Mrs. Viveash see in the garish, idiotic electric advertising signs in Piccadilly Circus symbols of the utter pointlessness of modern life, the antic hay in which they are engaged.

Amid all this idiocy, Gumbril finds two possible sources of meaning. One of these is art: late Latin verse for one character and Wren's architecture for another. Music, too, has possible meaning: "The twelfth sonata of Mozart was insecticide; no earwigs could crawl through that music." But these are drugs only, and one awakens to find the world as meaningless as before. The second source of meaning, though Huxley does not press the matter, offers at least the possibility of a means for finding some lasting purpose in existence. In a remarkable passage, Huxley presents an experience that is to recur in *Time Must Have a Stop,* one of the clearly mystical novels. Possibly it describes something that Huxley himself experienced, or perhaps it is merely his "sensuous analogue" of some inexpressible intuition.

In any case, the experience can only be described as mystical. Gumbril is speaking to Emily: "There are quiet places also in the mind," he said meditatively. "But we build bandstands and factories on them. Deliberately —to put a stop to the quietness." The trivial preoccupations of everyday life, Gumbril says, serve to break the quietness; but at times the quietness "re-establishes itself, an inward quiet, a growing, expanding crystal. . . . It is beautiful and terrifying, yes, terrifying as well as beautiful. For one's alone in the crystal and there's no support from outside, there's nothing external and trivial to pull oneself up by or to stand on, superiorly, contemptuously, so that one can look down."

In this state, one's education, outward skepticism, sophistication fall away, says Gumbril; one is alone, undergoing an experience for which a rational twentieth century man is unprepared. "And at last you are conscious of something approaching; it is almost a faint sound of footsteps. Something inexpressibly lovely and wonderful advances through the crystal, nearer, nearer. And, oh, inexpressibly terrifying. For if it were to touch you, if it were to seize and engulf you, you'd die; all the regular, habitual, daily part of you would die. There would be an end of bandstands, and whizzing factories, and one would have to begin living arduously in some strange, unheard-of manner." And so one quickly thinks of "anything for a diversion"—business, jazz, gossip, politics. "And you lie tranquilly on your bed, thinking of what you'd do if you had ten thousand pounds, and of all the fornications you'll never commit.' He thought of Rosie's pink underclothes." (186–188)

Looking at Emily, who does not inhabit the same world as Mrs. Viveash and Mercaptan and Coleman, Gumbril muses. "There was quiet in her mind, he thought. She was native to that crystal world; for her, the steps came comfortingly through the silence and the lovely thing brought with it no terror." (188)

When Gumbril says that "there are quiet places also in the mind," he means that the mind, or at least some minds, have the ability to receive impressions directly, without the intercession of the senses. These impressions, which are of an unearthly, timeless serenity, presumably come from an order of being that is not perceptible to the senses; and so long as we continue to use only our senses to receive impressions, we shall never develop the ability to receive impressions by means of these "quiet places" in the mind—thus we shall never receive information about any order of being that cannot be apprehended by the senses, and we shall refuse to believe that any such order exists.

For Gumbril, knowledge of the existence of these "quiet places" comes when he is almost unconscious, "lying awake at night, sometimes—not restlessly, but serenely, waiting for sleep." One can use these faculties only, apparently, when one is not conscious of the distractions of the everyday world. Hence the statement that if the "something inexpressibly lovely and wonderful" and terrifying "were to engulf you, you'd die; all the regular habitual, daily part of you would die." The mystics, as Huxley later in his career points out, call this shedding of one's daily life "dying to self," i.e., discarding all that makes one a distinct personality, all that separates one from the Divine Ground. One would thenceforward have "to begin living in some strange, unheard-of manner." But Gumbril is not yet ready to "die to self," because "it's too terrifying, it's too painful to die." And so he creates any sort of diversion to drive away the "lovely and terrifying thing." Emily, on the other hand, is apparently by nature capable of using the faculties that in most people remain undeveloped. "She was native to that crystal world; for her, the steps came comfortingly through the silence and the lovely thing brought with it no terror."

Let us return now to the problem posed by Gumbril in the opening pages of the novel: is it possible to reconcile one's religious emotions and intuitions with one's intellectual awareness of the world as the senses describe it to one? Can one fit the information that one receives about an order of being not perceptible to the senses into the view of the world that an intelligent, educated, skeptical man of the twentieth century must hold? When one becomes aware of the "quiet places" in the mind and of the possibilities that those quiet places provide for entering into immediate, intuitive awareness of another order of existence, what does one do with that information? Having had a mystical experience, what move does a reasonable man next make?

Gumbril's answer is to put the matter out of his mind, to build bandstands upon the quiet places of his mind, because to pursue the matter would involve great changes in his life, changes of a sort that an intelligent materialist is taught by his society to consider absurd. And when by chance Gumbril meets a woman to whom the crystal world is familiar, who could presumably teach him to enter it at will, he destroys that possibility and with it all possibility of finding meaning in an otherwise meaningless world; in an afternoon of perfectly conscious and deliberate debasement and irresponsibility, he makes Emily's trusting him impossible. "Well, let everything go," he says. "Into the mud. Leave it there, and let the dogs lift their hind legs over it as they pass." At the end of the novel, when Gumbril contemplates the idiotic frenzy of the flashing electric signs and Shearwater's desperate pedalling on a bicycle that never gets anywhere, his consciousness of the pointlessness of existence is deepened by his knowledge that he has rejected the only possibility for meaning that his life offers. Given a choice between the absurdity of mysticism and the pointlessness of life without mysticism, Gumbril chooses the latter and resigns himself to continuing the antic hay.

Thus we may conclude that Huxley, the most autobiographical of novelists, had as early as 1923 seriously entertained the possibility of obtaining information by mystical means about an order of existence entirely hidden to the senses or the intellect. Indeed, there is good reason to believe that Huxley himself had had a mystical experience of the sort that Gumbril describes but that, like Gumbril, he was not yet prepared to make the tremendous changes in his view of the world that embracing anything so foreign to the Western mind as mysticism would involve.

Let us now skip over two novels, *Those Barren Leaves* (1925), in which the mysticism hinted at in the earlier *Crome Yellow* and *Antic Hay* is openly discussed, though Huxley draws no conclusions in the novel, and *Point Counter Point* (1928), in which, according to the received opinion, Huxley sees the error of his mystical ways and adopts instead D. H. Lawrence's doctrine of life-worship. *Brave New World*, which appeared in 1932, when Huxley supposedly was still under the influence of Lawrence and had outgrown mysticism, will illustrate the second of the two points of this paper, that a strong undercurrent of mysticism is to be found even in the novels in which Huxley had supposedly repudiated mysticism. The matter is a bit complicated at this point because Lawrence is also often thought a mystic; but Lawrence's doctrine prescribed living as fully as possible in the world of the senses and spirit and mind, being as fully human as possible, while Huxley's involved "dying to self," freeing oneself as much as possible from the burden of the body, the intellect, and the separate personality. Such a doctrine, as Huxley acknowledged at the time, sacrificed all aspects of man for the, sake of the spiritual; Lawrence's life-worship, on the other hand, gave all aspects of man their due, including the spiritual. In *Brave New World*, according to the received opinion, Huxley had abandoned his tentative explorations into mysticism and had embraced Lawrence's doctrines; we shall see however, that instead mysticism is not far below the surface of that novel.

In *Brave New World*, Huxley shows that any society that has set happiness and material well-being as its goals must, for the sake of stability, deliberately cultivate mediocrity and perpetual adolescence in all but a tiny portion of its numbers. If, on the other hand, it wants to make its members fully human, individual, and independent, it must abandon the economic, political, and social structures that impose conformity—in a word, it must revert to primitivism, with all of the attendant disease, intolerance, and ignorance. In the novel, the only two choices are the brave new world and the savage reservation; man has the choice, Huxley says in his preface, between insanity on the one hand and lunacy on the other. But Huxley hints at a third alternative.

The World-Controller, Mustapha Mond, like Huxley a man of prodigious intellect, discusses his reasons for suppressing a book on biology in which the author explained phenomena in terms of purpose: such speculation about the purpose of human life, Mond says in the novel, is unsettling because it may make people "lose their faith in happiness as the Sovereign Good and take to believing, instead, that the goal was somewhere beyond, somewhere outside the present human sphere; that the purpose of life was not the maintenance of well-being, but some intensification and refining of consciousness, some enlargement of knowledge. Which was, the Controller reflected, quite possibly true." (211–212)[5]

An odd statement: why should the alternative to happiness be "some intensification and refining of consciousness"? Nothing in the idea of happiness suggests such an alternative, as motion suggests rest or silence suggests sound. One might reasonably expect the alternative to happiness to be duty to society or obedience to a god's will; that Mustapha Mond seizes upon "some intensification and refining of consciousness, some enlargement of knowledge" as the purpose of life suggests that that idea might have been in Huxley's mind at the time as well. If so, Huxley was once again considering the possibility of man's cultivating his hitherto undeveloped ability to receive knowledge without using his senses. The "intensification and refining of consciousness" is what Gumbril in *Antic Hay* had hoped was possible after he became aware of the "quiet places" in the mind. It anticipates the statement in the passage from *Time Must Have a Stop* quoted above "that there is . . . a Tao, or Way, which must be followed, if men are to achieve their final end," that end being "to achieve . . . unitive knowledge . . . supreme identity" with the Godhead or Ground.

In speaking of "some intensification and refining of consciousness," Mond cannot mean mere exercise of intelligence: the brave new world provides for exercise of intelligence by a necessary few such as the World Controller himself and provides places of humane exile for those who cannot accommodate their intelligence to the infantilism of the planned society. Mustapha Mond, offered early in his career a choice between exile in the chaotic intelligent society and life in the orderly stupid one, does not regret having chosen the latter, despite his powerful intelligence. Thus in speaking of "some intensification and refining of consciousness" as the purpose of existence, Mond must mean something other than the free exercise of intelligence offered by the society of exiles. The goal, he says, lies "somewhere outside the present human sphere"; hence the goal cannot be anything now ordinarily available to intelligent human beings, but it must be something within their power to discover (note the word "present" in "somewhere outside the present human sphere"). Presumably Mond is speculating about the possibility, at least, of developing a latent faculty in man, his mystical intuition.

But like Gumbril in *Antic Hay,* Mond decides that attempting to develop one's latent mystical powers is so foreign to his view of the world that he will turn his attention to anything else. And the brave new world of which Mond is the Controller makes sure that its citizens will never develop this unsettling latent power, by systematically building "factories and band-stands" upon the "quiet places."

Another highly intelligent man in the novel—Huxley has always valued intelligence highly, and in his later novels makes it one of the three qualities needed for a man's salvation—is Helmholtz Watson, an Emotional Engineer, who rebels against the idotic drivel that his job requires him to write and shocks the authorities by writing a poem about an intuition received in solitude:

> Yesterday's committee,
> Sticks, but a broken drum,
> Midnight in the City,
> Flutes in a vacuum,
> Shut lips, sleeping faces,
> Every stopped machine,
> The dumb and littered places
> Where crowds have been: . . .
> All silences rejoice,
> Weep (loudly or low),
> Speak—but with the voice
> Of whom, I do not know.
> Absence, say, of Susan's,
> Absence of Egeria's
> Lips and, ah, posteriors,
> Slowly form a presence;
> Whose? and I ask, of what
> So absurd an essence,

That something, which is not,
Nevertheless should populate
Empty night more solidly
Than that with which we copulate
Why should it seem so squalidly? (216)

The "something which is not," the voice of silence, fills empty night more solidly than Susan or Egeria does. It is an absurd essence, and yet Watson says about his intuition of that essence "I feel . . . as though I were just beginning to have something to write about. As though I were beginning to be able to use that power I feel I've got inside me—that extra, latent power. Something seems to be coming to me." (217) Some kind of essence, that is, can be apprehended intuitively, can set free a latent power within some men, and makes copulation seem squalid. Evidently Watson has had a mystical experience. Having had that experience, Watson knows that he will be exiled, but he looks forward with pleasure to exile and the solitude that will make the operation of intuition possible.

Though Huxley does not develop the idea explicitly, he shows, by allowing his two most brilliant characters in the novel to admit the possibility of mysticism as a source of absolute knowledge and values in a world otherwise limited to useful but purely relative values, that mysticism was never out of his thoughts even at a time when he had supposedly, under Lawrence's influence, abandoned his tentative gropings toward mysticism.

To conclude: the examination of these two novels, one written at a time when according to the usual view Huxley had not yet become a mystic, and the other written at a time when according to the usual view Huxley had been convinced by Lawrence that speculation about mysticism was useless, shows that from the very beginning of his career Huxley has been strongly drawn toward the mysticism avowed openly only in the later novels. Thus the critics' contention that Huxley the skeptic and rationalist was saved from the absurdities of mysticism by Lawrence only to be seduced back into mysticism by Gerald Heard cannot be reconciled with the facts. Though he has certainly been influenced by Lawrence and others at various times in his career, as he has himself acknowledged, Huxley has shown in his career a steady and consistent development of mystical tendencies and has not undergone the two conversions of which the critics speak.

NOTES

1. "The Trouble With Aldous Huxley," *American Scholar* (Autumn 1942), 459.
2. *Mysticism,* 12th ed. (New York, 1930), xiv.
3. (New York, 1944), 294–295.
4. (London, 1928). Page numbers are given in parentheses.
5. (New York, 1950). Page numbers are given in parentheses.

JAMES H. QUINA JR.

The Philosophical Phases of Aldous Huxley

The philosophical phases of Aldous Huxley may be traced in terms of a cycle which ranges from negation to affirmation. The cycle begins with *Crome Yellow* and follows a descending path through *Antic Hay* and *Those Barren Leaves* reaching negative maturation in *Point Counter Point*. All the characters except Rampion in *Point Counter Point* drown in their own subjectivity. Rampion retains just enough contact with the natural world to be converted into a searching mystic in *Eyeless in Gaza*. In *After Many a Summer Dies the Swan,* Huxley gives us the gentle Mr. Propter who identifies time as evil and conversely identifies the timeless world of the mystics as the good in life. In *Time Must Have a Stop* and *The Genius and the Goddess,* the world outside of time is equated with love and becomes recognized as the ground of all religious experience.

Huxley demonstrates the human necessity for transcending time by showing in an ironic and often ludicrously funny way that modern man continually falls short of the very psychological and spiritual condition that he sets out to secure, and he falls short of it simply because he applies the wrong standards in attempting to attain it. What then, we may ask, is this condition Huxley believes modern man to be searching for? Huxley's wide reading in parapsychology and Oriental philosophy has no doubt influenced him considerably, but his criterion of spiritual health is something much simpler

College English, Volume 23, Number 8 (May 1962): pp. 636–641. Copyright © 1962 National Council of Teachers of English.

and a great deal more longlived than the revolving standards of the modern psychologists; it is simply *inner peace*. It is difficult to discover a Huxleyan character who does not demonstrate in his actions a search for peace.

Inner peace is secured only by abolishing the illusion of the identity. The identity must be annihilated by transcending time and by losing itself, so to speak, in the permanence of absolute reality—a reality which Huxley calls the Divine Ground.

The peculiar nature of the Huxleyan absolute has been dealt with rather technically by such critics as John Atkins and S. Nagarajan. But too much emphasis has been placed on the end product of Huxley's discoveries. Traditional criticism has been content to relegate Huxley's novels to that strange and somewhat monstrous category, the novel of ideas. The philosophic structure of the Huxleyan novel has been explained away by recording it as either a shift in Huxley's philosophy, arising out of some sort of irrational dabbling in a new metaphysical scheme, or, if any pattern has been noticed between one novel and the next it has, in general, been explained away on the basis that Huxley is a weak minded idealist who cannot bear the burden of hard facts, and who is therefore destined to withdraw into a mystical, but somewhat murky Oriental womb.

But because Huxley has done a great deal of research in Eastern mysticism and written books on the relationship of drugs such as mescaline to extra-sensory perception and has subsequently engendered some of these concepts into his novels, it does not follow that his important contribution to literature can be summed up in terms of his present philosophical scheme, nor does it follow that his novels have been merely projected images of a worn idealist carrying on a series of tautological grumbling sessions with himself without any causal connection between the grumbling sessions whatsoever.

I submit that Huxley does explore several metaphysical worlds before arriving at his present commitments, but that he does this in rational terms, that all the early philosophies that he examined are important in relation to his over-all method of structuring a complete metaphysics, that there is a clear line of cause and effect between each of his novels, ranging from *Crome Yellow* to *The Genius and the Goddess,* and that it is more important to examine the method Huxley uses in structuring his system rather than to attempt an analysis of his current beliefs.

By observing the methods used by the characters in attempting to secure inner peace, a trial and error system is constructed and the principles of finding inner peace are reached inductively. In Huxley's novels there are roughly six general methods by which modern man seeks to secure inner peace: (1) by a hypocritical identification with religious or metaphysical values, (2) by deifying the self so that all values become a projection of the self, (3) by identifying himself with nature, (4) by placing ultimate value on material gains,

(5) by suspending judgment, and (6) by transcending time and concretely identifying the self with the mystical world.

The first method, whereby man seeks to secure inner peace by a hypocritical religious position, is satirized unmercifully by Huxley in his early novels. In *Crome Yellow,* for instance, Mr. Barbecue Smith's theory as set forth in his book *Pipe-Lines to the Infinite* is shown in a ridiculous light because the theory was no more than an egocentric device which supposedly aided in his writing. In the same novel, Huxley presents Mrs. Wimbush in the same ludicrous manner. Her notion of immortality is constructed on rather shoddy pragmatic principles. Astrology, thinks Mrs. Wimbush, relieves the tedium of modern living, or as she puts it, "there's the next world and all the spirits, and one's Aura, and Mrs. Eddy and saying you're not ill, and the Christian Mysteries and Mrs. Besant. It's all splendid. One's never dull for a moment." In Huxley's world the hypocritically religious never achieve becoming anything more than an exaggeration of their inane selves. Their insights into the nature of reality tend to disclose that there is some kind of vague power present in the universe which at its best can help them write a better play or acquire wealth or even aid them in looking mysterious enough to be successful in seducing their next potential lover. Thus it is that the failure of an egocentric interpretation of the universe to give the truth-searcher inner peace may cause him to arrogate more and more power to himself and thereby attempt to control those outside himself by cultivating his supposedly specialized powers. This leads us to a consideration of the second method by which modern man seeks to secure inner peace: that of self-deification.

Self-deification is most prominently evidenced in the character of Theodore Gumbril, Jr. in *Antic Hay.* Gumbril, having committed himself to skepticism finds it difficult to trust in any ideological group. He becomes afraid of the loss of his identity and is driven by his need of internal strength to conceive of the complete man. The Complete Man is to be objectively characterized by his all-too noticeable, fan-shaped beard and his oversized, padded coat.

Sitting in his office one day, Gumbril glues the fan-shaped beard onto his face. He then undergoes a pseudo-spiritual metamorphosis:

> The effect, he decided immediately, was stunning, was grandiose. From melancholy and all too mild he saw himself transformed on the instant into a sort of jovial Henry the Eighth, into a massive Rabelaisian man, broad and powerful and exuberant with vitality and hair.—Great eater, deep thinker, stout fighter, prodigious lover; clear thinker, creator of beauty, seeker of truth and prophet of heroic grandeurs.

Such is the nature of the complete man. The process of deification is now complete. All that is left now is for Gumbril to assert himself in the form of the Complete Man. This he does by seducing (or being seduced by; it is difficult to tell) a very "fastidious" lady by the name of Rosie. Rosie, herself, manifests narcissistic tendencies. One evening, while contemplating her adulterous behavior, she slips her hands into her kimona and begins to fondle her own arms. Then she begins thinking of herself as a beautiful pink serpent. As long as Gumbril conceives of himself as the Complete Man, the Rabelaisian man, and as long as Rosie conceives of herself as a beautiful serpent, pink or otherwise, they cannot spiritually know one another. In Huxley's world, sensuality can only partially lift man above time, and what pleasure is gained is negated by the contemplation of the finality of sensual enjoyment. Gumbril, after having seduced another victim, the innocent and virginal Emily, is described by Huxley as "a man [who] on the night before his execution, [looks] forward through the endless present [and forsees] the end of his eternity."

Self-deification can take more demoniac forms than that represented by Gumbril. In *Point Counter Point*, for example, which Huxley described as his vision of hell, Spandrell is the supreme representative of Satanic evil. Spandrell is bored by ordinary evil. He therefore spends a great deal of his time trying to convert people to Christianity with the intention of later corrupting them. Thus it is that he speaks loftily of sensuality before the young and virginal Harriet, and equates in her mind the most exalted states of spiritual experience with "the most fantastic lubricities." After having kept her as his mistress for several months he then begins to turn spirituality against sensuality, to deplore the body and all its evil functions. Harriet leaves him, filled with hatred for him and for herself. Spandrell is left to meditate upon his own misery, which in his terms can be alleviated only by finding another innocent victim. Then the cycle will repeat itself, only to create more misery. In order to escape misery, in order to acquire inner peace in Huxley's world, then, man must ground his identity in something more permanent than his own ego.

The third method, considered by Huxley, whereby man might secure inner peace, is that of identifying himself with nature. Huxley has this philosophy verbalized in *Point Counter Point* by Rampion. Rampion recommends unmediated experience as a solution for stabilizing the identity. The hierarchical framework of traditional systems should be eliminated. Outside of abstract thinking, God simply becomes equated with life, or as Rampion puts it, "a quality of actions and relations—a felt, experienced quality." We find, however, that Huxley does not limit himself to naturalism, though he does use it as a base upon which to structure his later mysticism. Philip Quarles is intellect's representative in the same novel and though Quarles never packs the universe into a neat Hegelian synthesis, he intellectualizes enough to suggest the necessity of a more disciplined system than what Rampion has to offer.

In *Brave New World,* it is Rampion's primitivism which has been pushed to its logical extreme in the Savage Reservation. Here intellect has been sacrificed for feeling, and although there is some dignity in the freedom of the savages, they cannot be eulogized for having found inner peace any more than can the Brave New Worlders who represent the logical extension of placing ultimate value on material gains, the deification of pleasure, and the deification of themselves.

Since up to this point in Huxley's world man has not been able to find inner peace by turning his attention inward upon himself, we might then inquire whether turning his attention away from himself might be of some value. This brings us to the fourth method by which man attempts to secure inner peace; that of placing ultimate value on material gains.

Probably the most ridiculous example of placing faith in material objects is found in the character of Jo Stoyte in Huxley's *After Many a Summer Dies the Swan.* Jo Stoyte is completely identified with the temporal world, so identified in fact, that he is constantly tormented by the idea of death. Stoyte is a California millionaire who seeks to secure a kind of mortal immortality by taking hormone treatments from his private physician, Dr. Obispo. Dr. Obispo takes Stoyte to England with him where he intends to examine the home of a certain Earl who in the year 1797 had discovered the principle of increased longevity by eating the intestine of fresh carp. In the cellar of the old house they find the Fifth Earl:

> On the edge of a low bed, at the center of this world, a man was sitting staring, as though fascinated, into the light. His legs thickly covered with coarse reddish hair, were bare.—He sat hunched up, his head thrust forward and at the same time sunk between his shoulders. With one of his huge and strangely clumsy hands, he was scratching a sore place that showed red between the hairs of his left calf.

Obispo describes the creature as a foetal ape. The Fifth Earl's housekeeper had been immortalized along with the Earl, and together they carry on what Obispo believes to be hilarious antics. Obispo tells Stoyte that he can start taking the fish intestines the next day if he feels ready. Stoyte observes the creature before him, then replies:

> How long do you figure it would take before a person went like that?—I mean, it wouldn't happen at once ... there'd be a long time while a person ... well, you know; while he wouldn't change any.

And once you get over the first shock . . . well, they look like they were having a pretty good time. I mean in their own way of course.

In Huxley's system, an identification with the temporal world is considered evil because once the individual has grounded his identity in an object which is impermanent, the personality of the individual begins to decay. We have seen that in Huxley's world man will destroy himself by placing ultimate value on his own identity. On the other hand the identity cannot find stability in material objects because these objects are subordinate to time and will therefore decay. This brings us to step five in Huxley's scheme; that of positing skepticism as a method of securing inner peace.

Seemingly, the individual is trapped between placing emphasis upon himself or placing emphasis upon objects outside himself, neither of which methods produce inner peace. This explains why so many of Huxley's searching protagonists are skeptics: they are following the next logical alternative; that of suspension of judgment. They are afraid to ground their identity in anything, for they realize how easily they may be destroyed. The extreme disadvantage to this method is that the person becomes literally unable to act for fear of having identified himself with the wrong object. This explains why Anthony Beavis is unable to act in the first part of *Eyeless in Gaza;* he spends most of his time meditating. Huxley is not saying as Sartre has said that the meditation of religious verities leads to inaction. On the contrary, he is saying that meditation is crippling only when it leads the individual to vegetate on the nothingness between the deification of material objects and the deification of himself. The cycle must be broken somewhere and it is this necessity that leads us to the sixth and final method of securing internal peace; that of transcending time and concretely identifying the self with the world that is common to all religious experience.

In *Eyeless in Gaza, Time Must Have a Stop,* and *The Genuis and the Goddess,* Huxley equates the world outside of time with love. In *Eyeless in Gaza* Anthony Beavis has a mystical experience and gains the ability to act out of the spirit of love rather than restricting himself to his usual method of laborious abstraction. In *The Genius and the Goddess* Mrs. Maartens has an adulterous relationship with John Rivers in order to secure spiritual strength to save her husband from death. Paradoxically, Mrs. Maartens *does* derive spiritual strength from her act of adultery and the next morning she is able to save her husband from death. Old Beulah, who has prayed all night, insists that Mrs. Maartens has received grace from the Christian God. Rivers applies a Pickwickian interpretation; uses a hodgepodge of Christian and mystical terminology to explain the regeneration. To Mrs. Maartens, who is not a Christian, the new energy and psychic health is simply a function of life. Later Mrs. Maartens gets killed in an auto wreck. Huxley leaves the cause and effect sequences leading up to her death hanging on a tenuous thread which is suspended between naturalism and Predestination.

However God is interpreted in this novel, it is obvious that He acts, and His presence is most clearly manifested in the regeneration of Mrs. Maartens and her subsequent death. Her death is at once a martyrdom and an atonement. It is a martyrdom in the sense that her initial intention is to secure strength to save her husband from death; it is atonement in the sense that her naturalism evokes suffering, not only for her but also for her child and finally for Rivers.

In *Time Must Have a Stop*, as the title implies, Huxley again states that time must be transcended. In this novel, Sebastian Barnack, a young intellectual who has been haunted all his life by a desire for wealth and for sensual gratification gradually comes to realize the necessity of positing religious verities. Sebastian undergoes a spiritual transformation by discovering, among other principles, "that there is a Godhead or Ground, which is the unmanifested principle of all manifestation—and that it is possible for human beings to love, know, and virtually, to become identified with the Ground." Sebastian's conclusions are merely more concise statements of the philosophy already propounded by Mr. Propter in *After Many a Summer Dies the Swan* and Dr. Miller in *Eyeless in Gaza*.

In conclusion, it may be said that Huxley defines the world outside of time as absolute reality. It is the world of all the great mystics, and the principles that can be deduced by an identification with it embody the general ethics of Christianity, as well as some of the Oriental religions. It has been objected by some critics that the reality recommended for worship by Huxley is too cold, too inanimate, too impersonal. Such criticism, it seems, suggests a kind of theological or moral coercion on the part of the critic rather than an attempt at literary analysis. It is for this reason that it seems imperative that Huxley's philosophical *phases* be examined rather than a consideration of his present stage of philosophical development, and that his method of structuring a system and conveying it in literary form be deduced. We have no guarantee that his system has reached its final crystalline form, but whether it has or has not, it is doubtful that Huxley's final contention will evolve from the antecedent criticisms of merely segmented phases of his philosophy.

> *In all the historic formulations of the Perennial Philosophy it is axiomatic that the end of human life is contemplation, or the direct and intuitive awareness of God; that action is the means to that end; that a society is good to the extent that it renders contemplation possible for its members; and that the existence of at least a minority of contemplatives is necessary for the well-being of any society.*
>
> Aldous Huxley

JEROME MECKIER

Aldous Huxley: Satire and Structure

I

The unique existence led by Francis Chelifer in *Those Barren Leaves* (1925)[1] best illustrates the extent to which Aldous Huxley satirizes the majority of his characters for being escapists and eccentrics. The section entitled "The Autobiography of Francis Chelifer" informs us that the young poet has abandoned verse to edit *The Rabbit Fanciers' Gazette*, to live in wretched rooms in Gog's Court, and even to praise the unintelligent babbling of his fellow boarders at Miss Carruthers'. On the surface, Chelifer resembles the eccentrics who abound in Huxley's novels. He is apparently like Henry Wimbush in *Crome Yellow* (1921), an amateur historian who devotes himself to research on lavatory sanitation in the Middle Ages; or like Gumbril Senior in *Antic Hay* (1923), an architect who squanders his competence on plans to rebuild London according to the drawings of Christopher Wren. But Chelifer's eccentricity is conscious. He has seen, as has Huxley, the break-up of communal society into an amorphous collection of tangential egoists, each of whom inhabits his own private world. This break-up is, for him, such an actuality that to live anywhere except among eccentrics and as an eccentric would constitute escapism. Through Chelifer, Huxley shows that eccentricity and unreality have become so firmly established that the artist can only deal with life by becoming unreal himself. Chelifer insists that normality, centricity, and all who speak of such things

Wisconsin Studies in Contemporary Literature, Volume 7, Number 3 (Autumn 1966): pp. 284–294. Copyright © 1966 University of Wisconsin Press.

are the odd exceptions, they are irrelevant to the great reality, they are lies like the ideal of love, like dreams of the future, like belief in justice. To live among their works is to live in a world of bright falsehoods, apart from the real world; it is to escape. Escape is cowardly; to be comforted by what is untrue or what is irrelevant to the world in which we live is stupid.[2]

The world in which we live, Huxley's world, belongs to Lord Edward Tantamount and Old Quarles of *Point Counter Point* (1928). The first tries to graft a tail onto the leg of a newt, the second wants to write the *biggest* book ever written on democracy. Coleman summarizes the peculiarly modern situation that all Huxley novels deal with when he realizes that walking through London puts him in "the midst of seven million distinct and separate individuals, each with distinct and separate lives and all completely indifferent to our existence."[3]

Coleman's observation about the life led by modern society recalls the satiric parable of Hercules the dwarf which appeared in Huxley's first novel, *Crome Yellow*.[4] Only three feet, four inches tall, Hercules panics at the sight of normal-size dogs and suffers humiliation when the woman he asks to marry him picks him up and shakes him for his impertinence. Unable to cope with reality, Hercules sets up a private world built to his own dimensions: a dwarf-size house, a dwarf wife. He becomes increasingly fond of his limitations and writes poems exalting the small and classifying height as abnormality. But his hopes of filling the world with people his own size collapse when his wife gives birth to a normal-size son. After the son and two friends return from the Grand Tour and force Hercules' midget servant to dance on the tabletops, Hercules and his wife commit suicide. As he slices open his veins and allows the blood to flow freely in the warm water of his tub, Hercules personifies the futility of the eccentric escapism practiced by Gumbril, Wimbush, and all who fly off from the center to build up their own private world.

By reducing everything to their own limitations, Huxley's characters suggest an orchestra gone haywire. As Huxley observes in *Point Counter Point,* instruments meant for harmony emit cacophony:

The parts [of the orchestra] live their separate lives: they touch, their paths cross, they combine for a moment to create a seemingly final and perfected harmony, only to break apart again. Each is always alone and separate and individual. "I am I," asserts the violin, "the world revolves around me." "Round me," calls the cello. "Round me," the flute insists. And all are equally right and equally wrong; and none of them will listen to the others.[5]

Each member of the human orchestra is trying to drown out all the others, to establish himself and his private world as the focal point of the universe by sheer quantity of sound. Thus Shearwater's very name in *Antic Hay*, accentuates his insistence that life revolves around kidney research. For him, life is sheer water.

In addition to the orchestra image, Huxley continually presents society as a collection of parallel lines, none of which ever cross. Mrs. Viveash summarizes the eccentric's position when she suggests managing life "on the principle of the railways." For her, "parallel tracks" are a necessity. If you meet someone, "for a few miles you'd be running at the same speed. There'd be delightful conversation out of the windows." And when you have said all there is to say, "away you'd go, forging ahead along the smooth polished rails."[6] Denis, the young poet in *Crome Yellow,* becomes convinced that "we are all parallel straight lines" that never establish contact. He tries to confide in Mary Bracegirdle who is simultaneously trying to confide in him:

> *Denis:* The individual . . . is not a self-supporting universe. There are times when he comes into contact with other individuals. . . .
> *Mary:* True. . . . When one individual comes into intimate contact with another, she—or he, . . . must almost inevitably receive or inflict suffering. . . .
> *Denis:* One is apt to be so spellbound by the spectacle of one's own personality. . . .
> Mary was not listening. "The difficulty," she said, "makes itself acutely felt in matters of sex. . . ."
> "When I think of my own case," said Denis. . . . [7]

Spellbound by the spectacle of their own personalities, each insists on being the confider. Each is a parallel line talking about itself only. Though Denis realizes what is wrong with society, he is part of the problem rather than a solution to it. Beckett inserts his characters in ash cans, but Huxley, drawing on the novels of Thomas Love Peacock (1785–1866), puts his around a dining table or in a garden of some country house such as that of *Crome Yellow* and satirizes their isolation effectively.

Huxley's novels, then, are full of eccentrics whose egoism is continually the target of his satire. But in the Chelifer section of *Those Barren Leaves,* Huxley achieves an irony almost Swiftian in its convolutions, as reality and unreality, the normal and the deviant, the rule and the exception, all change places. The writing of poetry is a normal pursuit and hence to indulge in it would be eccentric. Like Keats, Chelifer exercises negative capability, but his capacity for sympathetic projection leaves him worse off than Descartes. To annihilate himself and become all that others are means he must become, like those around him, an egoist and an eccentric. By identifying with others, he becomes imprisoned in himself. His refusal to "run away from the reality of human life," leads him to subscribe to the main tenet of the eccentric's code: "Let each party stick to his own opinion. The most successful men are those who never admit the validity of other people's opinions, who even deny their existence."[8] Maartens, in *The Genius and the Goddess* (1955), makes an entire world out of his science. Jeremy Pordage, in *After Many a Summer Dies the Swan* (1939), lives between the covers of his books. And Chelifer, fully conscious of his predicament, makes a world from which everything extraneous to rabbit fancying is excluded. The world, as Huxley sees it, is without a center and its inhabitants are fragmentary. Each flies off from the center and sets up a world of his own in which be cultivates his ego. The oddball inmates of Swift's Academy of Lagado—the men who devoted their waking lives to projects such as the extracting of sun rays from cucumbers—now cover the earth.

II

Not only are Huxley's characters divided from each other, but they are also split within themselves. His scientists, painters, and writers—all of whom may be called "artists" in a broad sense—comprise, as the epigraph to *Point Counter Point* suggests, so many dichotomies of mind against body. In a disintegrated society, the artists, who should see life steadily and see it whole, are, Huxley complains, incurably split. They cannot converse with each other because they have all gone off on separate tangents and because each is in himself a battleground of mind against body. Each is either a Houyhnhnm or a Yahoo, all intellect or all genitals. Nineteenth-century ideals have broken down, and, with the exception of a spokesman whom Huxley inserts into some of his novels, no one calls for integration, for the creation of new standards.

The First World War stands as the culmination of the breakdown of nineteenth-century ideals, and characters such as Mr. Cardan in *Those Barren Leaves*, a man who functions like Mr. Hilary in Peacock's *Nightmare Abbey*, laments the loss of the nineteenth-century milieu. Calamy has just observed that he cannot imagine "a more exciting age" than the present, when everything is "perfectly provisional and temporary" and "nothing"—neither the Treaty of Versailles nor the belief in an afterlife—"is really safe." But Cardan replies that he prefers "a more quiet life." He says he was "brought up in the simple faith of nineteenth-century materialism. . . . We were all wonderfully optimistic then; believed in progress and the ultimate explicability of everything in terms of physics and chemistry, believed in Mr. Gladstone and our own moral and intellectual superiority over every other age."[9]

As in Peacock, contrasting opinions are presented by speakers both of whom believe in what they say. But the spokesman's opinion, here Cardan's, emerges as the superior one. The same topic is filtered through two or more characters of dissimilar outlook and is refracted in each case according to the sort of background the character represents. Of the two resultant opinions, one seems more reasonable and becomes more readily acceptable by contrast with the other. Huxley does not take Cardan's epoch as the ideal. Indeed, Cardan himself admits that most of his era's ideas were wrong or absurd. What makes the world Cardan fondly recalls superior to Calamy's is its possession of standards, beliefs, codes, self-esteem, and optimism, to all of which the era as a whole subscribed. The era believed everything to be explicable in terms of chemistry and physics. It was not a case of Shearwater explaining all in terms of the kidney, whereas Gumbril junior's panacea is pneumatic trousers with built-in cushions for humanity's posteriors. The age as a whole felt superior to its ancestors. Each individual's ego did not raise him above his contemporaries. The uncertainty Calamy finds so exhilarating about the present age encourages each person to seek security in a private world. Huxley and Cardan approve not the ideals of the nineteenth century but the desirability of a set of standards that serve as a blueprint for a communal society. What is needed, then, is not another Victoria, but a new set of standards and ideals that can invest society with a centric quality. Huxley agreed with Wyndham Lewis *(The Art of Being Ruled)* that the artist, as ally of the intellectual, must form and guide society; and that where he does not, intellectuals begin to pursue their specialties in ever-increasing isolation. The eccentric artist breeds eccentric intellectuals and an eccentric society. And an eccentric society, like the one that envelops Chelifer, produces more eccentric artists.

But the artist has clearly failed society. A thorough search of Huxley's novels turns up one eccentric artist after another. If, as we observed earlier, Huxley satirizes the eccentric in general, he satirizes the eccentric artist in particular. In *Point Counter Point,* Philip Quarles asserts that there is "less specialization, less one-sided development" in the artist and consequently he should be "sounder right through than the lop-sided man of science; he oughtn't to have the blind spots and the imbecilities of the philosophers and saints."[10] Yet Quarles' novels consist entirely of intellect, and his wife must seek sexual satisfaction from other men; whereas Burlap, who writes about St. Francis, really attains happiness only when he takes baths with women. The artist, even more than society, exists in a state of mind against body, is either a man of intellect or a creature of lusts. "Passion and reason," says the Fulke-Greville poem quoted as epigraph to *Point Counter Point,* are "self-division's cause."

Of several Huxley spokesmen who war against these split-men, two deserve particular mention: Mr. Propter of *After Many a Summer Dies the Swan* and Mark Rampion of *Point Counter Point*. Propter, whose name means "be-cause," cites eccentricity as the cause of man's predicament. Ironically situated in Hollywood, a city built on personalities, Propter calls on the individual to realize that his ego is "a fiction" which, when its frenzy has been quieted, is capable of being replaced by "a God conceived . . . as a more than personal consciousness." Without the attainment of this more than personal consciousness, man remains "doomed to perpetual imprisonment in the ego," and Hollywood remains the symbol of modern society.[11] Without such attainment, Huxley foresees a brave new world in which one finds regimentation but no solidarity, in which characters participate in pointless solidarity exercises:

> The group was now complete, the solidarity circle perfect and without flaw. . . . Twelve of them ready to be made one, waiting to come together, to be fused, to lose their twelve separate identities in a larger being.[12]

But of course the Great Ford whom the twelve wait for never comes.

Mark Rampion, who strongly resembles D. H. Lawrence, calls for a re-fusing of flesh and spirit that will permit man to join his animal with his rational functions. The strong and complete spirit must know what the heart knows as well as what the mind knows. Man is both Houyhnhnm and Yahoo and exists ideally when these two elements in his nature are balanced, when, instead of point against point, they are in the true counterpoint of equilib-rium. The caricatures Rampion draws of humanity's parade towards its goals show every marcher with either oversized head or oversized genitals. The early lizards died of having too much body, just as Old Bidlake is almost all flesh and no mind. But "sacrificing physical and affective life to mental life," as does the novelist Philip Quarles, also means disaster. Shearwater finally learns that one must "render therefore unto Caesar the things which are Caesar's," that body and mind must be "in proportion."[13] Gumbril junior, in the same novel, transforms himself into a reincarnation of the Rabelaisian or Complete Man. He grows a beard, becomes a "great eater, deep drinker, stout fighter, prodi-gious lover; clear thinker, creator of beauty, seeker of truth and prophet of heroic grandeurs."[14] By engaging himself in all directions, Gumbril junior re-mains perfectly balanced at the center. He becomes fully human. He obtains, as Rampion says the ancient Greek did, the benefits of his animality and his humanity. By refusing to kill any part of himself, he strikes a balance.

III

Huxley's unique achievement consisted in the development of a structure for his novels which would in itself carry out and support his satire. In the manner of Peacock, be accumulates characters at a country house or around a dinner table, and, as they talk, each reveals his eccentricity by trying to override the others, the way each instrument of the orchestra seemed to be doing in the image we examined earlier. In *Every Man Out of His Humour*, Ben Jonson defined a humour character as one whose spirits and powers all run one way. A typical Jonson play begins with the author conceiving a set of humour characters and then simply setting one off against another. Huxley's characters, each with his self-engrossing preoccupation, resemble Jonson's. And Huxley continually sets them off against one another. *In Point Counter Point*, the technique reaches perfection as Huxley employs Quarles' notebooks to comment on the structure he is using.[15]

The typical Peacock novel, such as *Nightmare Abbey* or *Crotchet Castle*, is a curiosity shop of characters gathered at someone's country estate. Mr. Chainmail *(Crotchet Castle)* wishes to live in the twelfth century. Mr. Asterias *(Nightmare Abbey)* searches for mermaids. When, in *Crotchet Castle*, the question arises as to what constitutes the *summum bonum* for society, each character unhesitatingly proposes his own brand of eccentricity. In the midst of the eccentrics, Peacock often inserts a spokesman whose voice is that of sanity and reason. The same confrontation device—the assembling of talkative eccentrics and the addition of one or more rational spokesmen—forms the basis of most Huxley novels. In *Point Counter Point*, Rampion glances around the assembled group and labels the eccentricity of each character: Spandrell is a morality-philosopher pervert, Quarles an intellectual-aesthetic pervert, and Burlap a pure little Jesus pervert. One sees everything in terms of morals and another transforms everything into mind and art. Each has made for himself an entire world out of one aspect of life. And every subject that arises in discussion will be twisted by each pervert until he makes it fit into his private scheme of things. Each of Peacock's characters talks almost exclusively about his particular preoccupation, but Huxley shows his eccentrics twisting any subject that comes up to make it coincide with their individual brand of egotistic eccentricity.

In effect, theme has become structure. What is being satirized and what makes the novel go are one and the same: the eccentricity of the characters. Quarles writes in his notebook: "A theme is stated, then developed, pushed out of shape, imperceptibly deformed, until, though still recognizably the same, it has become different."[16] Each character bends each theme to suit his own deformity. The novels not only insist on man's eccentricity but show it in operation. Structure, technique, and theme show the characters to be the uncrossing parallel lines Denis and Mrs. Viveash described.

Huxley referred to this structure as "musicalization," a device similar to the use of counterpoint in music. As a discussion topic passes through one eccentric after another, a series of variations appears as each eccentric bends the topic to suit his own eccentricity. Counterpoint in music occurs when a melody is added to a given tune until plurality results; that is, a melody not single but attended by one or more related but independent melodies. In the society the discussion group represents, no communal theme exists. Huxley's spokesman provides the main melody which all society should be playing (where there is no spokesman, the reader must provide the melody himself) and each eccentric plays a variation of it that is stubbornly independent and off center, as well as incomplete. Thus if Rampion speaks for a balance of mind and body, each of the other characters will pervert his statement to favor either mind or body since each is somewhat off center, being either all mind or all body or being more of one than of the other.

The Huxley novel is one of ideas in that "the character of each personage must be implied as far as possible, in the ideas of which he is the mouthpiece."[17] Huxley's characters are often little more than a series of ideas covered thinly with skin and given to talkativeness. But *Point Counter Point*, where the musicalization operates with maximum effectiveness, is the author's major achievement, even if, as Quarles confesses, we often feel we are watching characters rattle off "neatly formulated notions." By inserting a novelist in the novel, the musicalization is increased, for the novelist tells a part of the story along with Huxley and another refraction or variation results. Rampion is seen both as Huxley presents him and as Quarles describes him. And Quarles exposes his own limitations while writing about the other characters.

The abrupt transitions (as many as five or six a chapter) from one set of characters to another allow us to see all the parallels in operation even when they are not gathered at the same table. Though the characters cannot penetrate each other's private world, Huxley's technique can. In so doing, Huxley uses "multiplicity" to expose eccentricity. He shows us many layers of unsatisfactory love and inadequate wholeness. The absurdity of each layer that sets itself up as a totality is thus stressed, and each layer (or divergent melody) is continually and ironically juxtaposed with the others and with the ideal Mark and Mary Rampion represent. In them, Huxley personifies integral living. In them and through the variations on them, he attains another kind of wholeness: he treats his themes and events from all aspects, in every possible form be can think of. Thus Elinor and Philip Quarles, Burlap and Beatrice, Walter and Lucy are contrasted with the Rampions; and, within the same family circle, Philip's excessive intellectualism is displayed with the cheap sexual escapades of his father, Sidney, and the blatant sensuality of his father-in-law, John Bidlake, as the background. Philip uses art to protect himself against life, and his brother-in-law, Walter, expects life to resemble art. Thus, Huxley manages to get everything into the novel. Paradoxically, he sees the unity of life at the same time that he presents its complexities, for the divergent melodies, though off the beat, are clearly related to each other and to the central melody. Huxley becomes the re-integrating artist incarnate, the man without blind spots.

Huxley presents two of the modern novel's predominant themes—man's egocentric isolation and his inability to unify body and mind—and insists they are interrelated. The breach between mind and body must be closed before the egotism that separates one man from another can be quelled. Only then will the "grand march of intellect" perceived by Keats[18] become more than the caricature of humanity's progress sketched by Rampion. Through the use of image, parable, Swiftian irony, and musicalization, Huxley traces society's eccentricity to its sources and cities the artist as the person responsible for reintegration. Nowhere in the modern novel are the functions and failures of the artist subjected to such scrutiny. Like Peacock, Huxley examines romantic tenets. Like his own Mr. Propter, and Bruno Rontini in *Time Must Have A Stop* (1944), be condemns the materialistic craving that comprises this century's inheritance from the last and makes the ego shout "mine" as well as "me." And in his development of the confrontation technique into a highly convoluted musicalization, he fuses satire and structure and perfects a new form for the novel.

Notes

1. The title comes from Wordsworth's "The Tables Turned," line 30, and presumably refers to the lives led by the novel's characters. Huxley was fond of taking his titles from poets, using, among others, lines from Shakespeare and Tennyson. As in Wordsworth, Huxley's "barren leaves" are the books of Science and Art, in which we "murder to dissect."

2. *Those Barren Leaves*, Chapter V.

3. *Antic Hay*, Chapter V.

4. Chapter XIII.

5 Chapter II. It is interesting to compare this with Keats's statement (in a Letter to John Hamilton Reynolds for February 3, 1818):

How beautiful are the retired flowers! how they would lose
their beauty were they to throng into the highway crying out,
"admire me I am a violet! dote on me I am a primrose!"

6. *Antic Hay*, Chapter VI.

7. *Crome Yellow*, Chapter XXIV.

8. *Those Barren Leaves*, Part Four, Chapter VII. I find Chelifer's statement interesting in comparison with Keat's belief that if we all go our own ways intensely enough, we will all arrive at the same point (Letter to John Hamilton Reynolds, February 19, 1818). In Huxley, everyone does go his own way and the result is parallel lines. Several of Huxley's young protagonists are poets who recall Keats: Chelifer, of course, and Sebastian Barnach of *Time Must Have a Stop*.

9. *Ibid.*, Part One, Chapter III.

10. *Point Counter Point*, Chapter XX–VI.

11. *After Many a Summer Dies the Swan*, Chapters VIII, IX.

12. *Brave New World*, Chapter V.

13. *Antic Hay*, Chapter XI.

14. *Ibid.*, Chapter IX.

15. After *Point Counter Point*, though many of the same themes occupy him, Huxley seems to move from discussion novel or novel of ideas towards the more frontal approach of the essay. Though *Brave New World* (1932) and *The Genius and the Goddess* (1955) do not substantiate this view, I have in mind the last chapters of *Time Must Have A Stop*, which consist of essay-excerpts from Sebastian's notebook, the narrator sections of *Ape and Essence* (1948), and especially *Island* (1962), which makes only occasional attempts at being a novel. In the later novels, Lawrence's "blood philosophy," which Huxley modifies into a balance of body and mind, is abandoned for the mystical outlook of Bruno Rontini.

16. *Point Counter Point*, Chapter XXII.

17. *Ibid.*

18. Letter to John Hamilton Reynolds, May 3, 1818.

PIERRE VITOUX

Structure and Meaning in
Aldous Huxley's Eyeless in Gaza

The most obvious and disturbing feature of *Eyeless In Gaza* is the peculiar narrative technique used by Huxley. The life of the main character, Anthony Beavis, from childhood to the age of forty-two, and to his final adoption of a new philosophy of life, is not described in a continuous and orderly progression. The fifty-four chapters that make up the novel, each chapter being usually restricted to a simple scene or a brief episode, are disconnected, in the sense that Huxley does not provide transitions and leaves the reader to infer what happens in between. Besides, the time-sequence is completely subverted; the scenes belonging to different periods are all mixed up, as if the novelist had shuffled his pack of fifty-four cards and was now dealing them out one after the other as they turn up. The reader is thus placed in the unusual situation of having to travel back and forth in time and to re-order the chapters mentally if he wants to make sense of the novel—and he naturally wonders what can justify such a treatment of the story, and of him.

Some sort of justification will be immediately apparent. If he is at all responsive, he cannot fail to notice that the sentence (Chapter 3, p. 19):[1] 'One, two, three, four—counting each movement of his hand, he began to caress her. The gesture was magical, would transport him, if repeated sufficiently often, beyond the past and the future', is very similar to another sentence he reads soon after (Chapter 4, p. 20): '"Thirty-one . . . thirty-two", the boy said

The Yearbook of English Studies, Volume 2 (1972): pp. 212–224. Copyright © 1972 Maney Publishing on behalf of Modern Humanities Research Association.

41

to himself, and wished he had begun his counting when the train started.'
What is made clear in the context is (roughly) that the mechanical activity of counting was for the boy in 1903 an instinctive way of escaping from
unpleasantness and grief (at his mother's funeral), and has become for the
mature man of 1933 a conscious and systematic device to limit his consciousness to the palpable present. The technique clearly helps to show the points
of contact between different phases in a man's life.

But the reader may still find that the price he has to pay for some limited
artistic effects of that kind is too high. Such is in fact the conclusion reached
in a recent study of Huxley's novels: 'A curious but instructive undertaking is
to read the sections of *Eyeless In Gaza* not as they are arranged but in the exact
order suggested by the dates that are the chapter headings; no essential meaning is lost.'[2] But what constitutes the 'essential meaning' is by no means a self-
evident fact in such a complex novel. And to approach the problem I would
like to quote from one of the early critiques of *Eyeless In Gaza*, by the novelist
Phyllis Bentley, who is mostly concerned with the question of the structure.
She makes a detailed and convincing study of the effects (of the kind just
alluded to) achieved by the 'constant interweaving' of past and present, the
'subtle associations of character, time and place'. She remains rather doubtful,
however, about the net result: 'The disadvantages of the jumbling method
are obvious. It confuses the reader almost to the point of madness; after all,
a card index should not be necessary for the understanding of a work of art.
Also—and this I think Mr Huxley has not sufficiently discounted—it does
not permit the slow development of personality.'[3] But at this point I may simply state the two related ideas which this article is intended to demonstrate.
One is that Huxley is not concerned with showing 'the slow development of
personality', but wants to focus our attention on a crisis, psychological and
moral, leading to a conversion; his vision is not evolutionary but climactic or
mutative. And the second idea is that the technique is not imposed on the
story from outside as a clever device, but consistent with, and indeed evolved
from, Huxley's conception of time, consciousness, and change. Even so, some
readers will still object on principle or out of laziness to having to compile
a mental 'card-index' to Huxley (or requiring a skeleton-key to *Ulysses*); but
others may be convinced that the effort to reconcile and adapt themselves to
the development of the structure is worth making—for the form is significant,
it is part of the 'meaning' as well as connected with the intended suasive effect
of the novel (for Huxley has already entered into his proselytizing phase).

It is useful to start with a brief summary of the main events in chronological order. And, since the attempt may appear at first sight to be hopelessly
inconsistent with the ideas just expressed (about the inseparability of the
technique), let me say that there is some critical point in trying to see what
is left out, together with the technique, when the story has been laid out flat

in time; and also that Huxley never intended his reader *not* to reconstruct the time sequence, and in fact wanted him to have in mind both the past as past slowly reconstructed, and the past as present in the consciousness at some later moment. The chronological time-sequence is one legitimate result of the reader's activity. All the events recorded fall into six periods.[4] (A): 1902–1904, four chapters. Anthony Beavis as a boy: death of his mother, schooldays at Bulstrode, early friendship with Brian Foxe, his father's second marriage. (B): 1912–1914, ten chapters. Anthony is at Oxford, full of intellectual curiosity, and has already adopted the attitude of the detached, dilettanteish observer of life. He has an affair with Mary Amberley, a pleasure-loving divorcee—while his friend Brian, a conscientious idealist, overworks himself in the Fabian cause, and keeps away from Joan, his fiancée, in a desperate attempt to repress his 'base' sexual instincts which could endanger the purity of their relationship. But Mary, who has a twisted sense of fun, and also an urge to run down all high sentiments, blackmails Anthony into kissing Joan. Anthony's failure to confess to Brian has tragic results: his friend is informed by a letter from Joan, and commits suicide by jumping from a cliff. Anthony manages to cover it up as an accident, but breaks with Mary, who would pry out his secret. (C): 1926–1928, and again ten chapters. They describe Anthony at work on his *Elements of Sociology*. Mary is ageing, and in the hands of her callous young lover Gerry, who soon runs away, after making a profit out of her financial ruin and seducing young Helen, Mary's daughter, whom he leaves pregnant and helpless. The end of the period sees Helen's abortion in Paris, and her marriage with Hugh Ledwidge. (D): 1931, and two transitional chapters. Mrs Foxe dies and the unpleasant affair of Brian's death seems to be buried with her; and Helen, who is bored by her clumsy, ineffectual husband, accepts Anthony's invitation to dinner. (E): 1933—February 1934, in thirteen chapters. First, four non-consecutive but early chapters (1, 3, 8, 12) describe the events of a single, crucial day, that of 30 August: Anthony finding a pack of old snapshots—he and Helen sunbathing on the roof of the villa—the dog flung at them from an airplane, crashing beside them and splattering them with blood—Helen reacting with puzzling violence and breaking off with Anthony. Later, Anthony, feeling at a loose end, accompanies his friend Mark Staithes on an adventurous expedition to Mexico, but there he falls under the influence of Dr Miller, a 'religious anthropologist' and pacifist, and decides to become one of his active followers in England. In the meantime, Helen has taken up with a young Communist refugee, and seen him captured by Nazi agents in Switzerland. (F): April 1934–February 1934, and fifteen chapters, mostly very brief. The technique, here, is different: we are given slices of Anthony's personal diary, in which some facts and conversations are recorded, but where the narrative gives way to meditation, and to the private description of spiritual struggle and progress. The diary, however, merges into the narrative form for the final sequence, when Anthony is preparing to deliver a pacifist speech at Battersea under the threat of physical violence from a group of nationalists.

Let us make first a few remarks on minor formal points. There is discontinuity (gaps in time) not merely between the periods, but also between separate scenes: for instance, between July 1912 (Chapter 19) and May 1914 (Chapter 27), that is two consecutive scenes in what has been defined as period B. There would be a problem for Huxley even in a chronological arrangement; but, on the other hand, since he has no objection to speeding up the narrative (Chapter 15 moves in a few pages from January 1903 to January 1904) or even to putting in transitional chapters (Chapters 25 and 29, of 1931), the technical solution lies near at hand. And the rearrangement would not be too difficult, since the chapters forming each sequence are, if not consecutive, at least placed in the right order; a sequence, covering a period, can be defined as a series of chapters following one another chronologically, though they are mixed up with chapters belonging to other sequences. More serious, in the event of a reshuffling, would be the difficulty of having to throw together at the end of the novel fifteen sections, amounting to some thirty-seven pages, made up of extracts from Anthony's diary, that is, having the form of a fairly extended essay. It would have been necessary for Huxley to cast his material into another form, and a less suitable one, since whatever happens at that stage is interesting only for its impact on the mind of Anthony, and is interpreted in the light of his new philosophy of life. Huxley had already used the method elsewhere; for instance in *Point Counterpoint*, with the extracts from Philip Quarles's diary. But those extracts were few, and relatively scattered because the novel followed up different stories at the same time: the Quarles sequence (with the bits of essay) was interrupted by the Walter Bidlake sequence, and a few others. Here, the technical difficulty is that Anthony, at the end (when the essay form is needed), tends to become the focal consciousness, or conscience, so that any splitting-up of the diary is precluded. There will be more to say on the question of the 'point of view', but at this stage I may add one further remark. Even in a classical novel like *Point Counterpoint* (classical, that is, in terms of structure) the reader is expected to perform some mental gymnastics, jumping from side to side, from one strand of the story to another. In *Eyeless in Gaza*, he has to jump forward and backward in time, which is more unusual, but not really more exhausting. What he is likely to miss at first is, of course, the motivation, the sense of the purpose of the exercise; time gives us the reassuring feeling that things follow from, and because of, one another—and where are we if we get the effect before the cause? But Huxley's main purpose is to shift our attention from sequence in time to timeless patterns of causality, from the blurred logic of becoming (deceptive, because we are just as shortsighted and self-deceiving as Anthony about what has just been happening to us) to the clear evidence of being, and to the evidence, no less clear, that being must be transcended.

This takes us back to the first scene of the novel, on the morning of the epochal day. Anthony Beavis is now forty-two, and affected by a melancholy sense of the passing of time, as he looks at the old snapshots of his mother, of Mary, of Gladys who was his mistress in 1931. And he suddenly rebels against this intrusion of the past, of all the 'superfluous memories'. He bursts out in invectives against 'old Proust', 'that asthmatic seeker of lost time . . . for ever squatting in the tepid bath of his remembered past' (Chapter 1, p. 6). This is all the more striking as the scene could, at least superficially, be called 'Proustian'. For Proust, what we have experienced and felt is never really obliterated, and any chance incident (it could be just this coming across a pack of old snapshots) can suddenly bring back to life some fragment of the past: and it will not be simply remembered, but restored, giving us an intuition of the submerged but permanent past below the level of our present consciousness. But there, of course, is the difference. Anthony is not immune to emotions—but they are just faint echoes of the old ones, and the pictures have no power to bring the past back to life because they are connected with a 'has been', and in no way (except through man's mechanical capacity for storing up images in the memory) related to his present being. That this attitude of Anthony is the result of a deliberate effort to cut himself adrift, to divorce and desecrate his past, is made clear by his parody of Wordsworth's famous lines: 'I would wish my days to be separated each from each by unnatural impiety' (Chapter 1, p. 10). The intensity and the form of the wish are explained some time later (Chapter 9, p. 64) when Huxley is building up the background for the crisis: the lines about days to be 'bound each to each by natural piety' had been quoted by John Beavis as a profession of fidelity to his dead wife, and the child had squirmed with discomfort at the naked emotionalism, which his father's second marriage was soon to prove shallow. Meanwhile, in the first scene, Huxley has clearly set the central theme of time and memory, of continuity and discontinuity in the individual, and of the role of the will in the shaping of the personality.

All through the day, Anthony tries and fails to lay the ghosts of an importunate past. Helen's brown, naked body reminds him of a Gauguin he had seen with Mary in Paris, her sun-warmed skin carries him back to a day spent in Brian's company . . . His drowsy meditation on the flat roof of the villa is obviously the psychological equivalent of the narrative method of the novel, and its justification: the remembered pictures are forced upon his mind without any chronology, without any visible principle of selection and arrangement. He tries to shut them out, to transport himself 'beyond the past and the future, beyond right and wrong, into the discrete, the self-sufficient, the atomic present' (Chapter 3, pp. 19–20): and the connexion is clearly made between the wished-for separateness of the present and the escape from responsibility for the past. He manages to reassure himself to some extent by asserting that one can never remember the actual quality of pleasure and pain: 'There is nothing like a re-creation of the event, which is lucky ... Think if one could fully remember perfumes or kisses. How wearisome the reality of them would be!' (Chapter 8, pp. 60–61). And it is true that there is nothing fundamentally Proustian about the novel (apart from the process of association); but the past has other ways than re-creation for making its impact felt. Later in the day, he makes an effort to organize the pictures chronologically, and to place them safely away from him: 'He sat down and methodically began to sort them out [the snapshots] subject by subject, into little heaps' (Chapter 12, p. 103). But they insist on getting mixed-up and making their way into the nightmare that concludes the day: 'A huge accumulation of neglected memories broke through, as it were, into his awareness. Those snapshots. His mother and Mary Amberley. Brian in the chalk-pit, evoked by that salty smell of sun-warmed flesh, and again dead at the cliff's foot, among the flies—like that dog ...' (Chapter 12, p. 111). As it is, Anthony can still hope that this obsession is nothing but a temporary psychological accident due to his emotional state: but he has already had the disquieting suspicion that the pictures were brought up with a purpose and to affect his present, that the reason for all those random events was 'not before the event, but after it, in what had been the future', that their point was that 'he might be forced, in the midst of this act of detached and irresponsible sensuality, to think of Brian and of the things that Brian had lived for; yes, and had died for ...' (Chapter 3, p. 19). This will turn out to be true: not in the sense that a supernatural providence is at work, but because the past can be re-activated in a crisis and force us to become conscious of what we are. But before acknowledging the truth, Anthony has to work out the implications of the break with Helen.

Clearly, the four chapters dealing with the single day of 30 August 1933 are the focus of the novel; the occasion for the narration of the earlier episodes (in sequences A, B, and C), and the justification of the technique (the past welling up in fragments that do not cohere) are to be found in Anthony's state of mind on that day. And here one might expect the novelist to adopt the technique of the 'point of view', but Huxley does not, and the episodes are narrated in an objective omniscient way. The point has been well made by Peter Bowering:

> The return to the experience of the past, beginning with the snapshots and memories on his forty-second birthday is thus the start of a process which eventually restores meaning to his life. In spite of this, most critics felt when the novel appeared that the method was unjustified. It must be admitted that the device

of time-shift is too mechanical; that the events of the past are recorded from outside by an impersonal narrator, whereas the treatment of time in the first chapter suggests a psychological method more after the manner of Virginia Woolf's *Mrs Dalloway*, in which the 'remembrance of things past' takes place in the mind of the protagonist.[5]

But the fact is that in the early chapters Anthony is not the only centre of consciousness: Helen too is one, independently of her status as an element in Anthony's consciousness. Her problems are similar to his (the book has a real thematic unity below the technical ambivalence, or inconsistency, if one chooses to see it that way), but she lives them out on her own. So, quite naturally, there are things in the novel that do not come within his ken: it is obvious, for instance, even in the early pages, that he knows nothing of Helen's abortion, or else he would not make the remark that makes her wince (Chapter 8, p. 61). It is only at the end of the novel, in the diary parts, that the dramatic method (with independent focussing characters) is abandoned for the I-narrative, a dogmatic one, and Anthony becomes the all-engulfing consciousness. Obviously, then, all the scenes cannot be recorded as remembered by him. But there is another reason for the objective treatment. Anthony's images from the past are not absorbed and fused into the living tissue of his mind: owing partly to their own nature (they remain distinct as memories) and partly to his efforts to keep them separate, alien from his present self, they are broken fragments of unassimilated, uncompromising reality—and that is why they have power to impose themselves and in the end to force a change upon him.

Anthony's relations with Helen have been placed from the start on a plane of unsentimental sensuality, compatible with good-fellowship, and even with some affection tempered by irony, but firmly excluding any emotional involvement. This agreement was accepted by Helen, though she longed for more warmth and feeling, and really imposed by Anthony, because it fell in with his mode of life: intellectual curiosity, no time or energy for emotions and responsibilities, an epicurean determination to enjoy each passing moment. The connexion between this attitude and his conception of personality is obvious enough from the first, but it is made explicit in Chapter 11, inserted just before the last chapter of the focal sequence. Anthony, in 1926, is reading through the section of his *Elements of Sociology* that deals with 'the individual and his concept of personality'; and he reflects on the modern breakdown of the concept, and on the succession of historical concepts that have been used to hold together what in experience is nothing but a formless collection of states, to prop up the humanist notion of a coherent continuity, and to fight the social dangers of psychological atomism. Among the moderns, Proust is mentioned (presumably in his destructive capacity), and also D. H. Lawrence: 'One of the most powerful personality-smashers, incidentally: there are no "characters" in his books' (Chapter 11, p. 98). Obviously, Huxley here remembers the letter in which Lawrence says: 'You mustn't look in my books for the old stable *ego* of the character', but for 'another *ego,* according to whose action the individual is unrecognizable, and passes through, as it were, allotropic states. . . .'[6] Before that, Anthony had toyed with the idea of 'the total man': it will recur to him at a later stage, and we shall then have more about Lawrence. But for the time he falls back on the comfortable persuasion that fits his philosophy of the *carpe diem:* 'Each man a succession of states enclosed in the flesh of his own side. And if any other principle of coherence were needed, there was always some absorbing and delightful intellectual interest, like sociology, for example, to supplement the persisting body' (Chapter 11, p. 99). And so, he prepares to meet Mary Amberley, whom he had sworn never to see again after Brian's suicide: but 'what right had the man of 1914 to commit the man of 1926?' (Chapter 11, p. 100). He is in fact rather curious to see what she will be like at forty-three—not suspecting that at the same age he himself will have to face the main crisis of his life and reform his views about the individual.

Anthony's uneasiness on that fateful day is due to a vague feeling of guilt ('wrong, irresponsible sensuality', Chapter 3, p. 19): he has been unfair to Helen, forced her to stifle her desire for affection; and he is all the more uneasy as she is obviously in the wrong mood, sarcastic and remote by turns. He cannot foresee that a shocking but minor incident will unaccountably (to him) bring their relationship to an end. But the fact is that Helen herself is going through an identity crisis. She is fighting down the feeling that her 'real I' is absent from her present life, with its detached, meaningless sensualities (Chapter 8, p. 59). When the dog crashes on the terrace and covers her with blood, she is suddenly possessed by a nauseous revulsion—from the blood, but also from Anthony, and her whole life. The violence of her reaction is obviously related to an incident previously narrated (Chapter 6, of 1926), when she had forced herself, out of pride and defiance, to steal a kidney in a shop, in spite of her disgust for the blood-oozing, pulpy thing; and it will later emerge that the dog and the kidney are parts of a complex of images, with the dead kitten on the day Gerry seduced her, and the foetus after her abortion, associated with physiology and sex. What she suddenly realizes is that she has forced herself, and again out of pride and defiance, to play the game of life with the common rules, and to develop, instead of a real personality, a being that is both empty and degraded; and from then on her evolution is a significant counterpoint of Anthony's own quest for identity.[7]

Anthony's reactions to Helen's hysteria can be summarized, since the outline is what matters here. Moved by pity, by the sense of having done her wrong, and even by a stirring of the love that once could have developed between them, he tries, clumsily enough, to convey something of his new feeling. But when he is repulsed, he does not insist: 'Give her time, he said to himself, give her time' (Chapter 12, p. 103). When she leaves the house, he lets her go: 'Later on, perhaps; this evening, when she had had time' (Chapter 12, p. 106). He tries to recover his old sanity, to 'explain away . . . that uprush of tenderness, that longing to know and love the suffering person within that all at once irrelevantly desirable body', and thinks of having her again later on the old terms (Chapter 12, p. 106). When he drives to the hotel to tell her that he has been a fool, and that he cares for her, she is gone. When he sends his love-letter, it comes too late: Helen receives it in a mood of reckless cynicism and turns it into ridicule.

Later on, as the chapters present one after the other the pictures of the past, objectively seen in the novel, and also objectively present in the mind of Anthony, who has so far refused to recognize that they relate in any significant way (other than mechanical remembering) to his present being, he is slowly compelled to admit that all these pictures, as they are passed in succession, reveal the same pattern of response and behaviour that has been his on the decisive day, and the behaviour of an Anthony who is inescapably *him*. All the episodes tell the same basic story in different forms. Anthony as a boy hates as well as admires Brian, 'because Horse-Face [Brian's nickname] has the courage of convictions which Anthony felt should also be *his* convictions—which, indeed, would be his convictions if only he could bring himself to have the courage of them' (Chapter 6, p. 56). In 1928, when Mary, deserted and ruined by Gerry, needs his help, he retreats, fearing her demands upon him: 'Fool, hypocrite, coward! But it was almost at a run that he made towards the door and hurried down the stairs.' On the way out, he meets Helen, who is struggling with the appalling certainty that she is pregnant; he feels that she is unhappy, but is only too glad to take advantage of her shyness to ignore it: 'But when he made another gesture of inquiring sympathy, she only shook her head again and turned away. "You'd better go", she said. Anthony hesitated a moment, then went. After all, she wanted him to go. Still feeling guilty, but with a sense of profound relief, he closed the front door behind him . . .' (Chapter 24, pp. 288–289). Anthony will never taste to the full the bitter consequences of his escapism: he will have no way to know that, by leaving Helen to her own devices and to her squalid abortion in Paris, he has helped to build up the disgust that will shatter their relationship. But a pattern, based on moral cowardice and the incapacity to go out of himself in an act of generosity, begins to cut across the division in time, and Huxley uses the juxtaposition of scenes to good effect. To give just one more instance, the chapter just discussed (Chapter 24) is preceded by a chapter belonging to 1914, in which Anthony, after kissing Joan and feeling ashamed for it, wants to get out as cheaply as possible: "'I shall write a letter.' "Courageous, as usual!" She [Mary] patted his knee' (Chapter 23, p. 280).

For, of course, the main instance of Anthony's typical behaviour is to be found in the story behind Brian's death, that part of the past he most tries to bury, to dissociate himself from, as being not his: passivity, and letting himself be directed by others and the pressure of circumstances; the urge to get away to France, or to Italy, in order not to face his responsibilities; the procrastination that leaves Brian, in his morbid state, to receive the full shock of the news in a letter from Joan; the moral weakness, when chance gives him a way to destroy all evidence of the suicide. What stands revealed and naked is his personality, what has slowly usurped the place of a possible better self: and the wish to ignore it was the half-unconscious motivation behind his philosophy of mental discontinuity.

To some extent, he has been the victim of predisposition. There is for Huxley such a thing as a psychological type; and Anthony, like Huxley, is 'Phlegmatic' (see the type described in *Ends and Means*), naturally averse to emotions, predisposed to detached intellectualism, tending to be, like Philip Quarles, 'an exceptionally intelligent tourist in the realm of feelings'.[8] But character is not fate, and for the mature Huxley life is not a comedy of humours, but a drama of the will. And here comes the paradox which introduces us to the second aspect or layer of the novel, and the phase of development which follows the crisis: awareness is but one step towards conversion, 'taking stock' (and not only for Anthony) is counting one's losses, and so facing the necessity of another policy. Huxley, again in his contemporary book of essays, neatly sums up the theme, which also underlies the structure: 'It is clear, then, that if we would transcend personality, we must first take the trouble to become persons. But we cannot become persons unless we make ourselves self-conscious.'[9] The due order in time is from self-awareness to transcendance. Here, given the peculiar structure of the book, the two phases are made to overlap—but it is also true, in fact, that they are not separate phases, for guilt attends consciousness from the first, and is already part of the process of change.

After Helen's departure, Anthony finds himself in a state of baffled misery, and he is suddenly reminded of a passage in Lawrence's *The Man Who Died*, that story about Christ risen from his tomb and wandering in the world again, conscious of his past mistakes (chastity, asceticism, the denial of life), and aware of 'the everlasting resoluteness of life', that 'vast invisible sea of strength', coming forth and asserting itself in all creatures (Chapter 26, pp. 233–234).[10] But Anthony's thoughts about the novelist he called a 'personality-smasher' now take a different turn: by asserting the supremacy of the dark, impersonal, sub-individual forces that are released in sex, he surrenders man's right to be more than a higher animal. Life is just the raw material out of which the self must be built up, not in separateness, but as consciousness rising out of the unconscious stream of vital energy. Lawrence, in his own way, carries on the same dehumanizing task in which Anthony was engaged when he was trying to get 'rid of responsibilities, of the need for consistency', trying in fact not to be there as an *I* in his own life (Chapter 26, p. 238). The words said by Helen on the roof a few days before have been impressed on his mind. So, the only way now is to make himself a person: but he feels that he lacks, 'the necessary courage, patience, strength of mind' (Chapter 26, p. 236).

That state of mind explains the temporary attraction of Mark Staithes, whom Anthony is going to follow on his Mexican expedition. Staithes is only briefly sketched as a character, but his contribution to the meaning of the novel is important. One general remark by Gerald Heard, who was Huxley's friend and the model for Dr Miller, may serve to define what he stands for: 'At first, Huxley had felt that he could defend himself against involvement, and so be guarded against heartbreak . . . He soon recognized that no discipline of conduct, or even training of character was enough. The one led to automatism, *the other to that bleak pride which is at best tragic and more often ruthless.*'[11] Anthony calls Mark 'tough-minded, firm of purpose', and embarks on his adventurous trip, not because he believes any more than Mark that any political or social good can result from it, but as a deliberate experiment in personality-building. The outcome is made clear in two contrasted scenes. First, Anthony is threatened by a young Mexican, and paralysed by his cowardice, which assumes the form of abject physical fear (Chapter 41). Later (in Chapter 51, near the end of the novel) Staithes gives an account of the way he crushed out all fear in him, of his exhilarating sense of power when he stood alone in front of a hundred armed peons, and then turned his back on them to walk slowly back to the house, knowing that his will had mastered them, and that they would not dare to shoot him. He has reached the state which is not yet within the reach of Anthony, and made his will an instrument both of self-control and of mastery over others. But in the same scene, Miller denounces the sterility of a self rooted in pride and the scorn of others; and Anthony, to Mark's surprise and dismay, declares his allegiance to Miller's views.

The reader is far less surprised, for in the final time-sequence in the novel, consisting in the passages from a diary started in 1934 but scattered all along the novel (the first extract being Chapter 11), Anthony has been exploring his, and Huxley's, new wisdom. The themes of his meditation are many, and closely related. He reflects on the situation of the Western world, with the conflicts of nationalisms, ideologies, and economic interests, with the temptation to solve all problems by force and to use bad means that can never achieve good ends; he points out the necessity of a change in the nature of man, of love conquering the aggressive instincts; he analyses the theory and describes the practice of pacifism, and, in Chapter 32, Miller provides in advance the positive counterpart of both Anthony's weakness and Staithes's sheer will-power by demonstrating the efficiency of nonresistance to violence; he insists on the necessity for each man to restore in himself the balance between the levels of his being, body, intelligence, and soul—training the body to control the impulses through the mind, adjusting himself to action, and orienting his action through an increasing awareness of that being within him that is 'other than one's ordinary self and immensely superior to it' (Chapter 54, p. 331). We are back to the problem of personality, and to Lawrence's idea of an underlying impersonal force, but what is here predicted is the union with a spiritual (not biological) reality which is the root of the 'better self' and the ground of man's individual being.

I am not going to discuss these ideas for their own sake, though no reader should feel inclined to take them lightly; I only wish to note their relevance to the central theme of personality, and comment on the diary form and the way the diary is grafted on to the novel. One could obviously take a dogmatic stand and pronounce that any novel fails in so far as it does not exclusively rely on an objective treatment which leaves the meaning implicit in the action—or again uphold consistency, and maintain that a combination of different approaches (here, the narrative and the meditative) impair the integrity and the credibility of a novel. But such narrow views about a genre which has flexibility for its main asset would leave out of the pale of genuine fiction not merely Huxley, who uses the device of the diary several times and most notably in *Point Counterpoint,* but a score of others, including D. H. Lawrence with his very outspoken spokesmen. It is far more useful to accept the device, and see how well or badly Huxley uses it.

One of the advantages resulting from Huxley's technique is that the pages of the diary are not thrown together into an indigestible lump at the end of the novel. Besides, these short sections are not fragments of a systematic essay: they truly have the character of personal notes jotted down, connected with the central theme, but leading up to it in various ways. And the style is often racy, sometimes brilliant. The reader may complain that the later Huxley, as essayist, or indeed novelist, tends to become dull, with all the old sparkle gone. It cannot be the result of a decay of powers, since in *Ends and Means* already, one year later, the style tends to be colourless and repetitive. One feels that Huxley is making a conscientious effort to write plainly and usefully: and the result is hardly an artistic gain. But here, the writer, for all his seriousness of purpose, is still in touch with the old irresponsible, playful self whose conversion he is describing—and he is still pleasantly infected by his manner.

The main point of the technique, however, is that the novelist was facing a real difficulty, and we can turn to his friend Christopher Isherwood for a discussion of the problem in another context:

> How am I going to show, in terms of dramatic fiction, that decisive moment at which my hero becomes aware of his vocation and decides to do something about it? . . . Aldous Huxley's *Time Must Have A Stop* avoids the moment altogether—making a huge jump from Sebastian the precocious, cowardly, uninhibited schoolboy to Sebastian the mature, meditative man, already far advanced in the practice of spiritual discrimination . . . It is all very well to use words like 'conversion' in an article for a religious magazine. They belong to an accepted terminology. I know that my readers will understand what I mean. But this kind of shorthand is never permissible for the novelist, with his mixed and highly sceptical audience. He has to explain, as though they had never been explained before, his hero's motives and objectives; and this, in a religious novel, is particularly difficult. How am I to prove that X is not merely insane when he turns his back on the whole scheme of pleasures, rewards, and satisfactions which are accepted by the Joneses, the Smiths, and the Browns, and goes in search of super-conscious, extraphenomenal experience? The only way I can see how to do this is with the help of the Joneses themselves. I must show that the average men and women of this world are searching, however unconsciously, for that same fundamental reality of which X has already had a glimpse.[12]

The procedure suggested by Isherwood is that adopted in *Eyeless In Gaza*, with the difference that in this case the Joneses are X's former self. We see Anthony 'searching, however unconsciously', for the 'fundamental reality' which, by the time he writes his diary, he has been able to have a glimpse of; and his groping in the darkness appears as a necessary part of his progress towards the light. Clearly, this method has the disadvantage of destroying most of the suspense about what is going to happen, but Huxley does not intend to arouse that form of interest and rather wants his reader to concentrate on the psychological and spiritual processes involved. True, we are made to wait a long time before we are told the story behind Brian's death (in Chapter 52) and the reason why the picture of the body at the foot of the cliff obsesses Anthony's mind from the first: in fact, one may feel that Huxley is stretching out the 1912–1914 sequence artificially to have at least that one hold on our curiosity of the common, too human sort. Still, the bare facts of death and guilt are soon given, even if the details are not filled in; and besides there is some psychological justification for the delay, since the past is remembered as well as narrated, and these are the images of the past and the part of the truth about himself that Anthony tries most hard to fight down and keep buried; and of course the delay enables Huxley to place in significant juxtaposition, or close proximity, the moment of deepest guilt (Chapter 52) and the hour of victory (Chapter 54). But, to take another episode, what could have been managed as a minor *coup de théâtre,* Anthony siding with Miller, while Staithes is still confident that he is his disciple, and no sign of the change has been given within the time-sequence—that possibility of suspense and surprise is killed off by the diary in which Miller's influence appears very clearly. But what Huxley achieves instead is giving depth to our vision. The reader sees Anthony caught between Staithes and Miller, showing no reaction, but watchful and impressed by the newcomer; and he feels the invisible working of grace that prepares him for the final choice. Besides, the diary itself is not a cold statement of the wisdom acquired but the dramatic record of a struggle to master the principles of a better life and to put them into practice. In the first entry (Chapter 2, p. 13), Anthony notes: 'This journal is a first step. Self-knowledge an essential preliminary to self-change.' And indeed the journal is the record of a progress; it takes us through the difficulties of character-building, down to the final scene of the novel. Anthony is then preparing to give a pacifist speech in Battersea, when he receives a note of warning from 'a group of patriotic Englishmen' who threaten him with physical violence. His first reactions are those of fear: for his own safety, and lest his degrading weakness should harm the cause he wants to serve. But Anthony is able to recognize the small voice of temptation which he had heard before in 1914, now urging him again to stay away, to go to the South of France for a while (compare Chapter 36, p. 296, and Chapter 54, p. 394); he can acknowledge it as being his, the voice of his unworthy self developed through the years, and he is at that final stage prepared to disregard it and break up the pattern of response. So, after a short meditation which recapitulates the main themes of the diary, he feels serenely ready to face whatever may be in store for him.

What Anthony had suspected in the beginning, that the reason for the preservation of the past in his mind was 'not before the event, but after it, in what had been the future' (Chapter 3, p. 19) turns out to be true. The past finds its meaning, it makes sense, in the consciousness that embraces it and sees it as a puzzle where at last every bit of the record has fallen into its appointed place. And this finality which Anthony had tried to dismiss as unbearable, is in fact our best hope. The past is preserved not in order to torture us, but to lead us through self-torture to salvation. It must take us from the meaningless succession of our becoming to the consciousness of a pattern cutting across time, which we acknowledge as our consistent being in time, and to the conviction that this being is to be transcended by a timeless act of the will.

It is clear, I hope, that the structure of the novel is a projection of the theme, that it disposes the events according to the principle of finality, the ends rather than the means. I do not imply that the structure has been assembled and adjusted by Huxley with meticulous craftsmanship all the way. What he seems to have done is to put together in the beginning the chapters concerning the focal day (Chapters 1, 3, 8, 12), with some chapters from other sequences that could suffice to define the theme of personality: Chapter 7 of 1934 deals with Anthony's past satisfaction in 'the debunking of man' and his present conviction that man can be reconditioned, while Chapter 11 of 1926 is about the breakdown of the concept of personality. The early sequence, which is important as an introduction but has less bearing on the crisis, is dismissed quickly (Chapters 4, 6, 9, 15). After that, the chapters can be mixed more freely, and Huxley seems to have mostly in mind the principle of significant proximity, with a view to bringing out thematic connexions again (Chapter 24 of 1927, Chapter 26 of 1933, once more on personality), to stress a dramatic point (the contrast between the two pictures of Mary in Chapter 33 of 1914 and Chapter 34 of 1928), or to throw light on what is going to be important (Staithes explained in Chapter 22 before he begins to play a central role in Chapter 26 and after). A few similar instances have been mentioned earlier, and some others are indicated in Miss Phyllis Bentley's article. But all this is bound to be felt as being mere cleverness if the purpose of the thing as a whole is not clearly grasped.

And it is a pity that too many readers have been put off by a structure they held to be pointless and have refused to take the novel on its own very acceptable terms: for it has much to offer to those who are willing to get along with it. In comparison with *Point Counterpoint*, which remains Huxley's best-known novel, it comes out as richer and better even in some of its characterization. Mary Amberley is every bit as good as Lucy Tantamount, and is all the more effective for being tracked down to the bottom of her too credible degradation. Staithes is much more subtly and convincingly characterized than his melodramatic counterpart, Spandrell. More generally, the structure gives us the full shock, the pathos as well as the meaning, of getting older in moving from the gay twenties into the anxious decade of depression and international tension. But, of course, *Point Counterpoint* has its claims to greater popularity: a single narrative method, more variety in the stories, and more of the lighter tone of Huxley's early manner. And Lawrence may illustrate another difference: Rampion, in *Point Counterpoint*, is a very good animation of him as a living character, as the prophet against the iniquities of the civilized man; *Eyeless In Gaza* certainly goes much deeper, to the roots of Lawrence's view of life (even though some points might be questioned), but it does so by means of a discussion of ideas.

It would be wrong, however, to suggest that this novel is abstract and artificial. It offers ideas, true, and the story itself is organized for a purpose. But *Eyeless In Gaza* is a genuine novel, not an essay on good and evil using the narrative form to provide a fable. In his final meditation, Anthony remains acutely aware of the paradox 'that unity was the beginning and unity the end, and that in the meantime the condition of life and all existence was separation, which was equivalent to evil' (Chapter 54, p. 398). Transcendence is self-destruction, ultimately: there is a contradiction between the aspiration of the personality and the very condition of its existence as personal; pure being is unconsciousness, and all consciousness is self-consciousness, that is consciousness of a self in separation. There is no way out; and indeed the whole novel gives us the permanent sense that no pattern, however elaborate, can hold and contain life, that there are areas of experience that can never be fully rationalized and spiritualized, that the conquest of the self is an endless task, because it is a contradictory one, that there is more to life than is filtered through into the final wisdom. And the very fact that the structure of the novel, elaborate as it is, leaves room for chance in the arrangement and a superfluity of meaning besides or against the abstract purpose of the novel, which it is designed to bring home, shows that Aldous Huxley is still doing the job of a real novelist, describing people not in circumstances arranged to fit a preconceived interpretation, but struggling with a reality that can never be fully controlled, in the novel and beyond it.

Notes

1. All references are to the Penguin edition of the novel; but the number of the chapter is also given, and since the chapters are fairly short any quotation should be easy to trace.

2. Harold H. Watts, *Aldous Huxley* (New York, 1969), p. 90.

3. Phyllis Bentley, 'The Structure of *Eyeless In Gaza*', *The English Journal* (College Edition), 26 (1937), pp. 130 ff.

4. This division is to some extent arbitrary as well as convenient. What I call (D) consists of only two chapters and can be taken as a mere introduction to (E); there is only a gap of three months between (E) and (F), the difference between the two being technical (from narrative to diary) more than chronological. So, one can choose to lump together (D), (E), and (F) into a single period. But the only objective definition of a sequence is that given below (a sequence is in chronological order) and it does not apply if you take (D) and (E), or (E) and (F), as forming one sequence.

5. Peter Bowering, *Aldous Huxley: A Study of the Major Novels* (London, 1968), p. 117. Good books on Huxley being few, it is worth noting that this one is excellent. The chapter devoted to *Eyeless in Gaza* is a very perceptive and comprehensive study of more aspects than I deal with. Mr Bowering, however, does not stress the centrality of the theme of 'personality', and consequently does not see it (as I do) as the unifying principle underlying the structure.

6. Letter to Edward Garnett, 5 June 1914, about *The Rainbow*. Huxley had been co-editor of *The Letters of D. H. Lawrence* in 1932.

7. I have no space to develop this idea, but wish at least to refer the reader to Chapter 38, where Anthony in his phase of transcendence meets Helen who is in her phase of awareness.

8. *Point Counter Point* (1963 edition, p. 108).

9. *Ends and Means* (1937), (1966 edition, p. 325).

10. One realizes here that Eustace Barnacle's after-death stream of higher consciousness in *Time Must Have Stop* was probably conceived as a remake and correction of Lawrence's story in the light of the perennial philosophy.

11. Gerald Heard, in his contribution to *Aldous Huxley: A Memorial Volume*, edited by Sir Julian Huxley (London, 1965), pp. 103–104; my italics.

12. Christopher Isherwood, in an article published among other essays including some by Gerald Heard and Huxley himself, in *Vedanta For Modern Man*, edited by Christopher Isherwood (London, 1945), and collected in *Exhumations* (London, 1966), pp. 117–118.

JEROME MECKIER

Quarles among the Monkeys: Huxley's Zoological Novels

I

Aldous Huxley chose names for his characters carefully. Occasionally these names had an allusive quality. Bruno Rontini, Sebastian's Virgil for Rome and the spiritual life in *Time Must Have a Stop*, suggests Brunetto Latini, Dante's mentor, a meaningful suggestion in a novel full of references to *The Divine Comedy*. In *Point Counter Point*, Philip Quarles's name constitutes an allusion more esoteric but no less significant. It sounds like *quarrel*, appropriate for a character who argues with his wife and debates with friends. But it also refers to an anonymous eighteenth-century work entitled *The Hermit: Or, The Unparallel'd Sufferings and Surprising Adventures of Mr Philip Quarll, an Englishman.*[1] In this Robinson Crusoe story of a man shipwrecked on an island, Quarll has monkeys for companions instead of the dependable Friday. The relevance of the animal imagery in *Point Counter Point*, the most famous of Huxley's zoological novels, becomes clearer immediately. Though in London, Huxley's Quarles is still among the apes. Anti-evolutionary satire pervades Huxley's novel: man not only comes from the apes, he continues to act like one. In *Man's Place in Nature* (1863), T. H. Huxley wrote about the 'man-like Apes', but his grandson's subject is ape-like man. Simian situations also occur in several of Huxley's later novels. Quarles's plight (and Quarll's) apparently fascinated Huxley throughout his long career, for he treated the subject in a series of variations. In *Point Counter*

The Modern Language Review, Volume 68, Number 2 (April 1973): pp. 268–282. Copyright © 1973 Modern Humanities Research Association.

Point (1928), the animal imagery emphasizes the arrested development of alleged human beings; from then on, zoological conditions exist when a protagonist with spiritual awareness is trapped among unenlightened characters belonging to a prior stage of evolution.

But did Huxley read *The Hermit*? Anyone familiar with the range of his reading will find the question impertinent. Nevertheless, there is more evidence than the striking similarity in the names of Quarll and Quarles, both with the Christian name Philip. *The Hermit* first appeared in 1727, an obvious imitation of Defoe. Huxley could have examined this book in the course of his studies at Oxford, where he wrote a paper on the development of satire.[2] More likely, he discovered it through Dickens, who mentions it three times in ways that indicate it was still part of the popular culture. Mr Slug's educational survey in *The Full Report of the First Meeting of the Mudfog Association* (1837) states that 'the proportion of Robinson Crusoes to Philip Quarlls was as four and a half to one'.[3] Slug means that nearly five times as many students have read the former, but his clumsy report sounds like a census. Dickens refers to *The Hermit* again in 'A Christmas Tree', where a review of fanciful books includes 'Robinson Crusoe on his desert island, Philip Quarll among the monkeys'.[4] The crucial reference occurs in *Martin Chuzzlewit* when Tom Pinch, visiting Salisbury, looks into a bookstore displaying children's books: there 'poor Robinson Crusoe stood alone in his might, with dog and hatchet, goat-skin cap and fowling-pieces, calmly surveying Philip Quarll and the host of imitators around him' (Chapter 5).[5] The Dickens novel Huxley was reading in 1925 was *Martin ChuzzleWit*.[6]

For internal evidence, there is the early scene in India where Philip and Elinor, having dined with Mr Sita Ram, discuss Philip's emotional shortcomings on the drive home. Clearly, Philip has always been a hermit, no matter how populated his surroundings. 'All his life long', Huxley narrates, 'he had walked in a solitude, in a private void, into which nobody, not his mother, not his friends, not his lovers had ever been permitted to enter' (Chapter 6).[7] Huxley and Elinor conclude that Philip, 'in the ordinary daily world of human contacts . . . was curiously like a foreigner, uneasily not at home among his fellows, finding it difficult or impossible to enter into communication with any but those who could speak his native intellectual language of ideas'. The time then shifts as Quarles, still listening to his wife, recalls a prior discussion in which he told Elinor 'about Koehler's book on the apes'.[8] Elinor had retorted: 'You're like a monkey on the superman side of humanity . . . Almost human, like those poor chimpanzees. The only difference is that *they're* trying to think up with their feelings and instincts, and *you're* trying to feel down with your intellect. Almost human. Trembling on the verge, my poor Phil.' Like Quarll, Philip is a hermit. He has difficulty communicating with others and is as far above the human level intellectually as monkeys are below it. The monkeys are trying to evolve further, while Quarles wants to recover abilities his evolution has caused him to leave behind. Elinor places Philip among the monkeys. Compared to them, he seems to be evolution's apex; but the true ideal lies somewhere in between.

The above passage indicates that the and-evolutionary satire in *Point Counter Point* works two ways: against the other characters (or monkeys), who cannot match Philip's intelligence, and against Philip, who has lost all contact with his own animality, with half of his human nature. Autobiography is important here. The picture of Quarll among his monkeys became a satiric analogue for Quarles amidst the artists and bohemians of the allegedly 'bright' 1920s. In that same picture, Huxley also saw himself. With a mind capacious and erudite as any in the present century, he may have felt like another Philip Quarll. He may have seen himself as an advanced evolutionary product condemned to live among men so underdeveloped that they resembled apes. However, Quarles's advance in intellect and perhaps his own, Huxley feared, had been paid for by a loss of feeling and emotion. This loss makes Quarles's daily human contacts, whereby an intellectual could be influential, an ordeal and a failure.[9] Within the novel, Quarles remains 'trembling on the verge'; he fails to feel down to the human level or to make the animal-like characters think up to it.

The Hermit does not strike the modern reader as good satire, though it manifests some subtlety. Where shipwreck merely brought out Crusoe's practical Protestantism, Quarll's misfortunes produce a genuine spiritual transformation. There is a second slap at Defoe in the substitution of apes, particularly Quarll's beloved Beaufidele, for Friday. The parody reveals what Defoe's imitator thought of Friday's plausibility. Huxley does not borrow from this work in a literal sense. It is the notion of a man living out his existence among lower forms of life that appealed to his imagination. The narrator in *The Hermit* learns of Quarll from Mr Dorington. Book One recounts the discovery. Dorington, Alvarado, and a young boy explore what they assume is an uninhabited South Sea Island. They are impressed initially by the beautiful monkeys and then by Quarll, a venerable Englishman with a white beard who has spent more than half a century on the island. Books Two and Three, consisting of the manuscript Quarll entrusted to Dorington, tell of earlier events. Book Two chronicles Quarll's dissolute London life and moral decline. Born in a parish of St Giles, he is for a time the accomplice of a housebreaker in an episode that foreshadows *Oliver Twist*. At one point, Quarll marries a famous prostitute; at another he is sentenced at the Old Bailey for having three wives at once. Here the parody seems directed at *Moll Flanders*. Later, Quarll, now a merchant, is shipwrecked off the coast of Mexico. In Book Three, Quarll relates how he developed a sense of religion on the island. Many of his adventures, such as the raid by Indians, recall

Robinson Crusoe; but the stress falls on the regenerated Quarll who sees his entire life as an illustration of 'the wonderful effects of providence'. Naturally, Quarll remains behind when Dorington and his party depart.

Whoever wrote *The Hermit* was either inferior to Defoe or else made Quarll a terrible bore in order to satirize Crusoe's loquaciousness. Quarll's propensity for preaching, his insistence that his life provides a moral, endear him to few readers. Despite his isolation, Quarll still moralizes in the manner of a London gentleman as he formulates maxims that include prohibitions against drinking and gambling, activities for which he has had no opportunities in fifty years. More important for Huxley is Quarll's endorsement of a life 'remote from the world' and 'without human assistance'. Were he to be made emperor of the universe, Quarll insists, he would not be concerned with the world again. His statements remind one of the conclusion to Huxley's *Those Barren Leaves* (1925) where Calamy, a potential mystic, isolated himself from the world. But this is a solution to life's problems that *Point Counter Point* abandons, perhaps due to Huxley's friendship (beginning in 1926) with D. H. Lawrence.[10] Huxley's novel endorses what he takes to be Lawrence's ideal of the whole man, fully developed in mind and body. Therefore, although Quarll relishes his situation, Quarles appears trapped in the midst of a self-styled intelligentsia whose members Huxley equates with lower forms of life. While Philip satirizes the other characters by likening them to animals, Huxley classifies him, significantly, as a 'hermit-crab' (22), whose isolation is partially his own fault. By failing to develop into the complete man Rampion recommends, the unemotional Quarles earns himself an unattractive place in the animal kingdom. There is added irony in the fact that Quarles is truly among predators and sub-humans, whereas Quarll finds the island's monkeys a blessing.

II

Clearly, *Point Counter Point* is a zoo. Nearly every character exhibits animal traits, so that the novel approaches the traditional bestiary. It becomes impossible to tell whether these are humans behaving as animals or animals displaying some human attributes. Hilda Tantamount playfully calls John Bidlake a 'beast', and he seriously regards Mary Betterton, his former mistress, as a 'monster' (2). Lord Edward rushes towards the sounds of Bach as would a 'dog with the smell of rabbits in his nostrils'. To the startled concertgoers he appears to be 'one of those monsters which haunt the palaces of only the best and most aristocratic families. The Beastie of Glamis, the Minotaur itself could hardly have aroused more interest' (3). This motif reappears when Quarles notes that characters in a novel of ideas are 'slightly monstrous', and that 'living with monsters', as he must do, 'becomes rather tiresome' (22). Beatrice's speech rhythms are compared to pecks from a goose (11), but Willie Weaver classes her among batrachians. Walter Bidlake compares parties, like the one at Tantamount House that inaugurates the novel, to a 'jungle of innumerable trees and dangling creepers' where guests resemble 'parrots' and chattering monkeys' (5); yet Walter himself repeatedly displays 'dog-like fidelity' to Lucy (6).

Characters not only resemble animals but argue in animal analogies. Mary Rampion feels the upper classes 'live like ostriches', while Illidge justifies man's waste of resources by observing that after a battle or plague hyenas and vultures 'take advantage of the abundance to overeat' (11). As comparisons of this sort accumulate, one concludes that the characters, perhaps unwittingly, depict themselves as a species in no way superior to the animal kingdom. Old Bidlake's critique of women, for example, compares them to bloodhounds and oxen (4). Even Rampion, Huxley's sage, refers to Whitman's lines about the wise life-style of animals to prove his contention that one must be the perfect human and the perfect animal simultaneously (9). But the satire increases in complexity here since Rampion feels men have lost or perverted the natural, healthy animal element in their make-up. The novel agrees with him. Burlap is 'vulture', 'parasite', and 'leech' (16), and Spandrell a 'dung beetle's maggot' (17). Sidney Quarles behaves like a 'sepia' or cuttlefish (20) as he tries to cover up his cheap sexual escapades. Philip, watching Elinor interview Vicar and Mrs Truby, exhibits the pros and cons of the zoologist's stance by feeling 'like Fabre[11] among the coleoptera' (19): he can observe the oddity of the situation but cannot correct it except in the satiric novel he eventually decides to write. Even while dictating letters, Webley is predatory. He paces like a 'restless lion' (32). A believer in the right to rule of the fittest and strongest, Webley personifies Huxley's insight that English Fascism was the political perversion of Darwin's biological theory. Ironically, the lion-like leader of the Freemen is murdered by the dung-beetle Spandrell, thus upsetting Darwin's theory and Webley's simultaneously.

What takes time developing, however, is Quarles's awareness of his situation and his resolution to become a zoological novelist. Molly D'Exergillod refers to Quarles as a 'Zoologist of fiction' quite early (7), but not until Chapter Fourteen does Quarles begin sketching out the novel that will satirize the claim of his friends to human status. At first, the novel will centre only on Lucy 'the man-eater' and her victim, Walter. By Chapter Twenty-two, when the zoological novel is apparently well under way, Philip has become more ambitious. He informs Elinor that 'he shall really have to write a modern Bestiary' one of these days. The last detailed account of the progress of this bestiary shows Philip incorporating episodes about, among others, Spandrell and Webley (26). By the time Philip has decided to become a zoological novelist, *Point Counter Point* already is a zoological novel. The conclusions of Huxley outside the novel coincide with those of Quarles inside it.

Two additional similarities between Quarles and Quarll deserve mention. Both keep journals or diaries and both inhabit islands. Quarles, in fact, spends nearly half the novel sailing from India to England. He lands in Chapter Nineteen under the impression that he has come home. As he realizes he is actually shipwrecked among the less than human, Huxley's picture of Quarles among the monkeys becomes a metaphor for the tragicomic situation of the sane intellectual in a bestial modern world. Ironically, as the situation becomes clearer to Quarles, his plight appears more hopeless. Only Huxley, whose Olympian point of view places him outside and above the novel, can use anti-evolutionary satire to remind his readers of man's failure to realize his biological destiny. Only he can incorporate Quarles's savage satire, admittedly a strident melody, into a larger contrapuntal composition which includes Rampion's recipes for wholeness and, even if in ironic contexts, allusions to the kingdom of heaven.

Quarles's zoological speculations relate in large part to the novel's marriage theme. Chapter Twenty-one contains a delightful counterpointing. First, Marjorie Carling and Elinor discuss Walter's infatuation with Lucy. Walter is unkindly compared to a pig, but Elinor wishes her unemotional husband was less of a hermit-crab. The scene then shifts to Philip researching his novel. He is reading Tate Regan's 'account of pygmy parasitic males in three species of Cerativid Anglerfishes'.[12] He makes a note in his pocket diary to compare Walter chasing Lucy to female angler-fishes carrying dwarf parasitic males attached to their bodies. Once again, the conclusions towards which Philip works are already reflected in the novel Huxley is writing. None of the males in *Point Counter Point* escape classification as parasites. Walter, Burlap, Old Bidlake, Spandrell, Sidney Quarles—all have parasitic tendencies where women are concerned. Even Rampion learned much of his Grecian approach to life from Mary. Ironically, Philip is worst of all, since his entire emotional life seems to depend on Elinor's. As did Lawrence (who published *Lady Chatterley's Lover* in the same year that *Point Counter Point* appeared), Huxley laments the world's loss of masculine vitality. The counterpoint moves from talk about the enslaved Walter to Quarles's role for Walter in his novel, but the fact that Philip is himself a variation of the problem he is satirizing adds a fourth factor to the juxtapositions: Marjorie's Walter (pig), Philip's Walter (dwarf anglerfish), Elinor's Quarles (hermit-crab), and Quarles the parasite. *Point Counter Point* introduces one unsatisfactory marriage after another, all of them parodic variations on the relationship between Mark and Mary Rampion, the main marriage melody lost amid a cacophony of perverse alternatives. Instead of promoting harmony, the marriage relationship has become one-sided, a vehicle for dissonance and masculine deterioration. Long-term relationships, a differentiating factor between the human and animal kingdoms, suffer distortion or survive precariously. When Mellors realizes he has found in Connie a potential mate, he sees the two of them pitted against the 'monkeyishness of the world' (17); but in Huxley, nearly all the males who take sexual partners seem to regress to a less attractive stage of evolution.

III

Philip's zoological approach to marriage makes his research part of a larger composition in which he again becomes a suitable target for his own satire. Even as he invented the zoological stance, Huxley exposed its limitations. Like Quarles himself, the zoological perspective is incomplete. Though excellent for satiric purposes, it cannot furnish all the modulations of mood, the variety of scene and temperament demanded by Quarles's other obsession, his theory of counterpoint. The more he becomes a zoological novelist, the less he remains, except in theory, a contrapuntalist; the more eccentric and one-pointed his artistry, the more Peacockian a character he seems.

One of the ways of achieving counterpoint, Quarles states, is 'to consider the events of the story in their various aspects—scientific, economical, religious, metaphysical, etc.' (22). The novelist is supposed to 'modulate from one to the other—as from the aesthetic to the physico-chemical aspect of things, from the religious to the aesthetic to the physiological or financial'. The bestiary aspect is one of many for Huxley, but for Quarles it develops into the only one. Philip's obsession, in some ways a valid one, allows Huxley to entertain the idea that life's basis, in practice if not in theory, is physiological and biological, that men act as if they were determined and controlled by their physiology. Through Quarles, Huxley attacks romantic, aesthetic conceptions of life with an hypothesis that goes beyond Naturalism. The animal imagery supports this hypothesis as it demotes human beings from their paramount position in the scheme of evolution. Quarles observes with a shock that Lucy's tongue and gums, when she smiles, are remarkably pale by comparison with her painted mouth. 'And then', writes Quarles, 'without transition, I was standing in front of those sacred crocodiles in the palace gardens at Jaipur' (22). In Quarles's novel, Walter is to make this contrapuntal connexion. The *femme fatale* becomes an ugly crocodile; the personification of the liberated 1920s, the advocate of good times and no more moral baggage than the modern aeroplane allows per person, experiences a sudden metamorphosis that reveals her true nature as a predatory beast. By such 'abrupt transitions' is counterpoint realized and the 'musicalization of fiction' (21) given its satiric, anti-evolutionary melody.

Another method of attaining counterpoint is to include a novelist in one's novel. Quarles writes: 'Put a novelist into the novel. He justifies aesthetic generalizations . . . And if you have him telling parts of the same story as you are, you can make a variation on the theme' (21). Throughout *Point Counter Point*, Quarles's conclusions within the novel corroborate Huxley's.

But the novelist that Quarles puts into his novel is different from the one Huxley inserts in his. Where Huxley's Philip initially advances a number of theories about the novel, Quarles's novelist is as one-pointed as Quarles is becoming. In his notebook Philip writes that

> Since reading Alverdes and Wheeler[13] I have quite decided that my novelist must be an amateur zoologist. Or, better still, a professional zoologist who is writing a novel in his spare time. His approach will be strictly biological. He will be constantly passing from the termitary to the drawing room and the factory, and back again. (26)

Huxley's approach is never 'strictly biological'. The multiplicity of life, the complexity of 'the human fugue' (2), forbade such a narrow approach. Through Quarles, Huxley could gain all the satiric advantages of such a narrow approach while suggesting that a man who senses he is trapped among lower forms of life deteriorates if he does nothing but mortify his alleged peers. The move from drawing room to termitary is one Huxley also makes. That Quarles and his novelist also do so amounts to an aesthetic generalization about the life-style of the so-called bright, young moderns. Nevertheless, the potentially positive elements in Huxley's conceptions of life as an orchestra gone haywire or a musical composition badly played (2) never yield entirely to the idea of life as a zoo. The novel begins with Bach and ends with Beethoven. In between the music of these creators of synthesis and harmony, Huxley displays his menagerie. But the activities of the animals never completely cancel the music or the possibility of life recovering its harmony. Ultimately, there is something too ant-like in the constant passing Quarles plans for his novelist.

The satiric advantages of permitting Quarles to accentuate the zoological aspect are indeed numerous. First, the animal imagery undermines the ideas and intellectual pretensions of most of the characters. Huxley's novel of ideas exhibits one of its finest ironies in the continual contrast of the characters' lofty concepts with their base behaviour. Sidney Quarles does research on democracy, Burlap writes a life of St Francis, Walter Bidlake considers himself an idealist in the Shelleyian mode—but all three display unattractive animal qualities and possess perverse sexual tastes. Or consider the earlier instance of Mr Scogan in *Crome Yellow* (1921). He describes the Rational State of the future (22), but Huxley compares him to a bird-lizard with beaked nose, scaly skin, and the hands of a crocodile (3), an evolutionary throwback. Scogan also believes in a laissez-faire sexual code. Disguised during Crome's charity fair as the Sorceress Sesostris, a fortune teller, he informs one of his attractive customers of her imminent affair with a man she will meet next

Sunday at six o'clock on a certain footpath (27). He will, of course, keep the appointment himself. Secondly, then, the animal imagery allows Huxley and Quarles to register their disgust with the sexual conduct of the allegedly liberated moderns. Man's origins, the comparatively short distance he has travelled since, and his tendency to revert to them, are matters Huxley never lets his readers or characters forget.

Thirdly, by stressing the arrested development of the majority of the characters, the imagery completes a threefold pattern: base animality, childishness, criminals and victims.

The suggestion that the characters have made a mess of evolution ties in with the charge that they have never grown up. Lord Edward, for example, is 'a fossil child' (2), old and wise in the laboratory but so emotionally retarded that he appears to be an overgrown child or an evolutionary throwback. The famous scene that concludes the novel—Burlap and Beatrice taking their baths together—is an ingenious mixture of childishness and perversity on the part of the parasite Burlap and the frog-like Beatrice.

Animal characteristics indicate arrested development but do not rule out aggressive behaviour. An extensive criminal-victim pattern runs through the novel.[14] There are predatory characters and those who become their prey. Walter preys on Marjorie, whom he ignores after persuading her to leave her husband. But Walter is in turn Lucy's prey, so that he, like others in the novel, is both criminal and victim. He succumbs to Lucy, who is both man-eating crocodile and perverted zoologist, 'She enjoyed experimenting, not with frogs and guinea pigs, but with human beings' (7). The criminal-victim pattern—Lucy preying on Walter, Webley stalking Elinor—is Huxley's version of the struggle for existence. T. H. Huxley hoped to substitute the ethical process for the cosmic one, to replace natural man with ethical man. Human beings were to escape their place in the animal kingdom, where 'non-moral evolution' predominates, and 'establish a kingdom of Man, governed upon the principle of moral evolution'.[15] Aldous Huxley's animal imagery serves as a critical commentary on his grandfather's dream. The characters in *Point Counter Point* remain subject to 'diverse laws'. They belong to society, but their antics are those of the animal kingdom.

Finally, the animal imagery re-enforces Huxley's amazed awareness of life's multiplicity. Human beings appear so astonishingly various that the possibility of achieving harmony, of constructing a one from the many, seems slight. Progress, evolution, and the perfectability of man are interconnecting myths which the animal imagery challenges. To accentuate the contrapuntal, seemingly chaotic qualities of life, Huxley breaks down the abstraction 'Man' into a variety of animal types that shows one man as different from another and as hostile to him as the lion is to the lamb. If life is to become harmonious, it will have to strive towards a contrapuntal harmony—perhaps the most intricate kind—in which variations support rather than oppose one another.

That Huxley should have seemed to his initial readers the voice of a generation embarking on new freedoms while rejecting values of the past now seems incredible. The older generation in *Point Counter Point* is in the main foolish and hypocritical, but the bright young moderns are no improvement. Both generations remind Huxley of a zoo, even if he makes Quarles's zoology seem excessive. The tenor of the times has simply become more blatantly bestial and perverse, the lies the Victorians lived by, including T. H. Huxley's hope for controlled evolution, more clearly absurd. By their life-styles the characters in *Point Counter Point* imply that history displays no moral order or development. For every advance, there is a step backward, so that point counter point means, among other things, biological deadlock: the professed modernity of the characters is undercut by a biological slippage, a loss of ground.

IV

Several characters in Huxley's novel compete for the position of resident zoologist. Only Rampion establishes his philosophy as a possible alternative to Quarles's zoology. Mark, too, is among the monkeys, but he has both the insight and the life-style the human being must preserve if he is to survive and exert influence in the zoo of the modern world. The characters who resort to animal analogies in their discussions become ludicrous variations of Quarles. Lucy intimates that she will turn to science when she grows old: 'Isn't there such a thing as human zoology?' she asks (12). The real zoologist in the novel is Lord Edward. Yet his experiments seem pale by comparison with the remarks of Quarles and Rampion. Lord Edward tries to demonstrate the unity of life, despite its apparent diversity, by grafting a tail on to the foreleg of a newt (3). He unwittingly parodies the evolutionary process by reducing to absurdity the search for life's unifying principle. His absorption in futile studies of growth and development have ironically kept him from evolving into a mature human being. Philip is the zoological novelist as unmitigated satirist, whose outrage at the bestial behaviour of his friends compels him toward the dehumanization of his characters. Just as Philip likens human mating habits to those of animals (6), Rampion compares Walter to a 'rabbit' and Lucy to a 'cobra' (11). Huxley calls this 'Rampion's zoology'. However, Mark's zoology is 'wholly symbolical'; it has its philosophical and optimistic aspects. Rampion is virulently satiric, yet the animal imagery he employs is figurative, akin to its use in Shakespeare. Quarles's is scientific: he literally reduces characters to their pre-human ancestors. Philip's tone is more Ben Jonson's in *Volpone*. Though Quarles yearns toward the completeness Rampion advocates, in practice he condemns any trace of animality in his friends. For Mark, as for Lawrence, animality is often also vitality. Thus only Rampion can suggest how a human being can incorporate his undeniable animal nature into a personality that functions as a coherent whole; indeed, he insists that the characters *must* do this if they are to recover the vitality and balance they lost by neglecting their animal natures, thereby allowing those natures to become perverse. One can (and probably should) construe Quarles's satire as an effort to remind his readers of their position as the apex of creation. But the satire is so unsparing that one feels Philip himself is no longer sure of man's ascendancy. His satiric zoology needs Rampion's 'symbolical' variety to rescue it from despair, to humanize it; while Rampion's satiric sketches, though powerful, are not rooted in Philip's knowledge of science. Subsequently, when Huxley's infatuation with Lawrence, on whom Rampion is based, comes to an end, no return to purely satirical zoology occurs. The philosophical element is retained under a new guise. In the later novels, a character can choose to cultivate his spiritual essence instead of his ape-like qualities. Philosophical and satirical zoology are never separated again.

Rampion's zoology explores the connexions between evolution and the ideal of the complete, fully human man. Two of Mark's sketches become *Point Counter Point* in miniature. These satirical caricatures appear to have been modelled on Lawrence's allegorical paintings. 'Fossils of the Past and Fossils of the Present' rejects evolution altogether (16). Man is not depicted as life's end product but as an unsatisfactory species no more suited for survival than the ichthyosaurus. The evolutionary line, drawn as 'a magnificently sweeping S', is a 'procession of monsters', dinosaurs at the start, and in the van 'human monsters, huge-headed creatures, without limbs or bodies'. In Rampion's scheme, men, having forfeited the proper use of their physical natures, appear too cerebral to survive, just as the dinosaurs perished from an excess of body. Appropriately, Burlap, to whom Rampion shows the sketch, is a prime example of a character whose perverse sexual life is controlled by his warped mentality.

The sketch containing two outlines of history, one by H. G. Wells and the other by Rampion, is more intriguing. The small monkey at the start of the outline according to Wells yields to larger figures that terminate in the god-like personalities of the twentieth century. Rampion's version, one of peaks and declines, shows the monkey becoming a large Greek. Renaissance figures are also impressive. From there, stature declines: 'The Victorians had begun to be dwarfish and misshapen. Their twentieth-century successors were abortions' (6). The future promises 'a diminishing company of little gargoyles and foetuses with heads too large for their squelchy bodies, the tails of apes, and the faces of our most eminent contemporaries'. Where Quarles compares modern life to a zoo, Rampion negates the theory of evolution itself. Both are moralists who engage in anti-evolutionary satire, with Quarles the more savage of the two. Yet Quarles criticizes characters whose behaviour frustrates the process Darwin outlined, whereas Rampion overthrows Darwin completely. Mark's is not a scientific zoology. Although his sketch measures fluctuations in the realization of human potential, it also denies the biological evolution of species. Rampion shatters the comfortable optimism of Wells, yet his drawing is philosophical zoology: good satire, bad science.

Subsequently, Huxley settles on a compound of attitudes that combine philosophical and scientific zoology. This compound echoes the scepticism of Lawrence and Rampion while incorporating the optimistic possibilities T. H. Huxley discussed. Lawrence flatly disbelieved in evolution.[16] Darwinian theory contradicted all of his intuitions about the drying up of vitality in modern life. Rampion's second sketch reflects his scepticism. It also reflects, by implication, T. H. Huxley's insistence that steps forward in the evolutionary process can be the result of effort rather than chance. How else did the monkey become the Greek? Ultimately, Huxley sides more with his grandfather and with Quarles, whose zoology, though at times too pessimistic, rests on scientific assumptions. Aldous Huxley's anti-evolutionary satire thus takes the position that Darwin was not wrong, that man often frustrates evolution, but that the process makes headway here and there through the efforts of enlightened individuals. They combine Quarles's instincts for satire with Rampion's concern for an improved humanity. By the close of his career, Huxley awaits the next step in the evolutionary process, an advance of mind that could make mystical awareness possible for all men.[17] Rampion to the contrary, Huxley eventually returns to man's mind as the factor that separates him from the ape. In the Epilogue to *Time Must Have a Stop* (1944), Sebastian Barnack formulates Huxley's final position on evolution. Sebastian sees life as a 'progression from animal eternity into time, into the strictly human world of memory and anticipation; and from time, if one chooses to go on, into the world of spiritual eternity, into the Divine Ground' (30). The mystic who, while still alive, has learned to stop time by penetrating the world of spiritual eternity, becomes evolution's vanguard. The enlightened individual, though trapped among monkeys, performs a service simply by being.

Point Counter Point initially appears to satirize Julian Huxley's religion of 'evolutionary humanism'. In *Religion Without Revelation*, published the same year as Aldous's novel and three years after Julian accepted a chair in zoology at King's College, the author argues that evolution is the only acceptable modern religion because it alone explains man's origins and potential destiny. Both brothers struggle with the legacy of their famous grandfather and end with positions T. H. Huxley could have accepted. Aldous's novel simultaneously criticizes and supports his brother's views. Julian asserts that man's 'destiny is to be the agent of the evolutionary process on this planet'.[18] The only species still capable of 'further evolutionary progress', man must 'aim at fullness and wholeness of development'. He must 'face the task of growing up, of building a personality out of the raw materials of his infant self' (p. 195). The characters in *Point Counter Point*, whether judged by Quarles or Rampion, fall short of these ideals. Yet Aldous is attracted to his brother's beliefs. In light of their later development, the brothers seem, even in 1928, to have divided T. H. Huxley's role between them. Julian becomes T. H.'s exegete, applying 'Evolution and Ethics' to modern times. Aldous then assumes the critical, debating side of his grandfather, the learned wit that must deal in fiction with characters who impede evolution, just as T. H. dispatched opponents of evolutionary theory. An examination of Huxleyan views on evolution could produce a study in itself. The point at present is that Aldous's opinions coincided with Julian's at several points. Some of Lord Edward's experiments may poke fun at Julian's projects,[19] but in his brother's beliefs Aldous found clues for a more philosophical yet sufficiently scientific zoology with which to modify Rampion's and humanize Quarles's. Julian stresses that 'our meagre knowledge of mysticism and Yoga makes it clear that some regions of human potentiality remain virtually unexplored' (p. 201). This puts him in eventual agreement with Sebastian Barnack and *End and Means*. *Point Counter Point* exposed the ape in man but never denied he might also be potentially an angel.

    In 1928, Sebastian Barnack's conclusions are still to come and Rampion's theories prevail. Mark insists the individual must 'be a perfect animal *and* a perfect human' simultaneously (9). The ideal is the 'sane harmonious Greek man [who] gets as much as he can of both sets of states. He's not such a fool as to want to kill part of himself. He strikes a balance' (10). The 'conscious soul' and the 'unconscious, physical, instinctive part of the total being' are 'intrinsically hostile' and must be 'reconciled'. Within the novel, Rampion-Lawrence advances the only plausible solution to the counterpoint of mind against body, the conflict that disrupts the internal harmony of all the characters. None of them achieves Rampion's ideal. Quarles is the only character, besides Mary, to comprehend it; but hermit-crabs seldom evolve into harmonious Greeks. Rampion's zoology remains 'symbolical', without converts. The novel ends with the true counterpoint of unity amid variation in the background as an implied ideal and Quarles stranded in the zoo of the foreground. Passion and reason remain self-division's cause. The picture of Quarll among the monkeys persists as a satisfactory analogue for Philip's plight.

V

The misconception continues that *Point Counter Point* is Huxley's only zoological novel. His novels consistently employ animal imagery. In *Island* (1962), Will Farnaby laughs 'like a hyena'. Shearwater in *Antic Hay* (1923) has a bird's name and sighs 'like a whale'. Predominant amid the recurrent animal imagery is the satiric picture of man as ape. From the zoos in the early poetry[20] to the genius Maartens who resembles 'an overwound clockwork monkey', the ape is Huxley's symbol for man's anti-evolutionary energy. Man's 'double nature' fascinates Huxley: man's phenomenal ego (ape) versus his eternal self (essence).[21] In *Point Counter Point*, man is an amphibian (mind against body); later, he is a triphibian (mind, body, spirit). Animal imagery links the two halves of Huxley's career. In the early fiction, one finds man the egotistical animal who misuses his body and distorts his mind. Subsequently, he becomes the ape whose self-centred mental and physical preoccupations conceal from himself and others his spiritual essence.

In *After Many a Summer Dies the Swan* (1939), *Ape and Essence* (1949), and *Island* (1962), the image of Quarll among the monkeys returns as Mr Propter, Alfred Poole, and Will Farnaby succeed where Quarles failed. They escape from the monkey-house of modern life.

Mr Propter, Huxley's spokesman in *After Many a Summer,* is in the midst of men whose ape-like aspirations threaten to reverse the process of evolution. The novel emphasizes the difference between longevity and true fitness for survival. The swan of the title, Jo Stoyte, is fantastically wealthy but remains emotionally 'a great big kid' (Book I, Chapter 3). Symbolizing the Tithonus element in all humans, the preference for prolonged life over spiritual advancement, Stoyte has a fear of death so extreme it compels him to finance Dr Obispo's research on longevity. Evolution, Huxley thus reminds the reader, provides no answer for the inevitability of death. Only Propter has this answer. He formulates Huxley's new and final definition of man as a *spiritual animal* (I.2). Propter maintains that one fights for the good on the level below the human and on the level above, on the animal level and the level of eternity (I.9). It is the human plane, that of time, craving, and the ego, from which one must escape. By stepping down to the animal plane via D. H. Lawrence or up to the spiritual plane via the mystics, one experiences a truly extra-evolutionary sense of timelessness. By trying to make the human plane eternal, the egoist Stoyte and the scientist Obispo perform ape-like antics; Stoyte, in fact, embraces regression as the novel ends.

Beginning in Book II, Chapter 4 with selections from the notebook of the Fifth Earl of Gonister, Huxley maintains an interesting counterpoint: one chapter devoted to the Earl, one to Propter. As the Earl regresses, Propter points the way to increased awareness. The former speaks for the ape in man, the latter for his essence. The Earl notices that carp in his moat live two or three centuries. In the 1790s, he begins ingesting the raw viscera of these fish (II.6). Eventually he regains his former strength and appears younger than his heirs. At the age of eighty-one he fathers three illegitimate children (II.8) before taking to the cellarage with his housekeeper to escape rumours and an inquiry. Jeremy Pordage learns of the Earl's experiments from a diary in the Hauberk Papers he is editing for Stoyte. Pordage's researches and those of Obispo coincide as both focus on the longevity issue. In a climax which the reader anticipates too easily, Stoyte and Obispo discover the Earl still alive in his cellarage; the only drawback is that he has degenerated into an ape. Obispo finds the Earl's condition and Stoyte's decision to adopt a carp diet 'the finest joke he had ever known' (III.2). The Earl's activities constitute the most successful sections of the novel, for the antics of ape-like man are more amusing than the demanding prescriptions of Propter the philosopher. But evolution is not mocked, nor is longevity synonymous with fitness for survival. At the terminal point of his devolution, the Earl became a foetal ape which then grew to full size, making the Earl the most pronounced case of arrested development in all of Huxley.

Ape and Essence, allegedly a film script by a certain William Tallis, also counterpoints two sets of scenes: in one sequence a baboon-like society destroys itself; in the other, the survivors start the destruction process all over again. A scientific expedition from New Zealand, the only country to survive a Third World War, arrives in southern California in 2108. The baboons who once lived there and in opposing countries—Huxley never refers to them as humans—annihilated themselves with poison gas. Tallis's script recounts this fiasco. Two rival groups, each with an Einstein on a leash, destroy each other with gas in the names of Progress and Nationalism.[22] The Einsteins evidently stand for the enslavement of science by the ape in man. When Alfred Poole, a biologist with the expedition, is captured by the even more simian survivors of the gassing (p. 45), the situation of Quarll among monkeys is reproduced with sinister literalness.

Ironically, Poole's capture leads to the liberation of his spirit, as Quarll's shipwreck led to his. 'Only in the knowledge of his own Essence', the Narrator remarks, 'has any man ceased to be many monkeys' (p. 55). Poole, thirty-eight and a timid but oversexed bachelor, discovers his essence, the particle all men have within them of the Divine Ground, in a sexual encounter on Belial Day with the eighteen-year-old Loola. A surprising setting for spiritual experience, this orgy is the novel's climax (p. 109). The new simian city, inappropriately situated near the former City of the Angels, has adopted the breeding habits of animals. Periods of abstinence surround the orgies of Belial Day. By behaving for once like an animal, an indiscretion Quarles would never have been guilty of, Poole rediscovers the plane of the fully human and has intimations of the eternal one beyond it.

Though not one of Huxley's better novels, *Ape and Essence* represents a reconciliation of the plights and views of such diverse figures as Quarles, Lawrence, Shelley, Propter, Stoyte, and Sebastian Barnack. Poole's experiences on the animal plane take him out of himself and out of time while awakening him to the world of spiritual experience, just as Propter and Sebastian insisted they would. If Quarles could have become more pig and less hermit-crab, he too might have advanced. Like Constance and Mellors in Lawrence's novel, Alfred and Loola flee an arid society at the end of the novel. Huxley wisely creates a community of 'Hots' for them to flee toward. Among individuals too combustible for periodic mating seasons, a healthy, unlimited sexuality still survives. The stress Lawrence and Rampion placed on the physical, animal relationship becomes a crucial step towards awareness, but a stage, not a goal. Poole's readings from a volume of Shelley make this clear. Initially (p. 147), he reads from *Epipsychidion:*

> We shall become the same, we shall be one
> Spirit within two frames, oh! Wherefore two?

This summarizes the experience with Loola. But if the Narrator's suggestion is reliable, Poole already understands that 'beyond *Epipsychidion* there is *Adonais* and beyond *Adonais,* the wordless doctrine of the Pure in Heart' (p. 149). Poole quotes the latter poem on the last page when he reads about 'That light whose smile kindles the Universe'. This light, beaming on the poet, is described 'consuming the last clouds of cold mortality. Huxley connects Shelley's poems with the Divine Ground. In *Point Counter Point*, Rampion contended Shelley was filled with a bloodless kind of slime (10), and Quarles commented unkindly on *Epipsychidion* (1); but here Lawrence and Shelley blend into Huxley's final diagram of the ideal evolutionary process that every individual can re-enact: from the animal to the human to the divine, a process that begins among the monkeys yet need not end there.

VI

Point Counter Point virtually begins with this description of Marjorie's pregnancy:

> Six months from now her baby would be born. Something that
> had been a single cell, a cluster of cells, a little sac of tissue, a kind
> of worm, a potential fish with gills, stirred in her womb and would
> one day become a man—a grown man, suffering and enjoying,
> loving and hating, thinking, remembering, imagining. And what
> had been a blob of jelly within her body would invent a god and
> worship; what had been a kind of fish would create and, having
> created, would become the battle-ground of disputing good and
> evil; what had blindly lived in her as a parasitic worm would look
> at the stars, would listen to music, would read poetry.

Huxley calls this the 'astounding process of creation'. The passage vividly records his astonishment. This is not just an example of his ability to describe human events from an unexpectedly scientific viewpoint. That so much can come from so little is for Huxley perhaps the most awesome aspect of life. That the product of such a marvellous process should so often fail to continue the development begun in the womb is life's tragedy. Put in its context, the passage could be read as Huxley's cynical comment on man's pretensions. Taken alone, it has a blend of hope and sadness that goes beyond analysis. What was once a single cell can observe the stars or listen to music. When Quarles castigates characters who behave like lower forms of life, Huxley is supremely sensitive to the human possibilities that have been lost.

Next to the activity in Marjorie's womb one must place Bruno Rontini's description of the evolution of a mystic in *Time Must Have a Stop*. Huxley summarizes it:

> Out of ten thousand [herrings] only one would ever break out of his carapace completely. Not a high proportion. But out of all those galaxies of eggs, how many herrings ever come to be full-sized fish? And herrings, it was to be remembered, suffered only from external interruptions to their hatching and growth. Whereas in this process of spiritual maturation, every human being was always his own worst enemy. (Chapter 10)

The astonishment of the first passage yields to a sense of the hardships in the growth that the second recommends. Few are capable of emulating Rontini, of breaking out of their carapace completely and growing to full size. Evolution is a tremendously selective process. Yet Huxley feels these few are evolution's pioneers. They reach now the state that mystics in all eras enjoyed and that the race as a whole may one day attain. Bruno's summary contains some optimism, but it has its modicum of Quarlesian satire: the number of men who reach spiritual maturity is less than the number of herrings who survive to become full-sized fish. Huxley never quite leaves Quarles's zoology behind.

The image of Philip Quarll among the monkeys lodged itself permanently in Huxley's mind. Looked at through Huxley's satiric eye, the world always seemed to trap the enlightened man among contemporaries backward enough to appear simian. In Huxley's novels, the zoo functions as a credible, satiric metaphor for modern life. Initially, Quarll's situation became that of Quarles: the plight of the intellectual in a bestial world. Later, Quarll among the monkeys stood for the effort required to isolate one's essence from the ape-hood of society and self.

Huxley's final completed novel, however, fostered optimism. After a sailing mishap, Will Farnaby is washed ashore on the island of Pala, a society of fully developed individuals. In one sense, the novel becomes a variation on *Point Counter Point*. The melody of Quarles's predicament is, as it were, played in reverse. Farnaby is more fortunate in his choice of islands than the Savage, who is brought to England in *Brave New World*. Among the fully human, Will, who laughs like an animal, is the monkey; but his chances for development are excellent. To reverse the plight of Quarles, Huxley knew a utopia would be required. Since neither *Island* nor *Ape and Essence* are among Huxley's best novelistic achievements, *Point Counter Point*, where animal imagery produces a bitterly satiric, zoological view of man, may prove fittest to survive.

Notes

1. *The Hermit: Or, The UnParallel'd Sufferings and Surprising Adventures of Mr Philip Quarll, an Englishman. Who was lately discovered upon an uninhabited Island in the South Sea; where he has lived above Fifty years, without any human Assistance, still continues to reside, and will not come away* (London, 1727).

2. See his letter to his father for 8 June 1915 (*The Letters of Aldous Huxley*, edited by Grover Smith, (London, 1969), pp. 71–72). The essay on satire from Restoration to Revolution stopped about forty years short of *The Hermit*.

3. Slug's report is included in the critical appendages to George Ford and Sylvère Monod's edition of *Hard Times* (New York, 1966), p. 308.

4. Charles Dickens, *Christmas Stories*, Oxford Illustrated Edition (London, 1956 etc.), p. 9.

5. The volume Tom eyes was probably a shortened children's version (24 pages) published by Hodgson in 1823 with a folding coloured plate by George Cruikshank.

6. Letters, p. 241. The story of Quarll may first have attracted Huxley in 1922 when the British Museum acquired a rare first edition of *The Hermit* with variant preliminary leaves that apparently revealed the author's name for the first time (previously only his initials had been known). The acquisition prompted an essay by Arundell Esdaile, 'Author and Publisher in 1727: *The English Hermit*', *The Library*, Series 4, 2 (1922), 185–192. The author of *The Hermit* is now thought to have been Peter Longueville.

7. Bracketed references throughout this essay refer to chapter numbers.

8. This is probably Wolfgang Köhler's *The Mentality of Apes* (London, 1925), a revision of the 1917 edition. Huxley's use of animal imagery is supported, wherever possible, by his knowledge of science. Huxley fortifies his satire with an examination of contemporary scientists who were exploring parallels between the human and animal kingdoms. But where the scientists mentioned in this article pointed out ways in which the animal kingdom anticipates the human, Huxley and Quarles treat the human kingdom as just another and less pleasing variation on the animal.

9. Harold Watts is more cautious. He notes that 'Quarles' fears—perhaps expressive of Huxley's estimate about 1928 of his own capacities for establishing

human contact—were not realized in Huxley's later life (*Aldous Huxley* [New York, 1969], p. 17).

10. For a discussion of the Huxley-Lawrence relationship and the extent to which Huxley comprehended his friend's philosophy, see Jerome Meckier, *Aldous Huxley: Satire and Structure* (London, 1969), Chapter 4.

11. Jean Fabre (1823–1915), French entomologist.

12. Charles Tate Regan (1878–1943), whose work on fishes Quarles and Huxley both seem to have read. However, the knowledge of cerativid angler-fishes Quarles displays does not go much beyond what can be learned from one of Huxley's favourite books, *Encyclopædia Britannica*. In 1925 Regan 'first recognized for what they were the parasitic dwarf males in deep-sea angler-fishes' *(DNB)*.

13. Quarles has read any of several works by William Morton Wheeler on ants and insects, such as *Social Life Among the Insects* (London, 1923), *Foibles of Insects and Men* (New York, 1928), or *Ants: Their Structure, Development and Behavior* (New York, 1913). Friedrich Alverdes's contribution may have been *Social Life in the Animal World* (London, 1927). In *Foibles* and in *Emergent Evolution and the Development of Societies* (New York, 1928), Wheeler occasionally sounds like Quarles, who must have enjoyed Alverdes's chapter on 'Human Sociology from a Biological Standpoint'.

14. See Donald Watt's fine essay, 'The Criminal-Victim Pattern in Huxley's *Point Counter Point*', *Studies in the Novel*, 2 (1970), 42–51.

15. See 'The Struggle for Existence' (1888) and 'Evolution and Ethics' (1893), *Selections from the Essays of T. H. Huxley*, edited by Alburey Castell (New York, 1948).

16. Aldous Huxley, 'D. H. Lawrence', *The Olive Tree*, (London, 1947), p. 208.

17. Nor does he neglect to justify mysticism from a scientific point of view. As early as *Ends and Means* (London, 1937), p. 295, he attempts to prove that scientists and mystics share a common conception of the universe as a place where an 'ultimate identity underlies the apparent physical diversity of the world'. In the same volume he asserts his belief that evolution can be regarded as 'a genuine process'.

18. Julian Huxley, *Religion Without Revelation* (New York, 1957), p. 193. The chapter on 'Evolutionary Humanism' here quoted from is a 1954 lecture added when the book was revised in1957. It does, however, represent views held earlier. Future references to this book are included in the text by page number. Gerald Heard also taught that man's consciousness does and should evolve.

19. See for example the project of feeding thyroid to axolotls mentioned by Julian Huxley in *Memories* (London, 1970), p. 26,

20. See Charles Holmes, 'The Early Poetry of Aldous Huxley', *Texas Studies in Language and Literature*, 8 (1966), 391–406.

21. Huxley examines this duality in, among other places, his introduction to Swami Prabhavananda and Christopher Isherwood's translation of the *Bhagavad-Gita* (New York, 1968), p. 13.

22. *Ape and Essence* (London, 1949), p. 31. References to this novel are in the text by page number since there are no convenient chapter divisions.

JANET L. GOODRICH

Bringing Order Out of Chaos:
Huxley's Time Must Have a Stop *and Vedanta*

Ｈow does a finite mind confront the infinite? The question might stymie any but the most enterprising of intellects. When he dies suddenly of a heart attack, Eustace Barnack, the aging esthete of Aldous Huxley's *Time Must Have a Stop* (1944), has no choice but to face the question. Banished by his death beyond the confines of time and space, Eustace must find strategies for existing in the territory of pure mind. Consciousness, awareness, and knowledge all have a place in this unfamiliar dimension, but independent, self-interested action does not. Eustace grasps for a memory—the last vestige of the timebound, comprehensible life he has left behind. In so doing, he resists annihilation and opts out of mystical union with the infinite.

Huxley, in the writing of *Time Must Have a Stop*, finds himself in Eustace's position, for in much the same way he is stepping out into new territory. But unlike Eustace, who wants to return to the life he left behind, Huxley seeks what lies ahead: a test of the religious hypothesis proposed in many of his writings and explored in his novels. *Time Must Have a Stop* serves as an early treatment of this hypothesis, one in which Huxley faces daunting obstacles to the artistic process. *Time Must Have a Stop*, the resulting experimental novel, exhibits innovations that carry it over several of the artistic hurdles in its path.

Extrapolation, Volume 40, Number 2 (Summer 1999): pp. 145–153. Copyright ©1999 Kent State University Press.

79

The hurdles themselves emerge from the fusion of Huxley's interests in mysticism and his calling as an artist. In *The Perennial Philosophy*, he implies that the novel represents a feasible context for investigating the mystical experience he concludes to be the lowest common denominator of religion. "In studying the Perennial Philosophy," he writes, "we can begin either at the bottom, with practice and morality; or at the top, with a consideration of metaphysical truths; or, finally, in the middle, at the focal point where mind and matter, action and thought have their meeting place in human psychology" (1). What better place for a study of the human psyche than the novel, with its capacity to accommodate numerous individual minds acting and interacting? But according to mystical belief, these individuals merely skate across the surface of an underlying divine consciousness with which it is the aim of humankind to join.

The Perennial Philosophy, which Sebastian, the novel's protagonist, describes in his journal in the closing pages of *Time Must Have a Stop*, is essentially a restatement of Vedantic philosophy. Detailed in one of the oldest existing collections of religious writings, the Vedanta, this philosophy's elements can be reduced to three propositions: human beings' true nature is divine; humankind's goal is the actualization of this nature; and, as the Perennial Philosophy assumes, all religions agree (Isherwood, *Western* 1). The pursuit of mystical experience—that is, union of the Atman (the divine nature housed within an individual) with the Brahman (the divine nature without, or what Sebastian Barnack calls "the unmanifested principle of all manifestation")—is fraught with difficulty because it requires full surrender of an individual's defining traits. Self-interest must dissolve in its every form to permit the kind of detachment from material things that enables a self to merge with the infinite, expanding the individual consciousness so as to include all reality. This self-transcendence is sometimes termed "nonattachment," defined by Gerald Heard as "what [a person] can know without intending to do anything about it" (231). Knowledge, not action, is the aim.

Little wonder, then, that in such a scheme novel-writing poses a problem, for the novel is itself a self-conscious form that takes self-conscious individuals as its subjects. Further, fiction relies on action and plot. How then does a writer convey a philosophy of contemplative inaction such as mysticism? Still another problem emerges in the conflict between the novel's reliance on sequential time and the mystic's attempt to join with a timeless reality. And, perhaps the crux of the artistic dilemma, how is the artist to express a transcendent experience when such an experience is by definition inexpressible?

It would seem, then, that while mystical experience itself is difficult to achieve, writing a novel about it is simply impossible. In *Time Must Have a Stop*, however, Huxley's experiment yields successful results by surmounting some problems entirely and giving insight into all, thus generating the fuel for further experiments.

One way Huxley innovatively approaches the artistic dilemmas presented by Vedanta in *Time Must Have a Stop* may be seen in his treatment of time. Timelessness within the plot's temporal train of events poses a problem Huxley is well aware of, as the novel's title and epigram from Shakespeare indicate:

> But thought's the slave of life, and life's time's fool, And time, that takes survey of all the world, Must have a stop.

Sebastian's commentary on these lines in the final pages serves as both an appropriate frame and, even more significant, as a clue to Huxley's own estimation of the function of time in art and life: "It is only by taking the fact of eternity into account that we can deliver thought from its slavery to life. And it is only by deliberately paying our attention and our primary allegiance to eternity that we can prevent time from turning our lives into pointless or diabolic foolery. The divine Ground is a timeless reality" (266). We might view Huxley's manipulation of time in *Time Must Have a Stop* as his attempt to pay his primary artistic allegiance to eternity, for by disrupting the experience of events in chronological sequence, the novel thwarts the tyranny of time.

One such disruptive technique used to good advantage is to alternate between the worlds of timelessness, inhabited by Eustace after his death, and time, inhabited by the novel's remaining characters. Eustace dies in chapter 12; chapters 13, 15, 17, 20, and 25 describe his experience after death. In chapter 28 Eustace returns to life by entering the person of a little boy, and we hear no more about him. Interspersing these chapters with those relating to the ordinary, timebound lives of the other characters frustrates the reader's desire to learn of events in uninterrupted sequence and thereby challenges the assumptions of temporal experience that lead to that expectation. It is as though time has several small stops within the novel—to be exact, six. Each of them occurs when a chapter about Eustace begins.

Not only does this technique interfere with the regular, chronological movement of the plot, it underscores the unfamiliarity of the timeless. The Eustace chapters begin in such a way as to disorient the reader, usually making reference to something Eustace is sensing in his private hell that is strikingly irrelevant to the close of the preceding chapter. Chapter 13, for example, begins, "There was no pain any longer, no more need to gasp for breath, and the tiled floor of the lavatory had ceased to be cold and hard" (125). This is probably the most reader-friendly opening of a Eustace chapter. Contrast it with the first line of chapter 15: "'Backwards and downwards,' the laughter and the cigar" (141). Like the opening of chapter 13, this description of a moment in Eustace's posthumous experience comes without any initial preparation. Chapter 17 employs a similar strategy, plunging into Eustace's consciousness without first grounding the moment in its context:

> To the tune of "Under the Bamboo Tree," to the accompaniment
> of Timmy Williams' knowing laughter, again, again:
> Probably constip, Probably constip, Probably constipaysh. . . .
> But of course it wasn't true. He had always known that it wasn't
> true. (153)

Again, we are thrust into Eustace's chaotic memory as it tries to make sense out of eternity, but we are given no preparation or explicit reference to him. Thus we never quite lose the jolt of entering the timeless, though as our stock of associations accumulates we become quicker in reorienting ourselves there with Eustace. In this way, Huxley not only disrupts time sense but also stresses the comprehensibility it lends to ordinary human experience. By getting involved with the story, the reader approaches a sort of simulated version of mystical experience by being forced to release insistence upon a novelistic presentation more respectful of chronological time and pace. *Time Must Have a Stop* thus invites its readers into a controlled experiment in extending the boundaries of time.

Further disruption of time occurs in Huxley's presentation of events after Sebastian's conversion to mystical concerns (though the likelihood of mystical experience on his part is questionable). The events of chapter 30, for example, make a considerable leap in time from those of chapter 29. It is as though Huxley, in the final lines of chapter 29, were heeding the Queen Mother's advice to "make the best of such time as is left" (245). He does so by presenting, in a concentrated form, the effects upon an adult Sebastian of the childhood events we have just read. We learn of Sebastian's interest in mysticism, his married life, his care for the dying mystic Bruno Rontini, his Minimum Working Hypothesis, and his observations about various other subjects as understood from his mystical perspective. But the information comes to us in no particular order. Instead, it is related in memory and in journals, in a series of starts and flashbacks that makes a patchwork of chronology in much the same way Eustace's memory does once he tries to assert it as a defiant defense against eternity. It is ironic that such a similar technique might be used both by Eustace, who militates against the timeless, and by Huxley, who eludes the force of time in the final chapter of *Time Must Have a Stop*.

The book is not entirely successful, of course, in sidestepping time. Ultimately, it remains an account of events occurring in sequence; even Eustace, outside of time, seems to continue to move within it as his awareness proceeds through phases in sequence. But by the use of alternation, of disorientation, and of memory, Huxley nevertheless launches an ambitious and partially successful attack on time. As a tentative answer to the problem of writing about timelessness, *Time Must Have a Stop* clearly gives evidence of inventive craftsmanship.

Just as time presents a problem for any novelist interested in Vedanta, so also does action. For to the same extent that the novel requires action, Vedanta, rightly understood, requires inaction—at least of the dramatic variety most suited to the novel. Huxley sums the situation up this way: "Pragmatism regards action as the end and thought as the means to that end; and contemporary popular philosophy accepts the pragmatist position. In the philosophy underlying Eastern and Western spiritual religion this position is reversed. Here, contemplation is the end, action (in which is included discursive thought) is valuable only as a means to the beatific vision of reality" (Isherwood, *Western* 366–367). It is thus difficult to construct a novel that relies on external action to carry the plot, for non-attachment recognizes value only in those actions which, devoid of self-interest, in no way distort the Atman.

Huxley's approach to this problem is to focus less on narrated events than on the continuous stream of experience. Eustace, for example, takes no action at all after he dies—except to resist the fact of his death; without a body, discursive thought (exercised in this case to revive through memory a sense of individuality) is the only form of action accessible to him. We learn of his progress (or regress, as it were) from the inside out, by observing chaos through the eyes and through the filter of his distinct personality. Aside from the tremendous mental energy required to maintain a sense of self in eternity, action is not possible for Eustace. Thus we learn that even thought is an action that can distance the rebellious self from Brahman. Our confinement within Eustace's center of consciousness creates a sense of the flow of experience rather than of dramatic acts that keep a plot moving. Restricting action to discursive thought in Eustace removes the novel from the tyranny of such dramatic action and moves it a step closer to non-attachment.

A second technique that contributes to the novel's evasion of action is its distanced depiction of crucial events, especially those pertaining to Bruno Rontini. Such a technique makes sense, given that Bruno is the novel's mystic; having seen the beatific vision, having mastered the life of non-attachment, Rontini has to be removed, quite logically on Huxley's part, from the world of self-interested actions constituting the novel. Thus the dramatic actions in which he participates are related to us from a distance, even before he is removed bodily from his apartment. His meeting with Gabriel Weyl to recover Sebastian's sketch, for instance, rather than described as it takes place, is sketchily suggested through Bruno's memory: "Gabriel Weyl had ended by yielding; but the surrender had been anything but graceful. Against his will—for he had done his best to put them out of mind—Bruno found himself remembering the ugly words that had been spoken, the passionate gestures of those hirsute and beautifully manicured hands, that face distorted and pale with fury" (220). As is so often the case in Huxley, the action is significant primarily for its symbolic value as an encounter between good and evil. Relating it briefly and from a distance serves this purpose and, in the process, it shifts the attention from action to thought, bringing *Time Must Have a Stop* that much closer to contemplation.

Bruno's abduction removes him entirely from the novel for an interval, and this too is related after the fact. The testimony of Carl Malpighi, Bruno's friend, gives us a terse summary of this pivotal event in Sebastian's progress. Once again, cushioning the event in elapsed time, in Malpighi's memory, and in the narrator's persona undercuts the action. These distanced treatments of dramatic action, then, although they do not successfully depict the degree of inaction sufficient to propel the audience into the beatific vision, certainly take us a long way towards the lesser significance of action in Vedanta.

Closely related to the conflict created by Vedanta's value on contemplation and the novel's demand for dramatic action is the conflict between Vedantic self-abandonment and novelistic self-consciousness. Union with Brahman—the realization of the divine nature humans possess—necessitates a departure from self, a stripping away of all the markers of individuality. This poses a formidable challenge to the novelist: how does a self-conscious individual depict such an experience in a self-conscious work about self-conscious characters?

Huxley confronts the problem in *Time Must Have a Stop* by using a method not altogether successful. By filtering our consciousnesses through those of the characters, the novel in effect strips away our individual concerns and enables us to identify with the characters. Such an identification is a product of the underlying common denominator in people—the Atman—and not of the collections of traits possessed by unique individuals. Thus the story comes to us through the minds of many and varied characters: the Queen Mother, Susan, Veronica Thwale, Eustace, Bruno Rontini, Sebastian Barnack. Each character has a unique personal history, place of residence, and motivation. But by combining his focus on consciousness with his generation of widely varied characters, Huxley brings about the very departure from the distinctive self that mysticism pursues. Doing so by plunging into a welter of distinctive selves is remarkable in that it seems to run counter to the aim of avoiding individuality. The other choice, however—consciously to try to forget self—collapses in the attempt, since deliberate self-forgetting demands constant recollection of the self one is trying to forget. The "filtration" method of *Time Must Have a Stop* amounts, paradoxically, to exactly the purgation that enables the Atman to unite with Brahman.

Huxley is, of course, merely exploiting the novel's form, and we might argue that the connection between the dynamics of the novel's characters and mystical experience is incidental. But Huxley consciously chooses the novel form, even though on the surface it seems entirely unsuited to his purposes. The more direct addresses of the essay could more easily cloud the message with Huxley's own personal temperament than could fiction. Fiction leaves more room, too, for the free response of those who read, since its indirectness does not encourage an immediate commitment of the will. This is not what the mystic seeks, for knowledge of the Brahman lies beneath the will; as William Law notes, the Atman through which human beings experience oneness with God cannot be searched out with the reason, intellect, understanding or will (*Perennial Philosophy* 2). Propter, the resident mystic of Huxley's *After Many a Summer Dies the Swan* (1939), points out even more directly that "self-will is the negation of reality" (128). Thus we should read *Time Must Have a Stop* not as an evangelistic tract that expounds the virtues of mysticism and urges the reader to adopt its tenets, but as an experiment in the practice of mysticism, a working out of the hypothesis. To read it as though it were Huxley's religious counsel to us would grant more integrity to the will than the mystic would allow. The novel acts instead to exemplify its tentative mystical thesis and to elicit an approximation of expanded consciousness in careful readers.

In the same way that communion with God lies beyond will, so it lies beyond expression. This may be the greatest of mysticism's burdens on the aspiring novelist. *Time Must Have a Stop* does not convey such a moment of revelation. Sebastian's moment of enlightenment, if indeed he has one, is left out of the novel altogether. And even Eustace, who is depicted as in the presence of God, fails to experience anything beyond his power of expression in words.

The novel nevertheless conducts its readers toward such an experience through a frame device such as those traditionally used to make the unbelievable seem less so. In Mary Shelley's *Frankenstein* and Coleridge's *Rime of the Ancient Mariner,* bizarre tales come to us by means of internal narrators. These narrators serve to remove that which is unnatural from the probing of our natural reason, which can prevent the "willing suspension of disbelief" so vital to appreciating such works. Similarly, Huxley insulates within the frame of Sebastian's journal the novel's more direct closing flirtations with mystical experience. Sebastian recounts the landmarks of his spiritual journey within the larger tale of the events that have set this journey into motion. Thus placed within the novel, the experience comes to us some time after its writing through the successive frames of time, of Sebastian's consciousness, of the narrator, and of the novel.

Still, though distancing some of the novel's more dense philosophical content through these frames may help to make it more comprehensible to the Western mind, Vedanta seeks not understanding but the ineffable beatific vision. Such a vision the novel does not often. Though certainly it is ironic that the goal should remain ineffable, such is the nature of mystical experience; no matter how clever the author, it cannot be described. It defies language because it defies relationship to the nature of experience language is designed to describe. Leaving open the question of whether Sebastian has had a transcendent moment is the only strategy available to Huxley, since it invites us to consider the possibility we would dismiss if it were expressed.

Recognizing *Time Must Have a Stop* as an experiment on the religious hypothesis helps to explain its concluding chapter, which upon first reading leaves the impression that the novel suddenly deflates at the end, losing its momentum and continuity. For the reader seeking a clearly articulated wrap-up, the ending leaves questions open. But if we accept that the ending explores Vedanta from an appropriately oblique angle, we may gain an appreciation for Huxley's craftsmanship and ingenuity in *Time Must Have a Stop*.

Such a reconsideration is warranted, given Huxley's awareness of the pitfalls in writing this novel. He elaborates on some of them through Bruno Rontini, whose advice to Sebastian could as well be Huxley's to himself:

> Men of genius express their knowledge of reality. But they themselves very rarely act on their knowledge. Why not? ... A man of genius inherits an unusual capacity to see into ultimate reality and to express what he sees. ... But if he spends all his energies on writing and doesn't attempt to modify his inherited and acquired being in the light of what he knows, then he can never get to increase his knowledge. ... Most men of genius take such infinite pains not to become saints—out of mere self-preservation. (224)

That Huxley undertakes such a task knowing its dangers is bold in itself. The creative measures he uses in crafting *Time Must Have a Stop* endow the book with considerable artistic merit as well.

Unlike young Sebastian, Huxley does not merely observe and record. By conducting this experiment, he actively seeks mystical experience. As Jerome Meckier notes, Huxley might be described as "an intellectual with a mistrust of mind and language, an artist who prefers unpopular truth to artistic effect and whose search in art for standards to live by is accompanied by a mistrust of art" (7). *Time Must Have a Stop* indicates, however, Huxley's willingness to accept, tentatively at least, a hypothetical core of belief. Perhaps it is this sense of personal investment in the novel that leads Sybille Bedford to suggest that it and other of Huxley's later works function as journals of his process of self-transformation (3). In any case, our feeling that in *Time Must Have a Stop* Huxley writes about himself may be part of the book's appeal. "Words may cause confusion and create entanglements," he writes, "but the absence of words creates total darkness" (Isherwood, *Western* 282). Surely *Time Must Have a Stop* is evidence of his willingness to creatively confront confusion in his search for belief.

WORKS CITED

Bedford, Sybille. *Aldous Huxley: A Biography.* Vol. 2: 1939–1963. London: Chatto and Windus, 1974.

Birnbaum, Milton. *Aldous Huxley's Quest for Values.* Knoxville: University of Tennessee Press, 1971.

Chakoo, B. L. *Aldous Huxley and Eastern Wisdom.* Delhi: Atma Ram and Sons, 1981.

Heard, Gerald. *Is God Evident?* London: Faber and Faber, 1950.

Huxley, Aldous. *Ends and Means.* New York: Harper, 1937.

———. *Men and Tendencies.* London: Sheed and Ward, 1937.

———. *The Perennial Philosophy.* New York: Harper, 1937.

———. *Themes and Variations.* New York: Harper, 1943.

———. *Time Must Have a Stop.* New York: Harper and Row, 1944.

Isherwood, Christopher, ed. *Vedanta for Modern Man.* Hollywood: Vedanta Press, 1945.

———. *Vedanta for the Western World.* London: Allen and Unwin, 1948.

Meckier, Jerome. *Aldous Huxley: Satire and Structure.* New York: Barnes and Noble, 1971.

Ramamurty, K. Bhaskara. *Aldous Huxley.: A Study of His Novels.* New York: Asia Publishing, 1974.

ALEX MacDONALD

Choosing Utopia: An Existential Reading of Aldous Huxley's Island

The well-known etymology of "utopia" expresses a central problem in the interpretation of *Island,* eu + topos means good place, and is arguable that Pala is a good place which represents a triumphant positive conclusion to Huxley's life-long battle with dualism, that Will Farnaby's conversion, from cynicism to utopian faith is the culmination of the progression of the earlier novels. On the other hand, ou + topos means no place, and it is equally arguable that *Island,* especially its horrific ending, represents the return of Huxley's profound pessimism, as David Bradshaw has claimed: "*Island* is perhaps Huxley's most pessimistic book, his poignant acknowledgment that in a world of increasing greed, mass communication, oil-guzzling transport, burgeoning population, and inveterate hostility, a pacific and co-operative community, like Pala's 'oasis of freedom and happiness' has little hope of survival" (viii), *Island* is an important modern utopian novel and such radically different interpretations are worth considering. It is my contention that *Island* is not pessimistic, that in fact it is a profoundly optimistic book, optimistic not just about the possibility of individual enlightenment (the "eupsychian" view) but about the possibility of utopia in the social sense. The basis for this is what I call an existential interpretation of the text, which I shall try to explain.

Utopian Studies, Volume 12, Number 2 (Spring 2001): pp. 103–115. Copyright © 2001 Society for Utopian Studies.

Aldous Huxley wrote eleven novels in his career. It is interesting to note that the titles of all but one contain two or more words. The exception, of course, is *Island*, which illustrates clearly the movement toward, unity which is characteristic of Huxley's thought. It is arguable that the central trend in Huxley's novels was the movement from a view of reality which was thoroughly dualistic at the start of his career to one in which, at the end, dualism had been resolved.

The famous jazz age novels were constructed upon exploiting the splits in human nature, and they exemplify the condition described in the epigraph to *Point Counter Point*.

> Oh, wearisome condition of humanity,
> Born under one law, to another bound. . . .

Huxley took particular delight as a satirist in writing variations upon the duality of flesh and spirit: Theodore Gumbril Junior of *Antic Hay*, for example, who in the midst of a religious service develops the idea of inflatable underwear to ease the rigours of hard chapel benches (10), or the episode of the Lapith girls in *Crome Yellow:*

> They waved away whatever was offered them with an expression of delicate disgust, shutting their eyes and averting their faces from the proffered dish, as though the lemon sole, the duck, the loin of veal, the trifle, were objects revolting to the sight and smell. George, who thought the dinner capital, ventured to comment on the sisters' lack of appetite. "Pray don't talk to me of eating," said Emmeline, drooping like a sensitive plant. "We find it so coarse, so unspiritual, my sisters and I. One can't think of one's soul while one is eating." (107)

Of course, in the privacy of their room the girls gorge themselves. The duality reaches a less comical climax in *Brave New World*, in which John Savage whips his flesh for lechery and at the end hangs himself because there seems no resolution, no way out of the dilemma. The starkness of the dystopian alternatives gives *Brave New World* dramatic intensity, even though Huxley in his 1946 Preface regretted that the Savage was not given an option.

It was in the novels of the thirties and forties that a way between the horns of the dilemma began to appear, In *Eyeless in Gaza*, Anthony Beavis reaches a state of spiritual calm, suggesting the mystical experience which can transcend the duality of the world. The basis for the leap beyond satire to positive vision was elaborated in Huxley's spiritual anthology *The Perennial Philosophy* (1945). In this work Huxley noted that the etymology of the word, "two" contains the notion of badness and suggested the possibility and the necessity of moving beyond duality to awareness of the Divine Ground of Being which unifies creation. The futuristic fantasy of this period, the post-holocaust novel *Ape and Essence,* is obviously satirical, although at the end the hero escapes from a repressed anti-flesh society to a community of "Hots" who approve of lovemaking. Dr. Alfred Poole makes his escape with Loola, the slight rhyming of their names suggesting the oneness which is yet to be achieved. It is achieved in *Island,* which in terms of genre is the utopia among Huxley's speculative fantasies and in terms of ideas is the end of a lifelong search to resolve the dualisms of the earlier novels.

Huxley is explicit about the importance of overcoming dualism, in a passage Will finds in the *Notes on What's What:*

> Dualism. . . . Without it there can hardly be good literature. With it, there most certainly can be no good life.
>
> 'I' affirms a separate and abiding me-substance. 'am' denies the fact that all existence is relationship and change. 'I am.'
>
> Two tiny words; but what an enormity of untruth!
>
> The religiously minded dualist calls home-made spirits from the vasty deep: The non-dualist calls the vasty deep into his spirit, or, to be more accurate, he finds that the vasty deep is already there. (199)

An example, which echoes in an interesting way the eating passage in *Crome Yellow,* is the Palanese idea of "chewing grace". Chewing the first mouthful of each course as the way of giving thanks emphasizes the unity of spiritual and material which earlier had been lacking and emphasizes the importance of "attention" (the refrain of the mynah birds in Pala) in a small and practical way.[1] The progress from dualism to a unitary view can be seen in microcosm in the development of Huxley's protagonist Will Farnaby, who moves through psychological, relational and spiritual changes to his final enlightenment.

At the beginning Will is sailing in the Strait between Rendang and Pala, singing at the top of his voice:

> Three, three for the rivals . . .
> Two, two for the lily-white boys,
>   clothed all in green-oh . . .
> One is one and all alone . . .
> And ever more shall be so. (6–7)

The little song ends—it anticipates in a different key the novel's progress toward oneness—a squall comes up, and Will only just makes it ashore.

After a harrowing climb he collapses in a clearing where he is discovered by two children. The little girl, Mary Sarojini MacPhail, gives Will his first lesson in how to get there from here, in this case how to get from a state of nervous terror about the dangerous climb and the snakes to a state of relative peace. The answer is applied Freud, the talking cure, expressing the feelings of dread over and over until their power evaporates and the terror is gone. "So what's all the fuss about?" the girl asks, and Will Farnaby has to laugh indeed the "whole universe" seems to be "fairly splitting its sides over the enormous joke of existence" (14). In this preliminary encounter with utopia Will learns a technique for getting from the self to the not-self, paradoxically by going deeper into the self, that is paying attention to the self, and in this the first two chapters anticipate the spiritual journey of the novel.

Will spends a considerable part of the book recuperating from his ordeal, and the action consists mostly of his meeting and talking with two kinds of characters, the Palanese who explain utopian ways to him and the outsiders who are bent on subverting Pala for economic and political reasons. At the beginning Will is himself one of these utopia-wreckers, as he is prepared to engage in skullduggery and connivance to sell out Pala to the foreign oil interest of the suggestively named Lord Aldehyde (64). One of Will's partners in this exploit is Mr. Bahu, the cynical but cultured ambassador of neighbouring Rendang, whose leader Colonel Dipa wishes to annex Pala. Bahu's comment is that Pala is "perfectly wrong because all too perfectly right" (59), that its evident goodness is irrelevant to the real world, that its "hubris" is a "deliberate affront to the rest of humanity" (61). Will deals with Bahu and with the Rani—whose expression of "domineering calm, of serene and unshakable self-esteem" he "peculiarly distasteful" (53)—bur it is clear he does not like what he is doing.

It is Murugan, the young Raja waiting, who acts as primary foil to Will. Murugan's relationship with Colonel Dipa echoes the sensualism of Will's affair with the pneumatic Babs, and his lust for the consumer goods in the "Newest Testament" of the Sears Roebuck catalogue (162) parallels Will's more cynical decision to get money and freedom any way he can. One way to characterize Will's progress in the novel is as a rejection of these negative influences, culminating with the moment when Murugan grabs Will's arm and asks if he is coming to join the plotters. "What the devil do you think you're doing, you little fool?" (288) is the angry response, a response Will rationalizes to himself as aesthetic: "Conscience? No. Morality? Heaven forbid! But supererogatory squalor, ugliness, and vulgarity beyond the call of duty—these were the things which, as a man of taste, one simply couldn't be a party to" (290).

However, Will is also exposed to positive models, who teach him that we are not slaves to our emotions and our histories but that we have some choices, including choices about relationships in our lives—the core of Will's own anger and guilt. For example, his nurse Radha and her boyfriend Ranga demonstrate a happy and open attitude to sex which is the opposite of the agonized flesh-spirit dualism which characterized Will's earlier life and the lives of so many of Huxley's satirical portraits over four decades. "'What do you do with him,' Will asks Radha, 'when he plays these despairing miserable sinner tricks on you? Pull his ears?' 'That,' she replies, 'and . . . well, other things.' She looked at Ranga and Ranga looked at her. Then they both burst out laughing" (77–78). When Will visits the home of Vijaya and Shanta he sees a non-neurotic family in action. One of the themes is the resolution of the dualism between human beings and nature, as Will observes the use of conditioning techniques to establish a relationship of trust between humans and animals. Another exemplar is Dr. MacPhail, who not only tends to Will's physical injuries but shows how it is possible to deal with death in a heroic way, far different from Will's experience as a boy and later with Molly. But it is Susila MacPhail, who lost her husband in a climbing accident, who has the most important role as psychic healer and teacher. One of Will's major turning points comes when he and Susila are discussing "how to remember and yet be free of the past" and Will recognizes his problem of dealing with the duality of the past and present: "Will you help me?" he asks (119).

Clearly she does help him and it is appropriate that it be Susila who guides Will through the visionary episode which constitutes most of the final chapter. Elements from the beginning of the novel—colors, the clock ticking—are picked up here, as if to suggest that the reality being described is the same in certain ways yet very different. Huxley uses music, a description of the "Fourth Brandenburg Concerto," to suggest the experience as Will moves from the "luminous bliss" of perceiving the room around him as a transfigured paradise to a manifestation of the "essential horror": "an endless column of tinbright insects and gleaming reptiles marched up diagonally, from left to right, out of some hidden source of nightmare towards an unknown and monstrous consummation" (315). Finally, however, the music stops.[2] Will pays attention to Susila, to the shadows and lights on her face, and comes to the moment which resolves the dualisms of the novel in the mysterious reality of another human being: "What he was seeing now was the paradox of opposites indissolubly wedded, of light shining out of darkness, of darkness at the very heart of light" (322). At this moment the dualisms of the spirit and flesh, past and present, intention and action, are subsumed into the Divine Ground of Being. Here I think is what might be called the metaphysical climax of the novel and of Huxley's career, a vision of unity—expressed in terms of imagery of marriage—where before there had been dualistic separation:

He stood there motionless, gazing, gazing through a timeless succession of mounting intensities and ever profounder significances. Tears filled his eyes and overflowed at last onto his cheeks. He pulled out his handkerchief and wiped them away.

"I can't help it," he apologized.

He couldn't help it because there was no other way in which he could express his thankfulness. Thankfulness for the privilege of being alive and a witness to this miracle, of being, indeed, more than a witness—a partner in it, an aspect of it. Thankfulness for these gifts of luminous bless and knowledgeless understanding. Thankfulness for being at once this union with the divine unity and yet this finite creature among other finite creatures. (326–327)

Will's experience gives him first hand knowledge of transcendence, and the vision is so overwhelmingly positive that one might reasonably conclude that *Island* is that rare bird among twentieth century imaginary societies—a genuinely positive utopian vision.

However, turning now to the negative reading, just at the moment of transcendence and enlightenment, Will and Susila hear the sounds which signal the end of the utopian dream. Murugan rides into Pala at the head of Colonel Dipa's forces to announce the United Kingdom of Rendang and Pala. They stop at Dr. Robert's bungalow and there is "the sound of a single shot; then a burst of shots from an automatic rifle" (329). Pala is a small island which has not diverted its energies to militarization, a fact which helps to make its utopian reforms manageable; yet this same fact is what makes it vulnerable to precisely the kind of invasion pictured at the end. The realities of global economics and political power have easily overcome the fragile experiment in utopian goodness, as David Bradshaw suggests in the passage quoted at the beginning. Huxley was free at the end of *Island* to suggest a positive future for Pala—it could have come under the protection of the United Nations or a powerful nation, as model for world development. Or he could have left the situation unresolved, with the possibility of a non-aggression treaty. But he chose to bring the troops in and in this there is surely strong support for the view that the pessimism of the early novels has been restored with an ironic vengeance.

What other evidence is there for a pessimistic reading of the novel, beyond the ending itself? There is Mr. Bahu's view, of course, that we are all "demented sinners in the same cosmic boat—and the boat is perpetually sinking. . . . Pala doesn't have the ghost of a chance" (70). Bahu's opinion is contaminated by his cynicism, his envy and his status as an undesirable and yet his prediction for Pala is echoed by Dr. MacPhail: "'. . . whether we shall be able to persuade you people to follow our example, or whether we shall even be able to preserve our tiny oasis of humanity in the midst of your world-wide wilderness of monkeys—that, alas,' said Dr. MacPhail, 'is another question. One's justified in feeling extremely pessimistic the current situation ...'"(130). In turn, this seems to echo Huxley's own opinion. In a letter to his brother in 1960 he suggested that public prospects did not look "very rosy: but perhaps young Mr. Kennedy will be able to do something about them—tho' it seems doubtful" (*Letters,* 900). Such sentiments imply the view that history is not a progress to utopia but an endless cycle, as suggested in the prayer to Shiva in the children's initiation ceremony:

> O you the creator, you the destroyer, you who sustain and make
>   an end
> Who in sunlight dance among the birds and the children at their
>   play
> Who at midnight dance among corpses in the burning grounds,
> You Shiva, you dark and terrible . . . (186)

This also is essential to *Island,* this cosmic dance which is "everlastingly purposeless" (191) and which can indeed leave us with skepticism about the idea of progress and a bleak view of the prospects for utopia.

How are we to account for the deep contradiction between optimism and pessimism which seems woven into the novel, and what message are we to take from it? Huxley has succeeded in describing a place which blends spirituality with sophisticated modern science, a utopia in which there is poetry and exquisite landscape painting, and in which the music of J. S. Bach is treasured, a society in which making love is itself an art form—it is not surprising that many readers, including myself, would resist the negative and pessimistic interpretation. And yet there is the fact of the terrible ending, the murder of Doctor MacPhail and the frightening speeches of the pipsqueak dictator Murugan as the invasion commences.

One way to resolve the interpretive dilemma is suggested by Gorman Beauchamp, who in his excellent 1990 article offers a eupsychian reading. The approach is based upon Abraham Maslow's term which means an "ideal state of consciousness" (Manuel and Manuel, 4). Beauchamp suggests that the reason Huxley brings the troops in at the end of the story is "to elevate the importantce of the eupsychic over the eutopic": although there is little possibility of utopia "the individual can work his or her own salvation, in whatever social context" (70). This provides a kind of resolution to the contradiction between optimism and pessimism, a way beyond the conclusion that the novel is simply conflicted. It says that although we may remain pessimistic about the world at large we can be optimistic about the prospects for individual enlightenment. Such individual enlightenment consists, as Beauchamp notes, in the perception

of the "world's fundamental All Rightness", of "Love as the primary and cosmic fact" (71), and it is demonstrated in the novel by the progress of Will
Farnaby. This seems a good description of enlightenment as Huxley intended
it, and it is indisputable that the eupsychic is important in *Island*. It is only
necessary to think of Huxley's concern for how to bridge the gap between
intentions and actions and the strategies for the transformation of (which are
also at the centre of Laura Huxley's *You Are Not The Target*). Yet I am bothered
by the diminution of the importance of the eutopic because in a sense this
seems to invalidate Huxley's project—why didn't he write some other kind of
book? why a utopia?—and because I have returned, for somewhat different
reasons, to my first instinct that *Island* is a genuinely utopian vision and not
simply eupsychian, that it offers a social goal as well as the individual goal of
enlightenment, that the sense of Huxley's epigraph ("In framing an ideal we
may assume what we wish, but we should avoid impossibilities") is that utopia
is possible and worth working for. It should also be noted that *Island*'s position is that human beings become what they become in large part because of
their environments, so the idea of eu-psychic consciousness in a non-utopian
environment is not supported by the premise of the novel.

    One critical element which moves the book beyond eupsychia to euto-
pia is the rejection of determinism, the notion that the future is open, contin-
gent upon decisions yet to be made. Pala was a long shot too, and it happened.
A conversation between Will and Shanta (whose names suggest the positive
and negative will and shan't) captures this important subtlety. Pala "happened
with us" Shatna says, "it can happen with you". Will agrees "It *can* happen.…
But in the context of H bombs and nationalism and fifty million more people
every single year, it almost certain won't"…"You can't tell till you try"…"we
shan't try as long as the world is in its present state. And, of course, it will
remain in its present state until we do try"…"Pala isn't Eden of the land of
Cockayne. It's a nice place all right. But it will remain nice only if everybody
works and behaves decently. And meanwhile the facts of life are the facts of
life. Even here" (218). One effect of their conversation is to remind us that
pessimism or optimism about a future which has not happened yet is not the
point, that he point is to pay attention the there and now and to make choices
for enlightenment and for utopia. Or as the *Notes on What's What* put it "there
has never been a society which most good doing with was the product of
Good Being and therefore constantly appropriate. This does not mean that
there never will be such a society or that we in Pala are fools for trying to call
it into existence" (37). Utopia is possible and we are not fools for trying to
achieve it.

    Indeed, we have a moral responsibility to try, and in implying this posi-
tion *Island* might be called an existential utopia. According to Sartre one of
the premises of the existential is that existence precedes essence, that it is in

choosing, in acting, that we define ourselves and give meaning to our lives (13). This could be understood to mean that we are both free and responsible and can choose to make an existential "leap" to believe in utopian transformation of the world as a context in which to give our actions meaning, in the way the Kierkegaard described the "reason-transcending decision to believe in God" (Bullock 220): "If I wish to preserve myself in faith I must constantly be intent upon holding fast the objective uncertainty, so as to remain out upon the deep, over seventy thousand fathoms of water, still preserving my faith" (Kierkegaard 204). Here is indeed what it might take to believe in utopia in context of the ending of *Island*.

There can be no doubt that Huxley is recommending to us the basic principles and practices which he has embodied in Pala: a non-dualistic theology, an ecological perspective, a strong emphasis on education and social conditioning, a de-centralizse Kropotkinesque political economy, pacifism, and so forth. The ending does not disestablish or invalidate this particular utopian mix but it does direct our attention away from it, and toward the struggle and the challenge of the world-at-large beyond Pala. Because of the ending Huxley offers us not the romance of a single far-off place to which we could go and be happy, a Shangri-La, but the challenge of difficult and very practical choices in our own world, to pay attention, to be here and now, to choose utopia in whatever terms the choice presents itself in our different lives. (The theme of attention, noted above, is constant throughout the novel, from Will's learning to pay attention to his feelings at the beginning, to Lakshmi's paying attention to her dying, to the intense attention to nature and to Susila which Will achieves in the final chapter.)

Throughout the novel there are intimations of an existential stance on the part of the Palanese. Consider the passage in Susila practices healing suggestion or "button pushing" on Will. She beings by talking about England, about the peacefulness of the Cathedral at Wells, and moves into imagery about clouds, a sleeping river and the cool freshness of mountains. Once these suggestions about rest and temperature have been made she offers Will a choice about his injury, as she reports afterward to Dr. MacPhail: "I got him to be conscious of his body image. Then I made him imagine it much bigger than in every day reality—and the knee much smaller. A miserable little thing in revolt against a huge and splendid thing. There can't be any doubt as to who's going to win" (33). A central idea of the Palanese way is the redirection of energy, in this case redirection from worry and fear into positive imagery. Here Susila suggests the choice for Will, but he will learn to do as the Palanese do and make the choice for himself.

Later, Will recalls to Ranga his experience in the slums of Rendang-Lobo, particularly his experience of a little boy, a "tiny pot-bellied skeleton" he had picked up and carried home. He says that such poverty is the kind

of "cosmic practical joke that God seems really to enjoy." The response is instructive: "'God has nothing to do with it,' Ranga retorted, 'and the joke isn't
cosmic, it's strictly man-made. These things aren't like gravity or the second
law of thermodynamics; they don't *have* to happen. They happen only if people are stupid enough to allow them to happen, so the joke hasn't been played
on us . . . And the reason is very simple: we chose to behave in a sensible and
realistic way'" (88). The idea of choice is what needs to be underlined here,
that the Palanese considered alternatives in a hard-headed and unrealistic
way and chose to create a utopia rather than not to, chose not to give in to
despair. When Will asks Dr. MacPhail about despair, despite his justifiable
pessimism cited above, the response turns on the idea of having a choice:

> "We don't despair," he said, "because we know that things don't
> necessarily *have* to be as bad as in fact they've always been."
> "We know that they can be a great deal better," Susila added.
> "Know it because they already *are* a great deal better, here and
> now, on this absurd little island." (130)

This lesson about choosing is confirmed when Will visits the classroom of
Mrs. Narayan, who points out that "if one chooses to . . . one can always substitute a bad ready-made notion for the best insights of receptivity. The question is, why should one want to make that kind of choice" (250)? And because
this power of choice does exist Mrs. Narayan is an optimist, "for the simple
reason that, if one tackles a problem intelligently and realistically, the results
are apt to be fairly good. This island justifies a certain optimism" (253).

However, isn't the power of choice a delusion which is obliterated by the
ending of the novel? I do not think so. Pala is a model community which apparently ends (although another chapter showing the Palanese way of coping
with the invaders would be interesting).[3] The idea and possibility of utopia
does not end but remains to be worked for. Pala was the result of intelligence
and good luck. The ending suggests not that utopia is impossible but that we
have to keep choosing it, over and over again, and something like Pala, or
something different from but just as utopian as Pala, can happen again. Our
future is not deterministically programmed but depends to some considerable
extent upon the choices we make today.

One of the things which intrigues me about this position is that it en-
capsulates a central utopian question about whether imagining utopia is a
rational activity or some more or less benign form of lunacy. For in response
to the assertion that utopia is possible if we make the existential choice for
utopia, and that Pala suggests this, the determined pessimist could assert that
utopia is not possible and the end of Pala demonstrates the fact. On this balancing beam the issue can go either way and how we choose may, as Aldous

Huxley might say, be a function of our digestive systems or a reflection of our faith or lack of it. Setting aside luck and hard work, which are constants in the equation, the determining factor seems to be—as it always is in matters utopian—our take on human nature: are we as a species capable of acting in our own best collective interest, competing in a healthy and respectful way, for example, or are we doomed to try to destroy each other because that, we perceive, is our best way to survive? I prefer to think that utopia is possible. Or rather, I prefer to think that utopias are possible. Like Pala they may not last, and like Pala they may be partial, but they are none the less real. One reason I prefer to take this view is because I believe the evidence is all around us, precisely in the way that Susila suggests Pala as evidence that utopia is possible.

From the perspective of an abolitionist of 1850 how would the position of black persons in the United States look today? From the perspective of a child labor law advocate of 1844 how would today's universal compulsory schooling look? From the perspective of a mid-nineteenth century feminist, how would today's enrollments in law and medical schools appear? From the perspective of an early nineteenth century operating room, how would today's surgical techniques compare? From the perspective of a family riding a wagon train Westward in 1850 how would three hours on a jet aircraft appear? Of course there are many serious problems today: social, educational, environmental. Much of the world's population still lives in dire circumstances, impoverished, oppressed, exploited, and in light of these enormous problems our world does not look upon utopia. And yet the examples above suggest that if we take certain measures—the progress of democracy is one which comes to mind—compared to 150 years ago this very incomplete and badly flawed progress we have made could look nonetheless genuinely utopian.

To make this point is to risk being taken for an apologist for what many perceive as the corrupt and unjust status quo, whether that means massive government programs or today's preference for the "free" market economy. But the point, rather, is that it is possible to imagine the world being really better for people than it is now, and that our choices can make a difference. Today we might recall stories of children's pulling coal wagons through dark and narrow underground tunnels in the 1840s and we are horrified that such atrocities were allowed. It may be that a century from now others will be equally horrified that so many thousands of today's children roam the hungry streets of big cities or turn to prostitution for their livings. What choices we make now do matter, if we choose to believe that utopia is possible. Of course it is relative, not absolute. Relative to a world of extensive child prostitution a future world of universal protection for children would in a real and meaningful sense be a utopian world, even though the Hydra might grow more heads at the same time, in the form of new challenges.[4]

This is why I choose to read *Island* as positive and utopian. Although *Island* is a realistic statement that worse worlds than this one are possible it is much more powerfully a hopeful statement that better worlds are possible. We are always at that balancing point, at the moment of existential choosing, and the meaning of our lives will depend on what we choose to believe and to do. At the end of the 1946 Foreword to *Brave New World* Huxley, after sketching the positive and negative scenarios for our future, said "you pays your money and you takes your choice" (14). Despite the horror of the invasion I think there is no doubt that the ending of *Island* still leaves the future open and challenges us to choose utopia rather than disaster. Will puts his arm around Susila and holds her close, while the narrator reflects: "The work of a hundred years destroyed in a single night. And yet the fact remained— the fact of the ending of sorrow as well as the fact of sorrow."

Notes

1. Chewing With Aldous
    in *Island* he makes
    utopia seem Palatable—
    no mean feast
    (A. M.)

2. The musical motif of dominant to tonic is one of the ways Huxley ties the end of the story (318) to the beginning (6), the music of Bach to the chanting of the Mynah bird. Music also connects East and West: according to the *Notes on What's What* "Buddhism and modern science think of the world in terms of music" (195).

3. Or there could be another novel, about occupied Pala. Perhaps there are three ways the plot of such a novel could go. The invaders might ruthlessly crush and exterminate the Palanese and replace them with their own people. The story could be a drama of controlled force versus non-violent resistance and end with an open question. Or the resilient Palanese might through their emotional and spiritual maturity convert the invaders to sanity and a re-established utopia.

4. UNICEF estimates that some 250,000,000 children world-wide are involved in child-labor (that is, work which goes beyond mere work to interfere with schooling, health and family life). See "City Streets and Children's Rights" for an account of the urban explosion of recent decades and the phenomenon of street children (Black 119ff).

Works Cited

Beauchamp, Gorman. "*Island:* Aldous Huxley's Psychedelic Utopia." *Utopian Studies* 1.1 (1990): 59–72.

Black, Maggie. *Children First. The Story of UNICEF, Past and Present.* Oxford: Oxford University Press, 1996.

Bradshaw, David. "Introduction." To Huxley, *Island.*

Bullock, Alan & Stallybrass, Oliver, eds. *The Harper Dictionary of Modern Thought.* New York: Harper & Row, 1977.

Huxley, Aldous. *Antic Hay*. Harmondsworth: Penguin, 1948 [1923].
————. *Brave New World*. Harmondsworth: Penguin, 1955 [1932].
————. *Crome Yellow*. Harmondsworth: Penguin, 1964 [1921].
————. *Island*. London: Flamingo, 1994 [1962].
————. *Letters of Aldous Huxley*. Ed. Grover Smith. London: Chatto & Windus, 1969.
————. *The Perennial Philosophy*. Cleveland: Meridian Books, 1969 [1944–1945].
————. *Point Counter Point*. Harmondsworth: Penguin, 1955 [1928].
Huxley, Laura Archera. *You Are Not the Target*. Foreword by Aldous Huxley, New York: Avon Books, 1976 [1963].
Kierkegaard Søren. *The Difficulty Of Being Christian*. Notre Dame: University of Notre Dame Press, 1968 [1964].
Manuel, Frank E., and Fritzie P. Manuel. *Utopian Thought in The Western World*. Cambridge, Massachusetts: Harvard University Press, 1974.
Sartre, Jean-Paul. *Existentialism and Human Emotions*. New York: Carol Publishing Group, 1995 [1957].

ACKNOWLEDGMENT

Thanks to Rob Luzecky and George Marshall for helpful comments, and to the editorial readers for Utopian Studies who raised a number of excellent questions and made suggestions for improvement.

BRAD BUCHANAN

Oedipus in Dystopia: Freud and Lawrence in Aldous Huxley's Brave New World

Freud's role in Aldous Huxley's *Brave New World* has been much discussed, but little consensus has emerged, partly because of Huxley's apparent ambivalence about Freud's ideas and his growing reluctance, after he had written the novel, to admit that he had ever been in agreement with Freud's conception of human nature. In a 1960 interview, Huxley said, "I was never intoxicated by Freud as some people were, and I get less intoxicated as I go on."[1] Although some have taken this statement as an unequivocal denial of any affinity Huxley may have had for Freud,[2] it reads less as a repudiation of Freud than as a confession that Huxley was indeed "intoxicated" by Freud to a certain extent when he was younger, although he certainly never reached the stage of feverish zealotry achieved by some of his contemporaries.[3] Indeed, Huxley's half-hearted protestations against Freud have prompted insinuations about the motives behind them. For instance, Charles Holmes claims: "throughout his life Huxley rejected Freud, though the tone and intensity of his rejection varied. Given Freud's emphasis on sex and Huxley's near-obsession with it, the rejection implies unconscious resistance incompletely understood."[4] Philip Thody has undertaken to explain this "resistance" in biographical terms:

> Huxley's adoration of his mother implied feelings of intense jealousy
> for his father, and . . . these were translated into the subconscious

Journal of Modern Literature, Volume 25, Numbers 3–4 (Summer 2002): pp. 75–89. Copyright
© 2002 Brad Buchanan.

notion that Leonard Huxley was at least partly guilty for his wife's death. . . . [T]he hostility which Huxley always shows for Freud's ideas . . . [is] an indication of the fear which he had that such a diagnosis might be true, and the fact that almost all the fathers in Huxley's fiction are caricatures would lend weight to this view.[5]

My concern, however, is neither to confirm nor refute such descriptions of and speculations about Huxley's ambivalent attitude to Freud, but to show how this attitude manifests itself in *Brave New World*, in which Freudian ideas are plainly on display. I also suggest that any account of Huxley's reaction to Freud should take into account the probable influence on Huxley of D. H. Lawrence, who attacked Freud's views yet whose life and work present clear examples of many Freudian theories.

The most prominent of Freud's ideas, at least for my purposes, is his notion of the "Oedipus complex," which, according to Freud, describes a male child's feelings of incestuous desire for his mother and parricidal aggression towards his father. Oedipus' story is potentially every boy's, according to Freud, because all boys see their mothers as love-objects and their fathers as rivals.[6] This was perhaps Freud's most controversial and unpopular theory, and one that Huxley might have been particularly eager to debunk. Yet on 24 August 1931, shortly after finishing *Brave New World*, Huxley wrote a letter to his father in which he describes his new book as "a comic, or at least satirical, novel about the Future . . . and adumbrating the effects on thought and feeling of such quite possible biological inventions as the production of children in bottles (with [the] consequent abolition of the family and all the Freudian 'complexes' for which family relationships are responsible)."[7] This letter shows that Huxley was willing to discuss the "Freudian 'complexes' for which family relationships are responsible" very seriously indeed and with his own father, no less. If Huxley had any doubts at all about the truth of the most famous of these complexes, he would certainly have assured his father that he harbored no such "complex," with its attendant murderous and incestuous feelings, or at least would have palliated the unpleasant thought that his own family was to blame for imposing these emotions on him. The fact that he did not, I propose, says a good deal about his opinion of the fundamental truth of Freud's theory of the Oedipus complex.

This opinion is shown even more clearly in *Brave New World*, in which the Oedipus complex is deemed such a dangerous and powerful force that it (along with the family structure that produces it) has been eliminated from civilized life, as far as possible. Children are no longer born to a set of parents but produced in an assembly-line process from fertilized eggs, which are then "decanted" into bottles and subjected to endless chemical alteration and conditioning.[8] By controlling all aspects of a child's birth and upbringing and by keeping adults in a condition of infantile dependency on a larger social body, Huxley's imaginary state has taken over the role of parent and robbed the child of his or her Oedipal potentialities. Indeed, it could be argued that the active suppression of the Oedipus complex is the principal tool of social stability practiced in this future. Yet this state of affairs is really just an extension of principles that have helped to form twentieth-century life, according to Freud. After all, in *Totem and Taboo* Freud postulates that the reason Oedipus' parricide and incest shock us so much is that we have constructed civilization precisely to discourage the two crimes of which Oedipus is guilty, the "only two crimes which troubled primitive society."[9] In Huxley's futuristic utopia, the prohibitions against parricide and incest are simply taken to their logical extreme, so that even the unconscious energies produced by repressing such desires are dissipated. The solution to the problem of Oedipal desire is to make everyone so infantile that he still feels as if he were in the womb/decanter. A popular song within the novel expresses this pre-Oedipal state: "Bottle of mine, it's you I've always wanted! / Bottle of mine, why was I ever decanted?" (*Brave New World*, p. 91).

Freud himself is treated as a prophet in this pseudo-paradise; indeed, he is elevated to near-divinity, along with Henry Ford (the similarity of their names comes in handy): "Our Ford—or Our Freud, as, for some inscrutable reason, he chose to call himself whenever he spoke of psychological matters—Our Freud had been the first to reveal the appalling dangers of family life" (p. 44). These dangers have to do not with incest or parricide but with "the prohibitions they were not conditioned to obey" and which force them to "feel strongly" (p. 47). Strong feelings, of course, are unpleasant enough to the denizens of the "brave new world," but the Director of London's Central "hatchery" supplements this already grim picture with the horrible thought of emotionally suffocating parents who once clung desperately to their children: "The world was full of fathers—was therefore full of misery; full of mothers—therefore of every kind of perversion from sadism to chastity" (p. 44). He sums up the plight of past generations vividly:

> home was as squalid psychically as physically. Psychically, it was a rabbit hole, a midden, hot with the frictions of tightly packed life, reeking with emotion. What suffocating intimacies, what dangerous, insane, obscene relationships between the members of the family group! Maniacally, the mother brooded over her children . . . like a cat over its kittens; but cat that could talk, a cat that could say, "My baby, my baby," over and over again. "My baby, and oh, oh, at my breast, the little hands, the hunger, and that unspeakable, agonizing pleasure. . . ."
> "Yes," said Mustapha Mond, nodding his head, "you may well shudder." (pp. 42–43)

The people of Huxley's future have not read Freud, quite clearly, but they have been indoctrinated with a Freud-influenced awareness of the possibility of illicit relations between mother and child. This awareness, which manifests itself in Lenina Crowne's distaste for the "indecent" spectacle of "two young women giving the breast to their babies," the sight of which makes her "blush and turn away" (p. 130), is exploited to inculcate a less visceral but nonetheless strong suspicion of any private or emotionally intense relationship between two people. Indeed, any individualized, personalized sexual feelings are branded as essentially incestuous, and the language of forbidden passion is essentially a disgusting outgrowth of the obsolete love-talk between mother and child: "My baby, my mother, my only, only love" (p. 49). An "only love" is an incestuous love, in Huxley's futuristic world, because it tends to work against the social solidarity which is the key to peaceful life.

Despite all this revulsion towards the very possibility of Oedipal crimes or Oedipal urges, the mythical figure of Oedipus returns to Huxley's novel with a vengeance, in the form of John ("the Savage"), a man who was born (in the traditional "viviparous" way) into an Indian tribe on a reservation in New Mexico. John's father is the Director of the London Hatchery, who leaves John to be raised by his mother, Linda, after he has impregnated her in the once-traditional but now unthinkable way. Like Oedipus, John grows up without knowing who his biological father is, but finally, with the help of his mother, he learns the truth. He also unintentionally ruins his father by embracing him publicly, kneeling before him, and addressing him as "My father"—a scene that no doubt functions as Huxley's satirical rendition of Oedipus' unwitting murder of his own biological father. Yet John is more of a Freudian case study than a reincarnation of Oedipus himself; his sensibilities have been formed by a battered edition of Shakespeare which he finds (rather improbably) in the squalor around him, and he identifies strongly with Hamlet's rage about his mother's marriage to Claudius. He experiences some classically Freudian Oedipal jealousy of the native man who sleeps with his mother, spurring his anger with apt quotations from *Hamlet:* "He hated Popé more and more. A man can smile and smile and be a villain" (p. 156).[10] Finally, as if to complete the Freudian cliché, John tries to kill Popé as he is "drunk asleep" (p. 158); he fails, but Popé is mildly impressed with his attempt and says laughingly but affectionately: "'Go, my brave Ahaiyuta'" (p. 159).

As if belatedly following this directive, John and his mother eventually leave the reservation with Bernard Marx, an insecure would-be intellectual who seeks to win approval and social status by parading them as curiosities back in London. Yet even after he has encountered the many attractive and available women there, John remains obsessed with his mother. He fondly remembers the intimate moments between him and Linda fondly, recalling "those times when he sat on her knees and she put her arms about him and sang, over and over again, rocking him, rocking him to sleep" (p. 244). Linda's own behavior towards John has contributed heavily to his fixation on her; she has been neglectful, sentimental, abusive, and affectionate by turns towards John. For instance, when John was little, she slapped him for calling her his "mother" and then, in a matter of moments, repented and kissed him "again and again" (p. 150), as if he were a suitable replacement for the lovers whom she has lost temporarily because of other women's jealousy. John never understands the nature of his feelings towards Linda, conflating his incestuous desires and violent impulses towards Popé with the trappings of heroism (after all, both traits are found in *Hamlet*). The fact that such powerful attachments are not normal any longer in a world of obligatory contraception and institutionalized promiscuity simply reinforces John's sense of tragic self-importance. Direct exposure to Freud's writings might have informed John that his feelings are not symptoms of some extraordinary powers or responsibilities, that they are normal emotions (at least in Freud's mind) to be recognized and overcome. Yet as we can readily see, no one any longer reads Freud, or if people do, they fail to apply or explain his theory of the Oedipus complex to John, the one human being to whom it is still relevant.

John finds it difficult to renounce his mother or sever their emotional connection (as he shows throughout the novel), and this leads him to be extremely censorious of any lustful impulse in himself, since all of his erotic attachments seem charged with the unsatisfied desires of his childhood love for Linda. When he calls Lenina an "impudent strumpet" (p. 232), he is not only censuring her evidently promiscuous behavior (which she, ironically, seems at times to be willing to change for his sake); he is projecting his revulsion at his own lusts onto her. We get a sense of how deeply John's libido has been repressed when he attends a "feely" (a futuristic movie which allows spectators to feel as well as see the actions onscreen) which features scenes of lovemaking between "a gigantic negro and a golden-haired young brachycephalic Beta-Plus female" (p. 200). No doubt prompted by memories of Linda and Popé,[11] John is revolted by this interracial love story; he "start[s]" violently as it begins and later terms it "horrible" (p. 202), although he is struck by the similarities between it and Shakespeare's *Othello*. Long afterwards, John's desire for Lenina become inextricably linked to the mixture of sexual arousal and disgust that he feels while watching the feely: "he felt her [Lenina's] lips soft against his own. So deliciously soft, so warm and electric that inevitably he found himself thinking of the embraces in *Three Weeks in a Helicopter*. Ooh! ooh! the stereoscopic blonde and aah! the more than real blackamoor. Horror, horror, horror . . . he tried to disengage himself" (p. 229).

John seems to identify with the possessive "negro" (whom he links to Shakespeare's nobler *Othello*), just as he had once identified with Popé, and yet he reacts with predictable disgust at the depiction of his own incestuous fantasies on the screen (just as he comes to hate Popé for having sexual access to Linda). Like Linda, the heroine of the "feely" is a blonde Beta who makes love to a man from a different, darker-skinned race. Lenina, who accompanies John to the "feely," is herself associated in John's mind with the "brachycephalic blonde" and, by extension, with Linda herself;[12] thus, as Freudians might well argue, he cannot imagine having sexual relations with Lenina before he has exorcised the unconscious incestuous demons that plague him and make him mistrust all sexual activity. These demons seem to determine his reactions to many of the everyday features of the world he has entered; for instance, he is outraged by the docile subservience of a group of identical Deltas awaiting their *soma*. He sees such twins as "less than human monsters," asking them why they do not want to "be free and men" and challenging them to throw off their dependence on drugged bliss: "Do you like being babies? Yes, babies. Mewling and puking" (p. 254). Here Huxley's keen sense of irony is at its most forceful: the Savage accuses the cloned workers of the same infantilism he has managed to confront only (and that partially) through his violent and unresolved "Oedipus complex." There may be more than Freudian theory at work here, however; as anthropologists have observed, twins frequently symbolize the results of incestuous activity. As René Girard writes in *Violence and the Sacred*, "Incestuous propagation leads to formless duplications, sinister repetitions, a dark mixture of unnamable things. In short, the incestuous creature exposes the community to the same danger as do twins . . . mothers of twins are often suspected of having conceived their children in incestuous fashion."[13] Thus, it may be that Huxley wants to indicate that John associates these twins with his own unfulfilled urges, which he must then repress all the more violently, or sublimate into radical activity (witness his act of throwing the Deltas' long-awaited *soma* out the window). After Linda's death, the link between her and these twins remains prominent: "he had sworn to himself he would constantly remember . . . Linda, and his own murderous unkindness to her, and those loathsome twins, swarming like lice across the mystery of her death" (pp. 296–297).

Haunted by such memories, John finally commits suicide, having failed to live up to the standards of chastity and morality which he has set for himself, yet he is not the only one who finds himself unable to live within the parameters of Huxley's imagined society. Bernard Marx and Helmholtz Watson share a sense that "they were individuals" (p. 80) and chafe against the conformity imposed on them, however pleasant its trappings may be. Like John, both of these heroes have a certain amount in common with Oedipus; both end up in exile, Bernard for his obstreperousness and Helmholtz for his refusal to live by the usual rules enforcing indulgence, promiscuity, and sociability.[14] They are friends but are conscious of a major difference between them: "whereas the physically defective Bernard had suffered all his life from the consciousness of being separate, it was only quite recently that, grown aware of his mental excess, Helmholtz Watson had also become aware of his difference from the people who surrounded him" (p. 80). While Bernard's show of resistance to the permissive status quo disappears once he has gained the self-confidence to get what he wants,[15] Helmholtz' desire to impose a measure of austerity on himself, especially with respect to his sexual relationships, is genuine.

John's and Helmholtz' moral objections to the amorous goings-on around them have long been assumed to be an expression of Huxley's own disapproval of promiscuity, and understandably so. After all, a few years before writing *Brave New World*, Huxley had claimed that "Nothing is more dreadful than a cold, unimpassioned indulgence. And love infallibly becomes cold and unimpassioned when it is too lightly made."[16] In a 1931 essay, Huxley argues that "No reasonable hedonist can consent to be a flat racer. Abolishing obstacles, he abolishes half his pleasures. And at the same time he abolishes most of his dignity as a human being. For the dignity of man consists precisely in his ability to restrain himself . . . to raise obstacles in his own path."[17] This view is remarkably close to that expressed by Freud in *Civilization and its Discontents*,[18] a book translated into English and published in 1930, which Huxley may or may not have managed to read before or during the composition of *Brave New World* (from May of 1931 to August of that year). Nevertheless, Freud is certainly to be numbered among the "reformers" mentioned by Mustapha Mond in *Brave New World* when he addresses his charges: "Has any of you been compelled to live through a long time-interval between the consciousness of a desire and its fulfilment? . . . And you felt a strong emotion in consequence? . . . Our ancestors were so stupid and short-sighted that when the first reformers came along and offered to deliver them from those horrible emotions, they wouldn't have anything to do with them" (pp. 52–53). Yet passages such as these have caused some of Huxley's readers to lump Freud in with his supposed followers in the novel. For instance, Philip Thody[19] argues that "In *Brave New World* it is . . . the implied ethical teachings of Freudianism that attract his scorn, the rejection of complex and mature emotions in favour of instant gratification and the pleasure principle. His disapproval is, in fact, almost Victorian in its moral intensity."[20] Nevertheless, critical opinion on this issue has been divided; Peter Firchow points out that "In *Brave New World* excessive restraint, like the Savage's, still leads to self-destruction."[21] Firchow not only contests the claim that Freud is a spokesman for libertinism in Huxley's eyes, he even goes so far as to argue (without much evidence, it must be said) that "Freud . . . is the closest the new world's science comes to having a conscience."[22]

Another, more clear-cut area in which Huxley and Freud have been deemed to disagree irreconcilably has to do with artistic creation. We know that, in Huxley's view, Freud was guilty of implying that art is (as Huxley puts it) a "happy efflorescence of sexual perversity."[23] In an article called "Formulations Regarding the Two Principles in Mental Functioning," first published in 1911, Freud did make the somewhat insulting claim that "The artist is originally a man who turns from reality because he cannot come to terms with the demand for the renunciation of instinctual satisfaction as it is first made, and who then in fantasy-life allows full play to his erotic and ambitious wishes."[24] Yet this position is a long way from the simple choice presented by Mustapha Mond (or "the Controller"), who states the official position: "'You've got to choose between happiness and what people used to call high art. We've sacrificed the high art'" (p. 264). Some have inferred that this passage means that in Huxley's mind Freud is the opponent of high art, since his theory of the "Oedipus complex" is meant to induce people to accept their lot and to be happy, rather than continue being neurotic and creative. Whatever the merits of this characterization of Freud's position, its assumption about the straightforwardness of Huxley's views does them a disservice. Huxley was deeply ambivalent about "high art," especially tragedy, which he regarded as an outdated genre. In his essay "Tragedy and the Whole Truth," Huxley argues that there is something inherently false about a tragic narrative: "To make a tragedy the artist must isolate a single element out of the totality of human experience and use that exclusively as his material. Tragedy is something that is separated from the Whole Truth, distilled from it, so to speak."[25] In this essay, Huxley uses *Othello* as an example of a tragedy which must exclude realistic details which would make it more truthful in order to achieve its dramatic effect. Of course, *Othello* is also mentioned prominently in *Brave New World*, where its interracial sexual themes resurface in the pornographic "feely" attended by John and Lenina. Mindful of John's habit of viewing everything in Shakespearean terms, Mond admonishes John that "our world is not the same as Othello's world . . . you can't make tragedies without social instability'" (p. 263). We may infer that in Huxley's eyes the "Whole Truth" lies somewhere between tragedy and pornography and that John's tragic vision of reality is an oversimplification of what Huxley recognizes as the complexities of modern life.

Huxley even seems to endorse one element of Freud's characterization of the artistic impulse, insofar as it is related to the Oedipal energies represented by John. In *Group Psychology and the Analysis of the Ego*, a monograph published in 1923, Freud creates a scenario to explain the role of creativity, or more specifically, of epic narrative, in primitive society just after the parricidal crisis in which the famous band of brothers has slain the tyrannical father: "some individual. . . may have been moved to free himself from the group and take over the [dead] father's part. He who did this was the first epic poet; and the advance was achieved in his imagination . . . He invented the heroic myth."[26] This formula of original creativity is extremely tendentious, to say the least; as Richard Astle puts it in his article "Dracula as Totemic Monster: Lacan, Freud, Oedipus and History," Freud is "projecting the Oedipus onto an earlier age to explain the origin of myth and, more generally, of narrative."[27] Nevertheless, Huxley seems to endorse something rather like it in his description of Helmholtz Watson's artistic difficulties. While John has no difficulty expressing his emotions (even if only through Shakespearean tags), Helmholtz, although a would-be artist, seems to be searching for an objective correlative with which to express his sense of difference and his ambitions; he has "'a feeling that I've got something important to say and the power to say it—only I don't know what it is . . . If there was some different way of writing . . . Or else something else to write about'" (p. 82). He is looking for something "'important'" to say, something "'more intense'" and "'more violent'" (p. 83), but he cannot countenance John's suggestion that he look to family life for his subject matter. Helmholtz refuses to see family life as a possible source of what he lacks: "'You can't expect me to keep a straight face about fathers and mothers . . . We need some other kind of madness and violence'" (p. 221). It seems clear that Helmholtz will never be a real artist, nor will he ever be able to understand his friend John, as long as he cannot accept that there is some validity to the Oedipal narrative.

Another disagreement that has been noted between Huxley and Freud has to do with their attitudes towards religion. Huxley plainly deplored Freud's implication that religion and other mystical experiences were a product of neuroses or sexual repression, yet he seems to acknowledge the reality of what Freud referred to in *Civilization and its Discontents* as "the oceanic feeling." If Huxley had not read this book, it must stand as an extraordinary coincidence that the religious ceremonies in *Brave New World* employ much of the same vocabulary used by Freud to describe a theory propounded by one of his correspondents (who turned out to be none other than the French writer Romain Rolland):

> I had sent him my small book that treats religion as an illusion, and he answered that he entirely agreed with my judgement upon religion, but that he was sorry I had not properly appreciated the true source of religious sentiments. This, he says, consists in a peculiar feeling, which he himself is never without, which he finds confirmed by many others, and which he may suppose is present in millions of people. It is a feeling as of something limitless, unbounded—as it were, "oceanic." This feeling, he adds, is a purely subjective fact, not an article of faith; it brings with it no assurance of personal immortality, but it is the source of the religious energy which is seized upon by the various Churches and religious

systems, directed by them into particular channels, and doubtless also exhausted by them. One may, he thinks, rightly call oneself religious on the ground of this oceanic feeling alone, even if one rejects every belief and every illusion.[28]

The quasi-spiritual rituals of "atonement" (p. 94) in *Brave New World* rely heavily on imagery very close to Freud's here; one song which features in these moments of group celebration is called a "Solidarity Hymn" and contains the lines: "'Ford, we are twelve; oh, make us one, / Like drops within the Social River'" (p. 95). Each participant drinks from a "loving cup" of *soma* after reciting a pledge of self-effacement—"I drink to my annihilation" (p. 95)—in a ceremony that seems like a parody of Christian self-abnegation.

This kind of water imagery is very much a part of everyday life in Huxley's dystopia; a group of ecstatic dancers is described as if "they might have been twin embryos gently rocking together on the waves of a bottled ocean of blood-surrogate" (p. 91). Yet, as if to register his awareness that this kind of mindless bobbing on the ocean's surface is not quite what Freud meant by the "oceanic feeling," he shows Bernard contemplating the ocean after participating in one of these liquefying moments. Bernard takes comfort in the ocean's inhuman wholeness, and he feels that his tenuous individuality has been strengthened somehow: "'It makes me feel as though . . . I were more *me*, if you see what I mean. More on my own, not so completely a part of something else. Not just a cell in the social body'" (p. 106). While Bernard's testimony of what this "oceanic feeling" means to him does not quite fit Rolland's description of a vague spiritual awareness, it does correspond rather well to Freud's judgment on the sources of such a feeling. Freud writes: "we are perfectly willing to acknowledge that the 'oceanic' feeling exists in many people, and we are inclined to trace it back to an early phase of ego-feeling."[29]

Another accusation made by Huxley against Freud is the not terribly original claim that the latter's emphasis on sexuality was "monomaniacal," as Huxley wrote in *Proper Studies*, published in 1927.[30] Yet Huxley himself reconsidered this verdict very publicly, in a newspaper article published 11 March 1933. In this brief piece, Huxley editorializes about the relative nature of Freud's insights about human nature, claiming that "It is only in the more prosperous sections of civilized urban communities that hunger loses its pre-eminence. Freud, who gives the palm to sex, worked in Vienna. . . . Love, as a wholetime job, has only been practiced by the more prosperous members of civilized societies."[31] Huxley admits that Dr. Audrey Richards is right to point out that sex does not assume the same importance in Bantu society as Freud claims it does in all human civilizations, but he goes on to say something that those who see Huxley as an unflinching anti-Freudian ought to find rather surprising: "That the psycho-analysts should be wrong about savages is not particularly important. The significant fact is that they are probably right about civilized people."[32] Huxley implies that Freud's "Pleasure Principle" is likely to triumph wherever social and technological "efficiency" prevails,[33] and he shows no signs of regarding this likelihood as anything to be lamented. In this respect, we may well wonder whether all the promiscuity which he portrays in *Brave New World* is to be regarded as the inevitable manifestation of otherwise desirable advances in human civilization.

* * *

Huxley was more than capable of making up his own mind about the relative merits of psychoanalysis, but around the time he began to write *Brave New World* he was still very much under the influence of D. H. Lawrence. Huxley first met Lawrence in December 1915 but did not become a close friend of his until 1926, when he and his wife, Maria, saw a good deal of the Lawrences in Italy. In 1920, Huxley had referred to Lawrence as a "slightly insane novelist" who had been "analysed for his complexes, dark and tufty ones, tangled in his mind."[34] As a result, Huxley cattily writes, "The complexes were discovered, and it is said that Lawrence has now lost, along with his slight sexual mania, all his talent as a writer."[35] Huxley soon changed his mind about Lawrence, but his conviction remained that literary talent cannot survive psychoanalytic scrutiny or successful therapy. Lawrence was a very important figure for Huxley during the years just before *Brave New World* was written;[36] Huxley visited Lawrence in Italy during the latter's final illness, and as his letters testify, he was profoundly moved by Lawrence's courage and his uncompromising (albeit frequently irrational) views about sex, social life, and the artistic vocation. Huxley was with Lawrence when he died on 2 March 1930 and witnessed his final struggles with great emotion, calling Lawrence "the most extraordinary and impressive human being I have ever known."[37] In memory of his friend, Huxley put together an edition of Lawrence's letters and even contemplated writing a biography of him, although the freshness of the memory and his own contractual obligations prevented him from writing a full-length work devoted to Lawrence.

Between the time Huxley renewed his acquaintance with Lawrence in 1926 and Lawrence's death in 1930, Huxley published *Point Counter Point, Proper Studies, Do What You Will,* and *Music at Night,* all of which contain references to Freud and/or psychoanalysis. Furthermore, while Huxley was writing *Brave New World* between May and August of 1931, he was still looking at Freud largely through Lawrentian lenses. Lawrence's deep attachment to his sensitive mother and his hostility to his crude father, the Nottinghamshire coal miner, might well have showed Huxley that at least one aspect of Freud's writing (the basic conception of the Oedipus complex) was very likely

true, or at least very plausible. In any case, Lawrence's own passionate engagement with Freudianism, as well as his dogged but rather confused attempts to
refute Freud's theory of the universality of the Oedipus complex,[38] certainly
made an impression on Huxley. In his essay on Lawrence, Huxley addresses
the question of Freud's relevance to Lawrence only once, and rather defen-
sively: "Explanations of him [Lawrence] in terms of a Freudian hypothesis
of nurture may be interesting, but they do not explain. That Lawrence was
profoundly affected by his love for his mother and by her excessive love for
him, is obvious to anyone who has read *Sons and Lovers*. None the less it is, to
me at any rate, almost equally obvious that even if his mother had died when
he was a child, Lawrence would still have been, essentially and fundamentally, Lawrence."[39] Huxley is no doubt reacting against the crudely Freudian
analysis of Lawrence's writing contained in John Middleton Murry's book
Son of Woman, which in the same essay Huxley dismisses as "destructive" and
"irrelevant."[40]

Huxley deemed Lawrence "a great man,"[41] and although he found Lawrence "difficult to get on with, passionate, queer, violent,"[42] he was generally
very loyal to him, and especially so after Lawrence's death.[43] In September
1931, Huxley was "making notes for a short study of [Lawrence] to serve as
introduction to the letters," a study which, as Huxley says, "cannot be specifically a retort to Murry" but will "try to undo some of the mischief that
slug has undoubtedly done."[44] The main symptom of Murry's mischievous
"cleverness" is his exploitation of "the psycho-analytical rigamarole" where
Lawrence was concerned.[45] Addressing this aspect of Murry's book, which
Huxley (showing an uncharacteristic taste for oxymorons) terms a "vindic-
tive hagiography," he admits that Murry's insights into Lawrence's psyche are
often accurate; Murry's Freudian analysis of Lawrence as a man in love with
his mother and in violent rebellion against his father "is able and in parts
very true."[46] *Son of Woman* was published in April 1931, and as a friend of
Lawrence's as well as a man of letters, Huxley might well have read it in time
for it to affect his portrayal of Freudianism in *Brave New World*. Whether this
was in fact the case, we may draw several analogies between John "the Savage"
and Lawrence himself, with whom Huxley was undoubtedly still preoccupied
regardless of his reaction to Murry's book. As a visionary (at least in Huxley's
mind) who remained true to his beliefs to the bitter end, Lawrence would
have provided an excellent model for John the Savage, whose ultimately self-
destructive moral absolutism is as unusual in the London which he visits
as Lawrence's was in his own bohemian circle (which included the notorious womanizer Bertrand Russell, his wife, Dora, Lady Ottoline Morrell, and
Gerald Heard). While John's apparent prudery seems to be fundamentally
opposed to Lawrence's worship of the phallic principle and emphasis on the
regenerative aspects of sexual activity, these two figures share an important

common trait in Huxley's eyes: they cannot countenance sex as a meaningless form of recreation. Both are convinced that sex bears a tremendous significance and that the purely recreational, hedonistic promiscuity of people such as Lenina and Bernard is deeply obscene.

The Oedipal themes in Lawrence's own life resonate deeply with John's struggles in *Brave New World*; Huxley's decision to have John direct his parricidal aggression towards Popé, a Native American, may have been inspired by Lawrence, who (having spent many years living among the native people of America) muses in a later essay about the notion of having a "dusky-lipped tribe-father" who, "like many an old father with a changeling son . . . would like to deny me."[47] Moreover, Linda's capricious yet ardent affection for John is entirely in keeping with Lawrence's pronouncements about the culpability of the mother in the development of incestuous desires in their sons. The over-affectionate mother, in Lawrence's eyes, "has not the courage to give up her hopeless insistence on love and her endless demand for love,"[48] and therefore "she provokes what she wants. Here, in her own son, who belongs to her, she seems to find the last perfect response for which she is craving. He is a medium to her, she provokes from him her own answer. So she throws herself into a last great love for her son."[49] Other familial situations found in Lawrence's work crop up in *Brave New World*; for instance, in Lawrence's *Sons and Lovers*, Paul Morel's aborted parricidal impulse seems to have been diverted and to have attached to Mrs. Morel. As her cancer worsens, Paul wishes that she would die and even goes so far as to administer a large dose of morphine to speed up the process. Huxley's John does not actually administer the gradual overdoses of *soma* that kill Linda, but, pressured by doctors, he agrees to allow her to take as much as she wants, and this leads to her demise (and to his crippling feelings of guilt).

Before he wrote *Brave New World*, Huxley denied having portrayed Lawrence in his own fiction, claiming that Mark Rampion, the Lawrence-like character in *Point Counter Point* is "just some of Lawrence's notions on legs."[50] Huxley felt that Lawrence was "incomparably queerer and more complex" than the dogmatic Rampion, whom Lawrence himself referred to as a "gas-bag."[51] Despite Huxley's diffidence about his fictional renditions of Lawrence, we cannot avoid suspecting that his portrayal of John in *Brave New World* is heavily indebted to his friend. Thus, Huxley repeatedly describes Lawrence's sense of humor as "savage," his "high spirits" are "almost terrifyingly savage," and his "mockery" is "frighteningly savage."[52] In both cases, Huxley remarks upon Lawrence's satirical intelligence (one of Lawrence's less well-known traits) and testifies to its power; it is therefore not surprising that he chooses a Lawrence-like hero such as John to be the explicitly "savage" vehicle of his own most biting satire. Although John does not display himself a terribly sophisticated sense of humor, his naïveté, intense earnestness, and plain-spokenness make for some mordant scenes in *Brave New World*. For instance, when John falls to his knees in front of the DHC and hails the horrified bureaucrat as "My father!" (p. 180), a word which is so "comically smutty" to the onlookers that they break into "hysterical" laughter (p. 181), Huxley is making the sardonic point that traditional family-based values have been completely turned on their head in his utopia.

Furthermore, like John opposing Mond, Lawrence stands in Huxley's mind for the integrity of the artistic impulse, as for the belief that it must be permitted to express itself even if the result is disastrous; as Huxley claims, "Lawrence was always and unescapably [sic] an artist."[53] In describing the difficulties of being an artist, Huxley quotes Lawrence's complaint that "At times one is *forced to* be essentially a hermit. I don't want to be. But everything else is either a personal tussle, or a money tussle; sickening. . . . One has no real human relations—that is so devastating."[54] Huxley echoes this lament after quoting it: "One has no real human relations: it is the complaint of every artist. The artist's first duty is to his genius, his *daimon;* he cannot serve two masters."[55] Huxley's remarks here imply that there is a split between the artist's task and his or her "human" relationships and that the true genius must finally lose faith in the "human" social setting that others depend on. We recall that, after making the rounds in London (visiting the self-declared intellectuals, much as Lawrence once did, to his own great disgust), the Savage tries to live as a hermit in the woods, and Helmholtz Watson decides that exile will serve his own artistic ambitions better than continuing to live in London.

Another odd detail that links Lawrence to *Brave New World* surfaces in a letter sent by Huxley to Lawrence in December 1928. Huxley describes a visit to a "night-bar . . . devoted to Lesbians" in which he witnessed "a wrestling match between two gigantic female athletes."[56] In *Brave New World*, we are told that Bernard and Lenina fly to Amsterdam to witness "the Women's Heavyweight Wrestling Championship" (p. 104). In 1928, the Huxleys contemplated spending six months on Lawrence's ranch in New Mexico, the Western state which would later become the location of the "Savage Reservation" on which John is born and raised in *Brave New World*. To this circumstantial evidence we may also add the fact that Lawrence's relationship with his wife, Frieda, struck Huxley as being highly unusual, not to say disturbing. Frieda Lawrence was older than her husband and behaved in a very maternal way towards Lawrence, at least in Huxley's eyes: "Lawrence was . . . in some strange way dependent on her presence, physically dependent."[57] Frieda's promiscuity came uncomfortably close to matching Linda's in *Brave New World*, just as Lawrence's possessiveness matched John's, as Huxley was well aware. He writes:

Frieda and Lawrence had, undoubtedly, a profound and passionate love-life. But this did not prevent Frieda from having, every now and then, affairs with Prussian cavalry officers and Italian peasants . . . Lawrence, for his part, was aware of these erotic excursions, got angry about them sometimes, but never made the least effort to break away from her; for he realized his own organic dependence on her.[58]

Frieda exasperated Huxley by her unreliability, indolence, and stubbornness and may have provided a model for Linda. Huxley confesses, "I like Frieda in many ways but she is incurably and incredibly stupid—the most maddening woman I think I ever came across."[59] Of course, Huxley realized that Lawrence too had his shortcomings; as he says, "I never understood his anti-intellectualism. . . . His dislike of science was passionate and expressed itself in the most fantastically unreasonable terms."[60] In this respect, once again, Lawrence is very like John, who dismisses the scientific and technological advances of supposedly civilized London with quotations from Shakespeare or some other irrelevancy.

Despite his sympathy for Lawrence, Huxley felt that his friend's illnesses, both physical and psychological, were "unnecessary, the result simply of the man's strange obstinacy against professional medicine."[61] Clearly, Huxley was deeply ambivalent about both Lawrence and Freud; while he felt a great loyalty towards and admiration for Lawrence, he could not suppress his feeling that Murry was in fact right about the "complex" that afflicted Lawrence and that the latter could have been happier and healthier, although not necessarily a better writer, if he had accepted Freud's insights to a greater extent. This feeling is perhaps reflected in *Brave New World;* indeed, it could well be argued that John desperately needs Freud to explain his own urges and hostilities before they destroy him. However, while Lawrence knew of Freud and disagreed strenuously (perhaps mistakenly, in Huxley's eyes) with Freud's assessment of the incestuous subtext of human sexuality, the real problem in Huxley's *Brave New World* as far as John is concerned is perhaps not that Freudianism has taken over the social structure, but that no one is any longer able properly to explain, remember, or apply Freud's theories, since the family structure that they assumed has been abolished in "civilized" circles.

Clearly, Huxley's distrust of Freud was by no means the typical antagonism felt by an artist towards a scientist who is treading on his or her toes; Huxley's own ancestry (his grandfather was T. H. Huxley, the father of so-called "Social Darwinism") made him rather more receptive to scientific principles than most novelists would be. Indeed, Huxley was often dismayed at what he took to be Freud's lack of real scientific rigor; as he once exclaimed, "How incredibly unscientific the old man [Freud] could be!"[62] Furthermore, although *Brave New World* seems to imply that the conflicts within human nature are worth preserving, since they make us interesting, heroic, and tragic, Huxley himself was committed to treating mental and emotional illness by any means necessary. He was a firm supporter of the use of drugs in psychotherapy, and despite the fact that he derided Freud's insistence on the value of his famous "talking cure,"[63] he shared Freud's urge to help individual people survive their psychological disturbances. What *Brave New World* shows us, however, is that Huxley was willing to mock his own (and Freud's) drive to limit or eliminate suffering from human existence. *Brave New World* may still be read as a parable about the difficulty of preserving anything we can recognize as "human" if and when Freud's theory of the Oedipus complex is taken seriously and acted upon by an authoritarian political system. Nevertheless, given Huxley's own documented assent to many of Freud's views on the subject of infantile desire and repression, it is difficult to disagree with Robert Baker's claim that "The Freudian family romance, despite Huxley's repeatedly expressed misgivings concerning Freud's emphasis on erotic behavior, is one of the principal satirical conventions of his social satire. *Brave New World* is no exception to this practice."[64] In other words, Huxley seems to have been using the "Oedipus complex" not as a target for mockery in *Brave New World*, but as a weapon in his satirical attack on the mores of modern life and on its utopian fantasies.

NOTES

1. Quoted in Jerome Meckier, "Our Ford, Our Freud and the Behaviorist Conspiracy in Huxley's *Brave New World*," *Thalia*, I (1978), p. 37.

2. Foremost among these scholars is Jerome Meckier, who argues that Huxley's novel is a rejection of Freud's theories. Meckier's article, while intriguing, is unsatisfactory, mainly because it dogmatically asserts that Huxley satirizes Freudianism for being part of what Meckier calls a "behaviorist conspiracy" that dominates Western thought, which Meckier deems mechanistic and materialistic (p. 41). Of course, as Peter Firchow points out, "Huxley knew very well [that] mechanistic psychologists . . . were adamantly opposed to Freud; for them, consciousness was the last refuge of the soul" (p. 47). Furthermore, as we shall see, Huxley was often more of a materialist than Freud ever was, recommending drugs and behavioral modification therapy rather than Freud's "talking cure" in cases of mental illness.

3. According to an oft-repeated anecdote, Huxley mocked these Freud-worshippers at a psychoanalysts' convention by crossing himself whenever their hero's name was mentioned.

4. Charles Holmes, *Aldous Huxley and the Way to Reality* (Indiana University Press, 1970), p. 147.

5. Philip Thody, *Huxley: A Biographical Introduction* (Charles Scribner's Sons, 1973), pp. 16–17.

6. For Freud, Oedipus (who kills his father and marries his mother) is "nothing more or less than a wish-fulfillment—the fulfillment of the wish of our childhood" (*The Basic Writings of Sigmund Freud* James Strachey, trans. [Random House, 1938], p. 308).

7. Aldous Huxley, *Letters of Aldous Huxley* Grover Smith, ed. (Chatto & Windus, 1969), p. 351.

8. Aldous Huxley, *Brave New World* (Harper & Row, 1946), p. 91. All subsequent parenthetical references to Brave New World are to this edition.

9. *The Basic Writings of Sigmund Freud*, p. 917.

10. Reading *Hamlet* intensifies and focuses John's anger towards Popé, as Huxley is at pains to indicate: "it was as though he had never really hated Popé before; never really hated him because he had never been able to say how much he hated him. . . . These words . . . gave him a reason for hating Popé; and they made his hatred more real" (p. 157). Here Huxley implies that literary examples of human behavior—for instance, the Shakespearean representation of a son's jealousy about his mother's relations with another man in *Hamlet*—anticipate the Freudian theory of the Oedipus complex. His portrait of John shows how the Oedipus complex is produced partly through natural boyish pride and jealousy and partly through John's aesthetic enjoyment of Shakespeare's language. This is no doubt a sidelong jab at Freud, and certainly adds resonance to Huxley's remark that "All that modern psychologists . . . have done is to systematize and de-beautify the vast treasures of knowledge about the human soul contained in novel, play, poem and essay" (Aldous Huxley, *Music at Night* [Chatto & Windus, 1970], p. 292).

11. John has memories of "white Linda and Popé almost black beside her, with one arm under her shoulders and the other hand dark on her breast, and one of the plaits of his long hair lying across her throat, like a black snake trying to strangle her" (p. 157).

12. The link between Lenina and Linda remains strong in John's mind, even after Linda dies from an overdose of *soma:* "He tried to think of poor Linda, breathless and dumb, with her clutching hands . . . Poor Linda whom he had sworn to remember. But it was still the presence of Lenina that haunted him. Lenina whom he had promised to forget" (p. 302). John seems to have successfully transferred his love from his mother to Lenina, but instead of congratulating himself on his more adult object-choice (as Freud would likely have told him to do) he feels guilty for forgetting Linda, especially since he still blames himself for her death. It is difficult to avoid the suspicion that reading a bit of Freud might have helped John accept his adult sexuality.

13. René Girard, *Violence and the Sacred* (Johns Hopkins University Press, 1979), p. 75.

14. Oedipus exiled himself after discovering he was guilty of incest and parricide. While Helmholtz's genius with words and metaphors seems to recall Oedipus' facility in solving the riddle of the Sphinx which depends upon a metaphorical interpretation of the word "legs," Bernard's bodily defects—he is abnormally short—bear a resemblance to Oedipus' deformed feet. Both Bernard and Oedipus are forced to make their minds their most powerful asset; as Huxley remarks of Bernard, "a physical shortcoming could produce a kind of mental excess" (p. 81).

15. Bernard claims to want to delay his own gratification, telling Lenina that he wishes that their date had not ended "with our going to bed" (p. 109), but (unlike Helmholtz) he lacks the willpower to impose real obstacles on himself.

16. Aldous Huxley, *Do What You Will* (Chatto & Windus, 1956), p. 137.

17. *Music at Night*, p. 167.

18. In *Civilization and its Discontents*, Freud makes it quite clear that in his view all pleasure is only the release of tension, or the overcoming of obstacles and impediments; without the unpleasant uncertainty of anticipation or fear, there is no real enjoyment: "What we call happiness in the strictest sense comes from the (preferably sudden) satisfactions of needs which have been dammed up to a high degree . . . When any situation that is desired by the pleasure principle is prolonged, it only produces a feeling of mild contentment" (Sigmund Freud, *Civilization and its Discontents*, James Strachey, trans. [W. W. Norton & Company, 1961], p. 23). There is no essential contradiction between Freud's view and that expressed by Huxley: "Love is the product of two opposed forces—of an instinctive impulsion and a social resistance acting on the individual by means of ethical imperatives justified by philosophical or religious myths. When, with the destruction of the myths, resistance is removed, the impulse wastes itself on emptiness" (*Do What You Will*, p. 137).

19. Thody is eager to make Freud the main villain of the novel, as his analysis makes plain:

> . . . in *Brave New World* it is the declared aim of the authorities to translate into the sexual behaviour of adults the total irresponsibility and immaturity which supposedly characterize a child's attitude to its own body . . . The Freudian idea that we should avoid repressions and frustrations, that the way to happiness lies in the satisfaction of those primitive, instinctual, sexual drives which previous societies have been compelled to inhibit, is thus criticized first and foremost for the effect that it has on people's emotional life. (Philip Thody, *Huxley: A Biographical Introduction* [Charles Scribner's Sons, 1973], pp. 54–55).

20. *Huxley: A Biographical Introduction*, p. 54.

21. Peter Firchow, *The End of Utopia: A Study of Huxley's* Brave New World (Associated University Presses, 1984), p. 55.

22. *The End of Utopia: A Study of Huxley's* Brave New World, p. 47.

23. Aldous Huxley, *Proper Studies* (Chatto & Windus, 1933), p. xvi.

24. Sigmund Freud, *A General Selection from the Works of Sigmund Freud*, John Rickman, ed. (Doubleday & Co. 1957), p. 44. Freud goes on to mitigate this slight against artists: "But he [the artist] finds a way of return from this world of fantasy back to reality; with his special gifts he molds his fantasies into a new kind of reality, and men concede them a justification as valuable reflections of actual life. Thus by a certain path he actually becomes the hero, king, creator, favorite he desired to be, without pursuing the circuitous path of creating real alterations in the outer world" (*Freud: A General Selection*, p. 44).

25. *Music at Night*, pp. 12-13.

26. *A General Selection from the Works of Sigmund Freud*, p. 203.

27. Richard Astle, "Dracula as Totemic Monster: Lacan, Freud, Oedipus and History," *Sub-Stance*, XXV (1980), p. 99.

28. *Civilization and its Discontents*, p. 11.

29. *Civilization and its Discontents*, p. 19. Characteristically, Freud denies that this feeling is truly the source of religious emotions, which he attributes directly to one's relationship (or lack thereof) with a paternal figure: "I cannot think of any need in childhood as strong as the need for a father's protection. Thus the part played by the oceanic feeling, which might seek something like the restoration of limitless narcissism, is ousted from a place in the foreground" (*Civilization and its Discontents*, p. 19).

30. *Proper Studies*, p. xix.

31. "The Bantus and Dr. Freud," quoted in *Huxley's Hearst Essays*, ed. James Sexton (Garland, 1994), p. 161.

32. *Huxley's Hearst Essays*, p. 161.

33. Huxley concludes his essay with the remark: "Men and women under high biological pressure arrange the pattern of their life in one way; under low pressure, in another way. With every increase in the efficiency of social organizations, more individuals will come to live under low biological pressure" (p. 161).

34. *Letters of Aldous Huxley*, p. 187.

35. *Letters of Aldous Huxley*, p. 187.

36. As Huxley's biographer Sybille Bedford argues, Huxley was very much under Lawrence's influence when he was writing *Do What You Will*, a collection of essays published in October of 1929: "Much of *Do What You Will* was a continuation of ideas turned up in *Point Counter Point*. Mark Rampion is talking on. The impression of the Lawrentian ship was still upon the water" (Sybille Bedford, *Aldous Huxley: A Biography* [Chatto and Windus, 1973], p. 219).

37. *Letters of Aldous Huxley*, p. 332.

38. Lawrence was convinced that Freud was wrong about incestuous desire, claiming there was in fact a natural antipathy between parents and children where sex was concerned, and that "The incest motive is a logical deduction of the human reason, which has recourse to this last extremity, to save itself" (D. H. Lawrence, *Fantasia of the Unconscious: Psychoanalysis and the Unconscious* [Penguin, 1975], p. 206.

39. Aldous Huxley, *The Olive Tree* (Harper & Brothers, 1937), p. 206.

40. *The Olive Tree*, p. 205.

41. *Letters of Aldous Huxley*, p. 88.

42. *Letters of Aldous Huxley*, p. 288.

43. After Lawrence died, Huxley visited Nottingham to see some of Lawrence's relatives, then in January of 1931 Huxley went to the coal fields in Durham, trying to understand more about Lawrence's background as the son of a miner, and researching the problem of unemployment. By 18 May 1931, he had begun writing *Brave New World*, which he at first described in a letter as a "revolt" against "the Wellsian Utopia" (*Letters of Aldous Huxley*, p. 348). The initial anti-Wellsian flavor of the book soon receded in importance and by the time he was finished the book he was more concerned about its "Freudian" and "Pavlovian" themes, as we can see from the letter he wrote to his father on 24 August 1931.

44. *Letters of Aldous Huxley*, p. 355.

45. *Letters of Aldous Huxley*, p. 355.

46. *Letters of Aldous Huxley*, p. 353.

47. D. H. Lawrence, *Phoenix: The Posthumous Papers of D. H. Lawrence* volumes I and II (Viking, 1964), vol. I, p. 99. Lawrence continues: "I know my derivation.

I was born of no virgin, of no Holy Ghost . . . I have a dark-faced, bronze-voiced father far back in the resinous ages. My mother was no virgin" (Phoenix I, p. 99).

48. *Fantasia of the Unconscious: Psychoanalysis and the Unconscious*, p. 126.

49. *Fantasia of the Unconscious: Psychoanalysis and the Unconscious*, p. 122.

50. *Letters of Aldous Huxley*, p. 340.

51. *Letters of Aldous Huxley*, p. 339.

52. *The Olive Tree*, pp. 238–239.

53. *The Olive Tree*, p. 203. Huxley is clearly directing this remark at Murry, who deemed Lawrence a kind of prophetic, almost messianic figure, but refused to call him an "artist" because of the intensely personal and occasionally didactic nature of Lawrence's work.

54. Quoted in *The Olive Tree*, p. 226.

55. *The Olive Tree*, p. 226.

56. *Letters of Aldous Huxley*, p. 305. Huxley says that this contest was "ghoulishly funny," and, evidently adverting to earlier discussions with Lawrence, adds that "It was just the place for the Brewsters" (*Letters of Aldous Huxley*, p. 305), the Brewsters being Earl and Achsah Brewster, two oft-mocked admirers of Lawrence's work.

57. *Letters of Aldous Huxley*, p. 364.

58. *Letters of Aldous Huxley*, p. 831.

59. Quoted in Sybille Bedford, *Aldous Huxley: A Biography*, p. 228.

60. Quoted in *Aldous Huxley: A Biography*, p. 192.

61. Quoted in *Aldous Huxley: A Biography*, p. 215.

62. *Letters of Aldous Huxley*, p. 837.

63. Huxley enunciates his dissent from Freud on this point in no uncertain terms: "Freud—although he did himself say that finally all nervous disorders would turn out to be organic—he did say that in the meanwhile . . . we could treat them successfully by purely psychological means—I think this is absolutely untrue" (Bedford, p. 641). Thus in *Brave New World* Freud's verbal therapeutic technique has been replaced entirely with drugs and Pavlovian systems of punishment and reward. Interestingly enough, in 1949 Huxley wrote a letter to George Orwell, congratulating him on the publication of *Nineteen Eighty-Four*, but explaining why he felt that his own vision of dystopia was more likely to prevail than Orwell's. He writes: "Freud's inability to hypnotize successfully . . . delayed the general application of hypnotism to psychiatry for at least forty years. But now psycho-analysis is being combined with hypnosis. . . . Within the next generation I believe that the world's rulers will discover that infant conditioning and narco-hypnosis are more efficient, as instruments of government, than clubs and prisons" (*Letters*, p. 605).

64. Robert S. Baker, *The Dark Historic Page: Social Satire and Historicism in the Novels of Aldous Huxley 1921–1939* (University of Wisconsin Press, 1982), pp. 141–142.

SALLY MINOGUE AND ANDREW PALMER

Confronting the Abject: Women and Dead Babies in Modern English Fiction

Bakhtin tells us that a key image in "grotesque realism" (*Rabelais* 3) is that of the dying mother giving birth: "One of the fundamental tendencies of the grotesque image of the body is to show two bodies in one: the one giving birth and dying, the other conceived, generated, and born" (*Rabelais* 26). Indeed, the mother's death enables the infant's birth: "Every blow dealt to the old helps the new to be born. The caesarean operation kills the mother but delivers the child" (206). However, there is no place in grotesque realism for that other operation which kills the child but delivers the mother. Miscarriage is inimical to carnival—dead babies disrupt its life-death-rebirth schema—and induced abortions are antithetical to it.

All other in-and-outpourings are celebrated as testament to the corporeal openness by which the body transgresses the boundaries between itself and the world (*Rabelais* 26). These challenge the sealed, smooth and completed "classical" body of official culture which isolates the individual. Grotesque realism presents the individual body as one part of a common social body which is endlessly regenerating itself. "The material bodily principle is contained not in the biological individual, not in the bourgeois ego, but in the people, a people who are continually growing and renewed" (19). This view of death as continuing re-birth, of the death of the individual body as being subsumed into the larger and ever-continuing "collective ancestral body of

Journal of Modern Literature, Volume 29, Number 3 (Spring 2006): pp. 103–125. Copyright © 2006 Indiana University Press.

all the people" (19), hides its face from the stark actuality of dead babies. The induced abortion, then, is not narratable in *Gargantua* or any other carnivalesque fiction. However, it becomes so in the twentieth century novel.

To write an academic article about the fictional representation of abortion requires some delicacy. Perhaps even to write about it at all might seem to reduce its gravity to the purely academic. However, this was certainly not the case for the novelists of the 1930s and 1950s/1960s who took the brave step of representing abortion at a time when it was (for the 30s writers) a taboo subject or (for the 50s/60s writers) still outside the law and seen as morally reprehensible. Jean Rhys's *Voyage in the Dark* (1934) and Aldous Huxley's *Eyeless in Gaza* (1936) were groundbreaking in that they represented illegal abortions openly and recognizably with no apparent disapprobation. Without a tradition of representation to draw on—abortion having been necessarily invisible in nineteenth century fiction—both writers found new ways of writing to represent the experience of abortion and, in doing so, drew it inexorably to the attention of a significant readership. Alan Sillitoe's *Saturday Night and Sunday Morning* (1958) and Nell Dunn's *Up the Junction* (1963)—now at least with some antecedents—pushed the limits further, placing abortion at the imaginative center of their novels and thus forcing the reader to engage with the woman's experience, while working within a predominantly realist genre that did not spare harsh details. In spite of the relentlessness of some of those details, these later writers seem to have been able to invest abortion with a normality absent from the overheated, almost gothic depictions of their 30s forerunners. And within this normalization it is possible for them sometimes to be playful, even comic, in their language and in their modes of representation in a way that can carry readers far beyond the stark specifics of realism and so place them outside the reductive restrictions of the polarized abortion debate.

Insofar as one of the central achievements of the twentieth century novel was its exploration of areas of human experience hitherto deemed unsuitable for artistic and imaginative transformation (a process begun cataclysmically by Joyce's *Ulysses* and developed powerfully by D. H. Lawrence), these writers were in the mainstream of that revolution, bit by bit forming a tradition until even the Obscene Publications Act, a powerful force for censorship, was subjugated to it following the *Lady Chatterley's Lover* court case.[1] It is in the spirit of these writers that we approach their fictional representations of abortion, not as a catalogue of grim tableaux, but as part of the continuum of the novel tradition in its representation of the full range of human experience.

It is likely that these writers played some part in changing social attitudes as well as changing the novel itself and here class becomes an influential factor, given the different historical and cultural contexts of the two groups of writers. The writers of the 50s and 60s were the first generation of their century to make working class life their central subject, and to reach a mass market and thus a genuine working class audience. Sillitoe was himself working class and Dunn, though she was not, lived with, and lived the life of, the Battersea working class women she refigures in *Up the Junction* before writing the novel. We shall consider to what extent their class situation and consciousness altered the way in which they wrote about abortion, in comparison to Huxley (who was both of and writing about upper middle class society) and Rhys (writing about a *demi-monde* but as someone who interacts with the upper echelons of society through sexual relationships). In making this comparison, we shall invoke Bakhtin's concepts of the carnivalesque and of grotesque realism to suggest that the earlier texts challenge and modify Bakhtin's cyclical theory of the body, while a more optimistic, regenerative spirit prevails in the 50s and 60s depictions of abortion.

The representation of abortion in 30s fiction—bodily, but grim—resonates with Bakhtin's argument that modernity can sustain only a denigrated version of the grotesque, a faint echo of the carnivalesque humour of Rabelais, in which laughter is superseded by fear:

> Bakhtin says that the ambivalence of grotesque realism is no longer properly understood. [. . .] [A]ny contemporary version of the grotesque will feature only its downward, not its regenerative, aspect. The reason Bakhtin gives for the current absence of the grotesque is the onset of capitalism and privatized, individual life. (Vice 162–163)

Sue Vice equates this corrupted grotesque with Julia Kristeva's notion of the abject. Kristeva sees experiences of maternity and death, which reiterate the messy openness of the body, as moments of horror for women. This horror, she argues, is imposed on women by the patriarchal "symbolic," once they progress out of the "grotesquely oriented semiotic" (Vice 169). Vice argues that "abjection is the grotesque of modernity, its darker version: it is equivalent not to the classical, which turns its back on the organic, but to a frightening grotesque" (175).

This can serve as a precise description of the elements of the grotesque which appear in the crucial abortion scenes in *Voyage in the Dark* and *Eyeless in Gaza*. These scenes are deeply disturbing—in each case, a young woman character who carries an illegitimate baby faces grim combat with official notions of morality. Rhys and Huxley locate the distress of their female protagonists in the inner consciousness—both characters' responses to their abortions take the form of delirious dreams or visions. The emphasis on consciousness, arising out of modernism, presents the individual as being isolated from the common social body, trapped in her own angst. And yet, these representations of abortion function subversively. Huxley and Rhys challenge an official culture that attaches shame to unsanctioned motherhood and forces women to make desperate choices. The illegal, life-threatening abortion is the result of an official morality that imposes oppressive rules as to who can legitimately give birth. Rhys and Huxley provide no carnival laughter, but there is defiance.

Voyage in the Dark and *Eyeless in Gaza* have little in common as novels other than the fact that each features an abortion. Yet the way in which the actual abortion is written about in both is strikingly similar. Rhys's abortionist is Swiss-French, Huxley's is French (and Helen's abortion takes place in Paris). This may reflect the actuality of the time, but in both cases it lends an alienating context, through the foreign language, in which both Anna and Helen suffer disturbing dreams or visions which involve grotesque images.

Official society in these novels prohibits abortion. It claims to do this because of a concern for the unborn child. However, if this were a primary concern, single women would be encouraged to give birth and helped in the task of caring for their child—and illegitimate birth would be divested of its shameful status. In practice, unsanctioned sexual pleasure is punished either by the shame attached to illegitimate babies or by the imprisonment of mothers who seek an illegal abortion. Abortion, then, is a site of contest between official culture and the carnivalesque. Anna and Helen are forced to choose between the public shame of unmarried motherhood and the private pain of abortion, and they choose the latter.

When Anna, an impoverished chorus girl who has slid into prostitution, realizes that she is pregnant, she is completely isolated. Sent from the Caribbean by her step-mother to be schooled in England following her father's death, she is alien to, and alone in, London. After the abortion, she embraces this isolation. Looking at the fetus, she says: "I lay and watched it. I thought, 'I'm glad it happened when nobody was here because I hate people'" (155). This is the antithesis of a carnivalesque birth in which the mother's corpse nourishes the soil while the baby arises as one part of the communal body. The baby is dead and the mother survives in isolation. As Mary Lou Emery, speaking of this scene, puts it:

> Grotesque realism depends upon the body and bodily life, but as collectively, not individually, experienced. It represents the cycles of fertility, pregnancy, deterioration, dismemberment and decay [. . .] This collectively experienced cycle of life is opposed to the European realistic convention of "character." (79)

Bakhtin speaks pejoratively of "degenerate, petty realism" (*Rabelais* 53) in which the grotesque is corrupted, but a medieval worldview cannot be expected or possible, let alone desirable, in fiction written in the twentieth century. Rhys is responding creatively to the structures of authority of her time.

Thus, whereas the bodily outpourings of carnival debunk and ridicule official notions of propriety through laughter, Anna's hemorrhaging, which continues for six hours, serves as an indictment of them through its horror. Further, whereas carnival insists on explicit description in place of polite euphemism, Anna's blood cannot be explicitly named. Like the fetus, it is referred to as *it*. Anna's landlady says, "it come on at two o'clock and it's nearly eight now," and Laurie replies, "It's bound to stop in a minute" (155).

And yet, Anna's experience of abortion is punctuated by her memories of her Caribbean childhood. For example, when she is first terrified by the possibility that she is pregnant ("It can't be that, it can't be that. Oh, it can't be that. Pull yourself together; it can't be that." [139]), she puts herself to bed and recalls a woman called Miss Jackson, who used to let her play in her garden.

> Colonel Jackson's illegitimate daughter—yes illegitimate poor thing but such a charming woman really and she speaks French so beautifully she really is worth what she charges for her lessons of course her mother was— (139)

The unfinished sentence suggests, perhaps, that her mother was black. In this memory, Anna seeks comfort by remembering less censorious attitudes to illegitimacy. Emery rightly suggests that Anna summons these memories to "shield her from what is happening in the present" (75), but when the events in the bedroom where she is bleeding, possibly to death, are intertwined with her curious dream about a Caribbean masquerade she witnessed as a girl, this is more than simply a protective "shield." Horner and Zlosnik argue that:

> the conflation of the masquerade with Anna's experience of abortion allows her to half perceive the parallel between the hierarchical and oppressive social system of the West Indies, based in colour and deriving from a slave society, with that of England in the years 1912–1914 in which women are exploited and constrained. (160)

The masquerade presents easy laughter, the openness of the body, the parodic up-ending of hierarchies—in short, carnival. The black participants dance, their bodies sweat, they wear masks that parody the pious whites—through which they stick their tongues. Bakhtin says that the carnival mask "reveals the essence of the grotesque"—it is "connected with the joy of change and reincarnation [. . .] with the merry negation of uniformity and similarity;

it rejects conformity to oneself. [. . .] It contains the playful element of life" (*Rabelais* 39–40). Further, "the masks of the carnival bring about temporary freedom and dislocation from cultural hierarchies" (Horner and Zlosnik 159). These masks, with an aperture for the outthrust, ridiculing tongue, oppose and overturn the sorts of masks bourgeois society forces women to wear in order to appear "ladylike."[2]

In recalling the masquerade, Anna remembers herself as one of many performers who are also their own audience. For a chorus girl, used to appearing on a public stage—that is, as an object of the male gaze—there is defiance in this vision. Bakhtin reminds us that carnival "does not acknowledge any distinction between actors and spectators. [. . .] [it] is not a spectacle seen by the people; they live in it" (*Rabelais* 7). Carnival spurns hierarchies and its audience does not watch it, they *are* it.

Edward Braithwaite explains that Caribbean masquerades of the eighteenth and early nineteenth century grew out of African celebrations and had a political function, "to dramatize or satirize aspects of slave society—their and their masters' condition" (qtd. in Horner and Zlosnik 159). Horner and Zlosnik rightly see the masquerade in Rhys's novel as a descendant of such events, conveying the same sense of being "threatening to, and subversive of, white European values" (160).

However, Anna is caught in between two positions. She is white and, as such, an object of ridicule by the masqueraders ("Like that time at home with Meta, when it was Masquerade and she came to see me and put out her tongue at me through the slit in her mask" [151]) but she wishes she were black, and taking part. She is initially separated from the festivities by the slatted blind, and her family's disapproval. But, Horner and Zlosnik suggest that Anna "glimpses though the slats of the blind a critique of the cultural assumptions in whose terms she is defined" (160) and, defying the opinions of her elders, she goes out to join the dance. Her ability to do this arises from her mixed upbringing. On the one hand, her step-mother, Hester, has imposed bourgeois propriety but, on the other, she has a black confidant in Francine and the example of her profligate Uncle Bo. Hester attempts to counteract the influence of both these figures. She tells Anna, "I tried to get you to talk like a lady [. . .] That awful sing-song voice you had! Exactly like a nigger you talked—and still do. Exactly like that dreadful Francine" (55). Uncle Bo (also known as Ramsay) horrifies Hester because, not only has he fathered several illegitimate children but "they are called by his name if you please." Anna remembers Hester's tirade:

And you being told they were your cousins and giving them presents every Christmas [. . .] I gave Ramsay a piece of my mind one day I spoke out I said, "My idea of a gentleman an English gentleman doesn't have illegitimate children and if he does he doesn't flaunt them." "No, I bet he doesn't," he said, laughing in that greasy way—exactly the laugh of a Negro he had—"I should think being flaunted is the last thing that happens to the poor little devils." (55–56)

Uncle Bo shows Anna that one may do other things with illegitimate children than conceal them—or abort them. Caught between these influences, (and with an apparently indecisive father), Anna occupies a dual position. When she steps out to join the dancing, she bravely chooses the identity that embraces carnival laughter and, in Bakhtin's terms, true grotesque.

It is highly significant that this is the memory that comes to her as she lies bleeding in a London bed-sit, following her abortion. Rhys sets up a number of echoes between the two intertwined scenes that create a strong sense of irony. In her dream somebody says of the masquerade, "it ought to be stopped [. . .] it's not a decent and respectable way to go on it ought to be stopped" (156). The words "it ought to be stopped" are then repeated by the landlady, Mrs Polo, referring to the flow of Anna's blood. "It ought to be stopped" becomes an ironic comment on the way bourgeois society has constrained, controlled, and oppressed young women like Anna. The comment works like one of the carnival masks which parody white faces, appropriating a phrase which has been used to condemn carnival and to refer to Anna's blood.

Anna replies to Mrs Polo by saying, "I'm giddy [. . .] I'm awfully giddy." This is the result of blood loss and, perhaps, the gin she has drunk. But when she repeats the phrase in her dream, her giddiness is due to "dancing forwards and backwards backwards and forwards whirling round and round" (157). Again, this is ironic: carnival merriment is a preferable cause of giddiness. The phrase "I'm awfully giddy" also carries a connotation of self-censure, anticipating the doctor's criticisms, but while Anna may be cajoled into self-censure, the reader recognizes that she is a victim of official culture.

The way the grim reality and the carnivalesque dream play off each other reaches a powerful (and powerfully ambiguous) climax in the last half-page of the novel. The doctor speaks sarcastically about Anna's promiscuity, laughing cynically with Laurie. Anna says, "I listened to them both laughing and their voices going up and down" (159). This echoes Anna's earlier description of Hester and Uncle Bo arguing, in her dream, about the masquerade: "their voices were going up and down" (157). Thus, as Emery points out, Anna "joins together two discussions of moral decency—that of the doctor and Laurie, who are laughing at Anna's (and Laurie's) moral condition, and that of her relatives, who are debating the decency of carnival" (81). Anna, however, has chosen to join the dance—she becomes, in her imagination at least, one of "a community of satirical revellers" (Emery 81). This imagined belonging is an act of defiance against her imposed isolation. She chooses the satirical laughter of the masquerade over the cynical laughter of Laurie and the doctor. Emery interprets this optimistically:

> Unable to give birth, she refuses the doctor's interpretation of her body as following a socially illicit pattern and, instead, returns to her island home as a participant in its carnival culture. Through her imagined return, she enacts another kind of cycle, beginning again and perhaps changing the meaning of the abortion into an event that regenerates her own life. (81)

This may be too positive a reading for Rhys's ambiguous ending, but the fact that it becomes one possibility, alongside less uplifting ones, suggests that the distant masquerade may have the power to temper the abject with the grotesque.

The doctor assures Anna wryly that she'll soon be able to "start all over again," meaning that she will soon recommence prostituting herself, but Anna appropriates the phrase and repeats it, imagining a new life of fresh, misty (Caribbean) mornings. This vision of renewal, a kind of rebirth, is coupled with the image of her miscarriage and outpouring blood. It is as if carnival itself, so adept in turning norms on their head, has itself been upended, flipped over, to produce an ambiguous concoction of abject horror and carnival laughter which responds defiantly to modern, rather than medieval, structures of authority.

Anna's delirium shows defiance in the unconscious of a character who, in her conscious life, is passive and unassertive. In Huxley's character, Helen, the situation is reversed: she is a strong and defiant woman in her conscious life, but during the delirium she suffers in the aftermath of her abortion, the societal pressures she has fended off for years crash out of her unconscious and overwhelm her.

Helen is seduced by her mother's lover, Gerry Watchett, and left to cope with her pregnancy alone. In contrast to Anna's desperate cry, "It can't be that, it can't be that," Helen's response is to look up the word abortion in an encyclopedia. To her annoyance, the entry contains no information about how terminations are effected, but rather focuses on the illegality of abortion and the likely punishment.

> "If a woman," Helen was reading in the encyclopaedia, "administers to herself any poison or other noxious thing, or unlawfully uses any instrument or other means to procure her own miscarriage ... she is guilty of felony. The punishment for this offence is penal servitude for life, or not less than three years, or imprisonment for not more

than two years. If the child is born alive [. . .]" But they didn't
say which the proper poisons were, not what sort of instruments
you had to use, and how. Only this stupid nonsense about penal
servitude. Yet another loophole of escape had closed against her. It
was as though the whole world had conspired to shut her in with
her own impossibly appalling secret. (291–292)

Where Anna Morgan is dreamy, vague and unassertive, Helen is practical
and decisive, but the official culture which makes it impossible for her to
contemplate motherhood in her situation would also criminalize her for
seeking to avoid it. (Gerry, of course, gets off scot-free.)

Helen risks punishment, arranging an abortion in Paris. Here she is
forced to confront, in extreme circumstances, the horror of corporeality with
which she has battled throughout the novel. Whereas, in grotesque realism,
"the bodily element is deeply positive" (Bakhtin, *Rabelais* 19), Helen experiences, in her delirium following the termination, a nightmarish vision of a
crowd of strangers discussing the possibility that her own body will balloon
to Rabelaisian proportions.

The possibility of Helen with enormous breasts, of Helen with
thick rolls of fat round her hips, of Helen with creases in her
thighs, of Helen with rows and rows of children—howling all the
time; and that disgusting smell of curdled milk; and their diapers.
(318)[3]

Helen has been conditioned by the elevated image of the sealed classical
body presented by official culture (she has been named for the classical icon
of female beauty). She is horrified by her body's potential for openness, for
outpourings of milk and babies and, by extension, babies' feces.[4] This is
the abject.

Throughout her life, Helen has been caught between the "Rabelaisian"
influence of her profligate mother, Mary, and the pressures of male adoration which impose upon her notions of purity and beauty. Mary takes lovers,
talks openly of sexual matters and delights in shocking polite company. The
novel's chief protagonist, Anthony Beavis, finds this a refreshing relief from
stuffy propriety.

To be able to talk freely about anything (*anything*, mind you) with a
woman [. . .] casually mentioning beds, water-closets, the physiology
of what (for the Saxon words still remained unpronounceable) they
were constrained to call *l'amour*—for Anthony the experience was
[. . .] an intoxicating mixture of liberation and forbidden fruit,

of relief and titillation. In his father's universe, [. . .] such things were simply not there—but not there with a painfully, glaringly conspicuous absence. (247–248)

Conversely, characters like Hugh Ledwidge demonstrate the attitudes of official culture to the body which would see it as sealed, pure and statuesque (Bakhtin, *Rabelais* 29). Hugh idealizes Helen as a fragile and precious angel of "bright purity" (320). He recoils from the idea of sex as this would breach the sealed body, wanting only "to touch [her] as though she were a statue." He imagines her crawling into his arms to be "comforted and made warm" where she would lie "a picture, virginal, ideal, but melting, melting" (340) and repeatedly imagines her as a work of art to be gazed upon.

He wanted her to be like Ariel, like the delicate creature in his own manuscript, a being of another order, beyond good and evil. [. . .] Like Ariel, he repeated to himself, like those Watteaus at Dresden, like Debussy. (341)

He is horrified by the capacity of women's bodies for outpouring. When Helen is ill, her vomit rudely imposes her corporeality on him and he cannot conceal his disgust. He is repulsed by her periods, which "each month [. . .] renewed his secret horror of her body" (258).

Helen is caught between these two attitudes. She is first introduced to the reader as a rebellious teenager (her mother's daughter) who delights in shocking her conformist and conservative sister, Joyce. To Joyce's horror, Helen announces she is going to steal something from every shop in the high street, and she does this with ease until they reach the butcher's. With much difficulty, but as a matter of pride, Helen steals some raw kidneys, but the feeling of triumph she desired is undercut by her revulsion:

The thing slithered obscenely between her gloved fingers—a slug, a squid. In the end she had to grab it with her whole hand. Thank heaven, she thought, for gloves! As she dropped it into the basket, the idea came to her that for some reason she might have to take the horrible thing in her mouth, raw as it was and oozy with some unspeakable slime, take it in her mouth, bite, taste, swallow. Another shudder of disgust ran through her, so violent this time that it seemed to tear something at the centre of her body. (33)

That last sentence seems grimly to foretell her illegal abortion. When she emerges from the butcher's, Joyce's criticism is forestalled by Helen's distress: "'Oh, too filthy, *too* filthy,' she repeated, looking at her fingers" (34).

In a second incident, seven months later, she holds a dying kitten in her hands. Its eyes are "gummy with a yellow discharge," its running nose has "slimed the beautifully patterned fur of the face." The limp creature in her hands reminds her of the raw kidneys and she automatically recoils from it. Immediately, she is ashamed of herself—"How beastly I am!" (222)—but she cannot overcome her disgust: "she [. . .] couldn't bear to touch him, as though he were one of those filthy kidneys—she, who had pretended to love him, who did love him, she insisted to herself" (222–223).

Later on, when she is married to Hugh, she is self-assured enough to see his evident horror of her body as "an intolerable insult," but his disgust echoes her own reaction to the dying kitten. Helen, too, has a horror of the body's capacity for messiness and these two experiences—stolen kidneys and dying kitten—foreshadow her experience of pregnancy and termination. Following her abortion, they enter her dreams. She imagines bending down to kiss the "adorable little fingers" of her sister's baby, but the baby suddenly transforms itself:

> the thing she held in her arms was the dying kitten, was those kidneys at the butcher's, was that horrible thing which she had opened her eyes to see Mme. Bonifay nonchalantly picking up and carrying away in a tin basin to the kitchen. (318–319)

The "horrible thing" in the tin basin is, of course, the aborted fetus, which she associates with the kitten and the kidneys. To punish herself for this thought, she goes on to make a connection between all three—kitten, kidneys and fetus—and her own body.

> Turning her head, she could see herself reflected in the wardrobe mirror. [. . .] she preferred her sick pallor and dishevelment. "Like the kitten," she kept thinking. Reduced to a dirty little rag of limp flesh, transformed from a bright living creature into something repellent, into the likeness of kidneys, of that unspeakable thing that Mme. Bonifay [. . .] She shuddered. (319)

There is a piling up of metaphors or equivalences here. Helen likens the dying kitten to the kidneys, she likens the fetus to both kitten and kidneys, and finally likens herself to kitten, kidneys and fetus. From her initial, practical defiance which recognized the injustice of official notions of the female body (that corner women into illegal abortions and then impose penal servitude) she has come to a state of self-loathing.

All this may seem to illustrate Bakhtin's critique of the deleterious effect of modernist individualism on grotesque realism (*Rabelais* 321) but Helen is engaged with a specific oppressive discourse unknown to medieval women. Her strategies following her abortion show her struggling heroically to find a path to recovery and survival. Her first idea is to conform to official culture's view of what a woman should be. She proposes marriage to Hugh Ledwidge believing that she can reject her sensuous nature. She writes to him from Paris: "You probably think I'm a fool, and flighty and irresponsible; and it's true, I have been up till now. [. . .] Now I want to be something else. And I know I *can* be something else. *Sérieuse*. A good wife and all that" (341).

The oppressive and repressed nature of Hugh's adoration leads Helen into an affair with the sensuous aesthete, Anthony Beavis. He insists on emotional detachment and refuses her the possibility of love, telling her: "I'm always perfectly frank about its being nothing. I never pretend it's a Grand Passion. [. . .] Just a bit of fun" (4). Helen accuses him of "getting something for nothing" (5) but puts up with this initially because, unlike the inept Hugh, "he knew how to give her at least a physical satisfaction."[5]

This situation provides no solution to Helen's pain, though she is seemingly trapped by the partial relief it provides. It takes the novel's most bizarre and gothic moment to force a crisis: while Helen and Anthony sunbathe naked on a rooftop, a dog falls out of a plane and smashes onto the roof, splattering them with blood.

> With a violent but dull and muddy impact the thing struck the flat roof a yard or two from where they were lying. [. . .] From head to foot both of them were splashed with blood. In a red pool at their feet lay the almost shapeless carcase of a fox-terrier. (98)

Anthony tries to make light of it, but Helen enters a state of shock. She stares "with wide-open eyes at the horribly shattered carcase," her face, with a streak of blood across it, is "very pale" before she covers it with her hands and begins to sob (99). This is a moment of epiphany for both characters. Anthony realizes that he does in fact love Helen and tries to tell her so, but he is too late. Her epiphany is a negative one: she sees that her affair with Anthony has been no solution and resolves to leave him. In his ignorance of her abortion, he is bewildered by her departure. He tells himself the dog's death, while unpleasant, was "not unpleasant enough to justify Helen in behaving as though she were acting Ibsen" (103).[6]

The beginnings of her recovery are finally effected through her affair with a German communist, Ekki Giesebrecht. She thinks it is because he has provided her with a political cause, but it seems more likely that the reason is that she has experienced intimacy and love for the first time. After Ekki is captured and murdered by the Nazis, she meets with (a reformed) Anthony, who describes the encounter in his diary:

[Helen said,] "I thought I could never see you again because of that dog. Then Ekki came and the dog was quite irrelevant. And now he's gone, it's still irrelevant. For another reason. Everything's irrelevant for that matter. Except Communism." But that was an afterthought—an expression of piety, uttered by force of habit. (212)

Anthony perceives the curative value of love and, by a different route (via the guru-like Dr. Miller), has come to understand this for himself. The novel ends ambiguously, but with a possibility of hope for Anthony and Helen.

Huxley's narrative presents a woman who is seduced, seeks an illegal and life-endangering abortion for want of other options, and struggles to overcome the experience. The abortion scene itself is revolutionary in that, in place of disapproval, it carries a sense of sympathy with Helen's suffering. It is true that Huxley shows the horror of the abject in place of the laughter of grotesque realism, but in doing so, he makes a powerful critique of current structures of oppression.

* * *

Rhys and Huxley sought to give an accurate picture of society as it acted upon the individual at that time. Here, class is certainly a factor, since it is quite possible that a working class woman of the same era wouldn't have experienced the alienation from her social community in the act of abortion as it is experienced by Anna and Helen. Her distress might have been similar, but the sense of separation that amounts to alienation in the depiction of Helen's and Anna's abortions might not have arisen in a working class context. But we have no British working class fictional depictions of abortion of the period to test this against.[7] Certainly when we do begin to see such depictions, in the post-war novels of Sillitoe and Dunn, it is in a still-ambiguous but potentially optimistic context in which there is space for defiant laughter. These authors and their characters were distanced by their class from the bourgeois structures of authority that oppress the 30s authors and characters; they are more closely associated with the carnivalesque tradition that survived in certain forms of working class entertainment and recreation. These novels, in their alignment against "official culture" (*Rabelais* 166) and in their celebration of "the life of the belly and the reproductive organs [. . .] acts of defecation and copulation, conception, pregnancy and birth" (*Rabelais* 21), do reinstitute a Rabelaisian voice into the novel. Of course, there can be no simple return to the grotesque realism of the medieval period. Instead, these texts can be read as positive, laughter-full responses to the modern denigration of the grotesque identified by Bakhtin, which at the same time engage with the ideological pressures on the modern individual human subject.

Key to these novels is their realist aesthetic, since it is this which makes their representations of working class reality socially and culturally significant; as we have argued elsewhere it is an elastic realism which allows plenty of room for the Bakhtinian grotesque (Minogue and Palmer). The depictions of abortion within such an aesthetic are necessarily specific to lived human experience and so present a special test for our putative reinstatement of the Rabelaisian within modernity, since for the contemporary reader those images which are closest to a Bakhtinian model may in their particularity carry negative meanings that directly contradict the larger positive meanings such images carry metaphorically. This inherent contradiction may not matter in comparatively trivial incidents as when in *Saturday Night and Sunday Morning* Arthur Seaton vomits on the couple in the pub. Here the comic momentum of the scene, and our narrative allegiance to Arthur at this point, carries the reader away from thoughts of what it might actually be like to be vomited on. It matters much more, however, in the abortion scene in that novel, where the narrative point of view shifts the reader's sympathy from Arthur to Brenda, and where, though it is in part represented through a comic consciousness, the gravity of what we are observing always lurks below the surface. In Dunn's *Up the Junction,* where the grotesque is less overt, and where the consequences of abortion are made graphic on the page, including a description of the dead fetus, the reader is brought up hard against the physical reality of the body, both the woman's and that of the dead baby. Nonetheless, Rabelaisian cheerfulness will keep breaking through in a form which we might call the modern grotesque.

The fullest expression of this comes in *Saturday Night and Sunday Morning* in the chapter dealing with Brenda's gin-and-hot bath abortion. Remarkably, the tenor of this chapter is comedic, mock heroic. Brenda lolls in her bath, a latter-day goddess worshipped by the acolyte Em'ler in "the ceremony of 'bringing it off,'" while Arthur waits in attendance, the obedient but sulky servant (Sillitoe 85). Here not class but gender roles are reversed, and Brenda can bid Arthur to do her service, even if it is only to stand and watch. Alternate libations of hot water and gin are poured, as Brenda's pink body is wreathed in steam. Something akin to pleasure permeates the room, its source Brenda herself whose eyes "turned good-naturedly on the room around her" (88). She brings both Arthur and Em'ler, in their different ways cross and concerned as she is not, under the benevolent spell of her fatalistic warmth. The anxiety of the earlier chapter in which, just before she tells him she is pregnant, "he felt the agony of her worry clinging about them, thick and tangible" (67) and where her "laugh went echoing bitterly along the empty road" when he suggests she might have the baby, is here dissolved in clouds of steam until "Arthur could not worry any more" (89). As Em'ler supports her step by step up the stairs, in an ironic reversal of Arthur's earlier drunken fall down the stairs of the White Horse pub, "A clear laugh came out of Brenda's drunkenness: 'I don't care whether it comes off or not. I don't care now'" (91). She has taken over the irresponsibility of Arthur's earlier "Couldn't care less, couldn't care less, couldn't care less" (17) and for once, though only momentarily, it is Arthur who is made to feel the burden of care, paradoxically heavier as Brenda generously absolves him: "You're a good-hearted lad, Arthur" (88).

The resonant echoes of Arthur's headlong drunken fall at the start of the novel take us back to the way Sillitoe pictures Arthur at this defining first moment as deliberately splurging his bodily energy. His excesses reflect and magnify those of his community, and to the extent that his disruptiveness mirrors a potentially uncontainable class energy (present in the room around him), his body mirrors the social body. Now, at a time when one might expect a downward turn into gloom, the abortion scene is used to elevate Brenda in turn to the embodiment of the mass of her people, to empower her as she decides what will happen to her own body, and to touch her with a generous beauty as she rises before Arthur and the reader, "her pink steaming body unfolding [. . .] like a rose in bloom" (90). The repeated motifs of abandonment, helplessness, and liberation, and the linguistic echoes of rolling, swaying, and laughing in this chapter recall Chapter One, not to link Arthur's original carelessness with Brenda's fate, but rather to eschew blame and to celebrate their final blissful unconcern. Both are reduced to helpless bodies, and just as Arthur has been earlier figured as "a fully-dressed and giant foetus curled up at the bottom of the stairs" (12) now Brenda, hauled up to bed by Em'ler, "fell back and lay perfectly still, giving a sigh and going immediately back to sleep" (91). There is a narrative equality between them here that outweighs either censure for the one or pity for the other. Sleeping like a baby in the bed where she conceived, Brenda will finish off what she had begun there, in a way that seems, in this narrative, perfectly natural. When Arthur next sees Brenda she has emerged looking "fresh and innocent, red-cheeked and relaxed," and praising Em'ler for her help "that night," signaling to Arthur that they can both "close their eyes" over it (121). In Sillitoe's representing the abortion in the same comic spirit as the first chapter, even as he sacrifices the terrible actuality of the dead fetus, the mock heroic ritual of "the ceremony of 'bringing it off'" combines with the routine ordinariness of the event to produce a mood of celebration representative and symbolic of a deeper reality than the surface events depicted.

The abortion chapter stands, like the Goose Fair chapter, at a key point in the first longer section of the novel, "Saturday Night." Both chapters are emblematic of abandonment and misrule, and both contain powerful elements of the carnivalesque and its celebration of the grotesque body. But they are underpinned by the novel's predominantly realist mode, and they must stand by the measures of realism at some level. Readers might feel that in these terms Arthur gets off scot-free and Brenda is represented as a mindless body, careless of actions which at best make a mockery of decent hard-working Jack (whom the hapless Em'ler is told is the father) and at worst show her as utterly callous about the fetus she aborts (by her casual mention that she hopes the wallpaper won't peel off like "the last time" [86] she reveals this isn't her first self-induced abortion). However, Brenda's attitude can be seen as accurately pragmatic for her time. As she points out to Arthur when he suggests she keep the baby, "What do you think having a kid means? You're doped for nine months. Your breasts get big, and suddenly you're swelling. Then one fine day you're yelling out and you've got a kid. That's easy enough though. Nowt wrong wi' that. The thing is, you've got ter look after it every minute for fifteen years. You want to try it sometimes!" (70). "Not me," is Arthur's reply, and indeed it is not he nor any of the other men depicted in the novel who have the care of the children. Brenda's practical attitude, strengthened for us by her direct Northern-accented speech, in no way undermines the fact that she is a loving mother, as we see from her treatment of little Jacky. But she knows the real world, and for her the choice is simple: to sacrifice an unborn child at an early stage by a non-dangerous method is far preferable to having to reveal her infidelity to her husband and saddle him with bringing up Arthur's child. Ada's attitude to abortion is similarly unsentimental, her perfunctory moralizing ("He'll just have to face the music" [76]) cancelled out by her advice to try the gin and hot bath method. Similarly the women's attitude to sex in the novel is as free and easy as the men's, and this is not seen as a cause for blame unless one is foolish enough to be found out. The woman is shown, however briefly, taking power to herself within what is otherwise very much a man's world and doing so in a way that proudly celebrates the female body and allows the pleasure of the sexual act to suffuse the act that deals with its consequences. Sillitoe's treatment of the abortion via the mock heroic grotesque is perfectly of a piece with the actual morality of the world he depicts.

If *Saturday Night and Sunday Morning* manages this difficult balance, it does so, however, by sparing the reader one particular sort of body, that of the dead baby. Characteristically of a novel whose focus is dominantly masculine, while Arthur vomits twice, noisily, and over two innocent people, we never see the blood on Brenda's sheets. Dunn's *Up the Junction* redresses the balance in the other direction. This novel is both less Rabelaisian than *Saturday Night and Sunday Morning* and more graphic in its depiction of the dead fetus. In that respect it is braver, more testing of the reader—and of our Bakhtinian analysis. Nonetheless, there remains a sense of liberation, though the scenes depicting still birth and abortion put considerable pressure on that liberation.

Up the Junction, even more than *Saturday Night and Sunday Morning,* shows a world in which pregnancy is a trial rather than a joy, where illegal abortion is a natural part of the culture, enabling girls to return to the source of true joy, sex (that the latter may lead to the former is seen as a little local difficulty). Even when girls go through with their pregnancy, as in the chapter "Sunday Morning" set in a home for single teenage mothers, there is no pleasure expressed at the thought of the coming child, perhaps because they will all be likely to give the babies up for adoption. Most of them have already tried to get rid of the baby and are going to full term only because that failed. Their conversation drifts laconically through the chapter, between those plodding to church and those left behind (Marion and Sonia) to look after the new babies. The topics alternate between the sexual encounters that led to their pregnancies, the attempts to get rid of the baby, and the desire to be slim and attractive once more and thus to start the process all over again. Here perhaps the nasty irony of the remark made by Anna Morgan's doctor would be a fair comment—but it would no longer be likely to be made, because in the world of these girls the irony has been flattened out into normality. Marion recounts that "I was having a good time till I started to get fat at about four months. Then I tried to get rid of it, but it was too late—I never thought I might not be able to get rid of it" (Dunn 45). Sonia's Dad had gone "up the chemist and tried to get a stick of something they used before the war [. . .]" (47)—the fact that her Dad participates somehow marking the pragmatism of attitude to abortion more than if it had been the mother, abortion traditionally being, and being represented as, an area of female knowledge, and Dads being more characteristically seen as protectors of their girl children. These reminiscences are interleaved with wistful memories of sex and hopes for more in the future: "Here—it'll be nice to be looked at again, won't it? I'm going to make myself a new dress—tighter than tight, like a second skin" (45–46) (pregnancy is primarily associated with being fat); "But they say it's marvellous when you're naked" (47). The babies "wrapped tight in their calico slings" are merely a backdrop to all this, until Marion's and Sonia's increasingly idealizing musings ("If you love a boy and you want to give him the best thing in the world there's only one thing, isn't there?") are cruelly interrupted by the screams of black Moira "standing by the bed bare-footed on the glazed tile floor, screaming while the baby's head emerged" (47). We are given to understand that Moira's baby is born dead ("she stood stiff and screaming till the black baby slipped out with a soft thud onto the stone floor") though even if it had been alive the Matron makes no move to tend to it. The implication is that it is better dead. The story is closed over (as Brenda and Arthur "close their eyes" over what might have been): "nobody ever saw black Moira again" (48).

The impact of Moira's dead baby and the image of it hitting the floor may stand as far stronger than anything else in this story, and its narrative placing, with the shrill screams of the reality of pregnancy piercing the rainbow bubble Sonia and Marion have been blowing between them, may be seen to contain a moral judgment. But the narrative technique of *Up the Junction*, as the many direct speech quotes above indicate, utterly eschews authorial comment. Nell Dunn herself, talking about the novel retrospectively over a distance of forty years, remembers vividly that in the Battersea world she lived in and depicted there was a "tremendous sort of liveliness [. . .] I had a sense of, almost of celebration of the liveliness." Her own aim as a writer was "witnessing, without any judgement, what it was like" *(Still Angry)*. If the fictional seems to disappear in these statements, the formal qualities of narrative, dialogue, and structure work strongly in favor of capturing the liveliness and celebration, and contribute to the lack of judgment she aimed for. Violent injuries and deaths at work or on motorbikes jostle with scenes at the washhouse, where the women tumble together in a happy collaboration of youth and age, while smells from the cow cake factory mingle with the soap suds; easy pleasure is taken from a walk up the junction, buying the latest fashion at the "Pay-As-You-Wear" shop, brown ales in the local pub, a stolen swim, a dangerous motorbike ride, while pain comes with getting caught (by the police or by falling pregnant), getting married (the chapter entitled "Wedding Anniversary" shows a couple laying into one another in fury), and getting old. But the pain and pleasure are placed almost indifferently side by side, suggesting perhaps the simple inevitability of their juxtaposition. Work, for the women, is often a communal activity, in the sweet factory or the washhouse, where play and teasing are in the air. And over and through all of it there are drifts and layers of talk. The young working class girls who are the central characters live a reckless life not unlike that of Arthur Seaton, with sexual pleasure their uppermost concern. While that pleasure itself is not directly shown, it emerges in the constant and often cacophonous and contrapuntal dialogue which is the book's characteristic mode. The free play of language, including the representation of accent, and the lack of an authorial commentary, makes this more like a drama than a novel, and that impression is reinforced by the short, often disconnected chapters, vignettes from the lives led "up the junction." The sense of disconnection thus produced might give the reader a moral view on these lives as ultimately dislocated and alienated, meaningless except for a certain hedonism. However, the girls themselves seem not to share this view, living their lives for the moment, enjoying their youth and freedom since they have before them in their worn and weary mothers the specters of what comes with age. Like Brenda, they see life for what it is, and where opportunity is limited and money is short, why not head for what pleasure there is? Like Arthur, they turn from pain when it appears and replace it with as much of its opposite as they can.

When the girls do reflect on their lives, rather than this leading them to look ahead and plan for a different kind of life, it reinforces their philosophy of the hedonistic present. One of the pregnant girls on her way to church determines: "Well, one thing's for sure. I'm not going steady no more. I'm going to sort meself out some one-night fellas with plenty of money" (44), while the worldly wise Marion ("I'm not like you. I've always had worries, so I'm used to it" [45]) concludes "Thing is one can't always be scheming. Them what are always planning and scheming don't live, do they?" (47). True, these comments come before the girls have experienced the death of the baby, and in a further poignant irony Moira is never given a voice—except to scream. But the contrapuntal, dialogic mode which has built up to this chapter and continues from it leaves little room for judgment. Readers who fancy they know better than Marion about the importance of planning, and who privilege the brutal moment of Moira's baby's death over the other moments of the story, may have got it wrong. As the old scrubber, Mrs. Hardy, says, giving her earrings to one of the young girls, "Here, love, you wear these. Go on. Yer a long time dead, girl! Get out and enjoy yourself" (102). As the chapter is entitled "Death of an Old Scrubber," we know what is coming. But crucial to many of the unexpected juxtapositions in this novel is that, while there is irony aplenty, it is not intended to produce a knowing or moralistic response. Similarly, while there is much bathos in this novel, there is so much that it ceases to be bathos. Rather, Dunn is laying before us the constant juxtapositions of an ordinary world, where a woman's epitaph can—with dignity, and without irony—be a note pinned to the laundry door: "Owing to the passing of Mrs. Hardy the bagwash won't be ready till Wednesday" (105).

Rube's abortion and subsequent delivery of her dead five-month old fetus is set precisely within this world. In the briefest of chapters (six pages), sandwiched between the near-prostitution of "The Clipjoint" and the female domesticity of "Wash Night," Rube goes through seven visits to the abortionist, Winny. There is a go-between, Annie, who makes the progression to the actual abortion easier ("Rube was cheerful now the first move had been made" [68]). Rube is accompanied by two friends in an act of female solidarity that is all the more solid for not having any such theoretical idea behind it. And this support continues throughout—unconsidered, natural, pragmatic: "But that wasn't the last time Rube and I trailed up to Wimbledon. She had to go seven times before anything happened [. . .] Later I'd cart Rube home weak-kneed and trembling on the bus" (69). The abortionist, like those in the 30s novels, is a suspect figure: "Winny was about forty-five. She wore a red dress above her knees showing her varicose-vein legs, ankle socks and gym shoes" (68). "Winny didn't eat anything all day. She was always on the bottle" (69). Dunn's democratic world is not quite forgiving enough to forgive the abortionist; but here again, perhaps, she simply reflects reality. The tough part of the representation comes in the later part of the chapter, when Rube eventually "brings it off." The narrator's suggestion that a doctor should be called is rejected because "they might try to save the baby" (70). In a page and a half Dunn lays Rube's agony, which could be life-threatening, against the Sunday dinner: "The smell of Sunday dinner cooking floated up the stairs. Rube bent up tight with pain. [. . .] Sylvie came in. 'I'll hold her now, Mum, if you want to go and have yer dinner'" (70). Rube's shrieks echo Moira's screams, while diverse threats are uttered against the baby's father Terry; the family eats their dinner, Ben E. King sings "Oh yes, she said, yes," and the narrator rings the doctor, finally. "When I came back from ringing, Rube was shrieking, a long, high, animal shriek. The baby was born alive, five months old. It moved, it breathed, its heart beat" (71).

There are elements of the comic in these bathetic juxtaposings—or there would be if it weren't for the inherently distressing subject matter. But this is surely the key to Dunn's style. As we have learnt from previous chapters, Sunday dinner may be as important as anything else—even an abortion. Rube is simply "relieved" to have the business over, while Sylvie and her mum peer in wonderment at the "tiny baby still joined by the cord"—a wonderment that has absolutely no consequence for their subsequent actions: "Later Sylvie took him, wrapped in the Daily Mirror, and threw him down the toilet" (71).

As with Sillitoe, representation may do something more here than the experience of the lived reality would. If we found ourselves in the room with Rube—as the narrating Dunn presumably did—we might be appalled. But Dunn seeks to represent the prevailing attitude as she observed it, and to valorize it, in the sense of showing where it comes from. The compassion lies precisely in the lack of judgment.[8] As with Sillitoe, Dunn's "celebration of the liveliness"—her phrase, ostensibly at odds with the abortion scenes described above—seems to rise above specific grimnesses and permeate the work as a whole. Central to this dynamic is the interplay of language we have discussed. And while Dunn's work seems almost relentlessly heteroglossic in the way it intercuts voices, relies so strongly on direct speech (and the narrative present tense), and allows full play to the democratization of language Bakhtin lauds, it is rather the way she represents a particular stratum of language that gives force to this novel as a challenge to official culture. "The speaking person in the novel is always, to one degree or another, an ideologue [. . .] A particular language in a novel is always a particular way of viewing the world, one that strives for a social significance" (Bakhtin, Dialogic 333). From the speaking persons in Dunn's novel comes a flood of language, but one which is made up of many small streams flowing into and out of each other. There is a richness and diversity in this back-and-forth of voices, but there is also a genuine equality. Not even the narrator's voice dominates, indeed her voice is carefully, politely, but clearly delineated as different from this "other" mainstream. When the girls are working in the sweet factory, the narrator calls Ruby: "Could you come over here a minute please?" The reply is "Listen to that. We've got to take her in hand—teach her how to speak. You say, 'Rube, fuck you, get over here, mate!'"(26). Elsewhere, off with a boy after the illegal dip in the swimming pool, he says to her "You must think I'm slow. I don't know what to say to a decent girl. If you was an old slag, I'd just say, 'Come 'ere [. . .]'" (13–14). This placing of Dunn within the social group but slightly outside their language adds authenticity to the representation of that language as expressive of a particular class and culture. It does not force her out but flows around her.

Clair Wills, acknowledging and extending a critique made originally by Peter Stallybrass and Allon White, argues:

> [I]t appears a mostly compensatory gesture when critics enthuse about the "carnival*esque*" they find in the latest (post-)modernist novel. Surely they can't really confuse reading a good book with the experience of carnival grounded in the collective activity of the people? What seems to be lacking in this textual carnival is any link with a genuine social force. (85)

Similarly, objections can be raised to Bakhtin's stress on the importance of heteroglossia; Gramsci for example argues that this emphasis on difference inevitably disempowers the "lower" speaker, holding him and his class back from the power that official language confers, and from the unity implicit in revolutionary struggle (183–187).

Up the Junction and *Saturday Night and Sunday Morning* provide counter-examples to Gramsci's analysis. For in these novels we see communities and the individuals within them using their own language with the confidence of its being complex and rich enough to challenge orthodoxy and thus make the transition into a fully literary language. But the question remains as to whether any of these novels has a link "with a genuine social force," or whether indeed the literary assumption of features of carnival into the carnivalesque weakens rather than strengthens any opposition it might have made to official culture, by subsuming it, through the process of reading, into that official culture. In the novels of the 50s and 60s, an inherent difficulty arises from their predominantly realist mode, which assumes a close connection between representation and reality, and which depends in part on readers seeing a relation between their own lived reality and that which the words on the page seek to represent. When elements of a different, though related, tradition—grotesque realism—are introduced, there is a break in that relation. So though the texts themselves may be illuminated by the Bakhtinian concepts of the carnivalesque and the grotesque body, and thus may stand against his relegation of the modern novel to the sphere of the privatized consciousness, it may be that as modern read- ers we are wedded to the individually human as opposed to the social body. The depiction of abortion, where we inevitably associate our own individuality both with that of the woman and by extension with that of the dead (but po- tentially alive) fetus, may be a step too far even for grotesque realism. Bakhtin's mantra that "the material bodily principle is contained not in the biological individual [. . .] but in the people, a people who are continually growing and renewed" (*Rabelais* 19) is, taken politically, an inspiring ideal. But his concept of the grotesque body depends heavily on fleshly actuality—protuberances, orifices, and all that goes in and comes out of them, are vital to his analysis that at these margins "the confines between bodies and between the body and the world are overcome" (*Rabelais* 317). The contemporary reader enjoys the benefits of making choices about the body and the self in distinction from the "cosmic whole"; she might celebrate her own privatization rather than regret it. Bakhtin's ideal, taken metaphorically, is wonderfully optimistic; but applied to the actuality of people's material selves and individual lives, it places the life and the death of the body on the same level. In the end this may come to seem annihilating rather than liberating.

But these texts, and the realities they represent, remain. Rhys's and Huxley's brave women undergo a bodily horror that is underwritten as ap- propriate by society, but they still, in their consciousness, put their tongue out at that society and that notion of propriety. Sillitoe's and Dunn's women are much more pragmatic about the necessity of abortion, and in that they have achieved a female independence and confidence in their place in soci- ety which seems to be a function of their class. For once the working class woman has a position of power, to decide without sentimentality or, indeed, society's opprobrium, the fate of her unborn child. But the bodily messi- ness—and the carryover of that into consciousness—remains. However, in the 50s and 60s texts these are displaced into modes of representation which are on the one hand relieved of the grimness of the 30s novels and on the other do not need to pay lip service to concepts of the abject. Brenda is the mock-heroic heroine of her own abortion; Moira and Rube have a far harder time, yet they float away from their dead babies, borne on the happy tide of sexual fulfillment. As members of society we may have learned to disapprove of such amoral liberation; as readers we may be carried along by their pleasure. If we think of the fetuses, we may be shocked by their laconic fate in the narrative; if we think like Bakhtin, we may see a resolving theory. But if we look at these 30s and 50s/60s texts together and as a whole, we see a careful, human, imaginative, non-judgmental attempt to understand the experience of any woman who chooses to abort her pregnancy. As with all fiction, what survives is a representation of something central to human experience.

Notes

1. All the novels we discuss were written when abortion was still illegal (though in the case of the 50s/60s novel the debate about the rightness of this was beginning to open up in the lead-up to the Abortion Act of 1967).

2. Anna has resisted Hester's attempts to make her "behave like a lady" (56) and says of the word lady itself: "some words have a long, thin neck that you'd like to strangle" (120).

3. Compare grotesque realism's emphasis on genitals, buttocks, belly, nose, and mouth (Bakhtin, *Rabelais* 318).

4. Her horror is intensified by the presence of the abortionist, Mme. Bonifay, whom Huxley describes as a woman of "Rabelaisian good humour" (319). Helen is disgusted by her stink of "garlic and dirty linen" (316). "She loathed the beastly woman but at the same time was glad that she was so awful. That cheerful, gross vulgarity was somehow appropriate" (319).

5. Due to Huxley's extreme disruption of chronology, the reader shares Anthony's ignorance of Helen's abortion at this point. The reader may feel that Helen's unhappiness is explained by Anthony's heartlessness. Only with hindsight can the reader reinterpret the true reason for her "resentful sadness" (3) and her "ordinary hell of emptiness and drought and discontent" (13). Similarly, Anthony is oblivious to the significance of her comments when they discuss his war wound.

> Helen shuddered. "It must have been awful!" Then, with a sudden vehemence, "How I hate pain!" she cried, and her tone was one of passionate, deeply personal resentment. [. . .]
> "One can't remember pain," he said aloud.
> "*I* can." (57)

6. If the reader has remembered the single passing reference to Helen's abortion (57), he will understand the source of Helen's horror, but it is more likely that the significance of the scene will become apparent only when the reader reaches the abortion scene itself much later in the novel's disordered time-scheme.

7. Nicole Moore points out that, by contrast, "many abortion narratives featured prominently in Australian realist novels of the '30s and '40s" (70).

8. K. J. Shepherdson shows that Tony Garnett's television play version of the novel took a far more judgmental view, foregrounding the abortion scene with perhaps the specific intention of contributing to a change in the law. Though Dunn later proclaimed her pride in the fact that "I helped to change the law" *(Still Angry)*, her aesthetic remained one of witness, which was subverted by Garnett's more polemical aesthetic (Shepherdson 64–71).

Works Cited

Bakhtin, Mikhail. *Rabelais and His World*. 1965. Trans. Hélène Iswolsky. Bloomington: Indiana University Press, 1984.

——— . *The Dialogic Imagination: Four Essays*. 1934–1935. Ed. Michael Holquist. Trans. Caryl Emerson and Michael Holquist. Austin: University of Texas Press, 1981.

Dunn, Nell. *Up the Junction*. 1963. London: Pan Books, 1966.

————. In conversation. *Still Angry After All This Time.* Programme 5. BBC Radio 4, London. 5 November 2004.

Emery, Mary Lou. *Jean Rhys at "World's End": Novels of Colonial and Sexual Exile.* Austin: University of Texas Press, 1990.

Gramsci, Antonio. *Selections from Cultural Writings.* Ed. David Forgacs and Geoffrey Nowell Smith. Trans. Willam Boelhower. London: Lawrence and Wishart, 1985.

Horner, Avril and Sue Zlosnik. *Landscapes of Desire: Metaphors in Modern Women's Fiction.* Hemel Hempstead: Harvester, 1990.

Huxley, Aldous. *Eyeless in Gaza.* 1936. London: Flamingo, 1994.

Minogue, Sally and Andrew Palmer. "Helter Skelter, Topsy-turvey and 'Loonycolour': Carnivalesque Realism in *Saturday Night and Sunday Morning.*" *English* 51.200 (2002): 127–143.

Moore, Nicole. "The Politics of Cliché: Sex, Class and Abortion in Australian Realism." *Modern Fiction Studies* 47:1 (2001): 69–91.

Rhys, Jean. *Voyage in the Dark.* 1934. London: Penguin, 2000.

Shepherdson, K. J. "Challenging Television: The Work of Tony Garnett." Dissertation. University of Kent, 2004.

Sillitoe, Alan. *Saturday Night and Sunday Morning.* 1958. London: Flamingo, 1994.

Vice, Sue. *Introducing Bakhtin.* Manchester: Manchester University Press, 1997.

Wills, Clair. "Upsetting the Public: Carnival, Hysteria and Women's Texts." *Bakhtin's Cultural Theory.* Ed. Ken Hirschkop and David Shepherd. Manchester: Manchester University Press, 2001. 130–151.

MAARTJEN N. SCHERMER

Brave New World *versus* Island— *Utopian and Dystopian Views on Psychopharmacology*

Aldous Huxley's *Brave New World* (1932) is a famous and widely known dystopia, frequently called upon in public discussions about biotechnological developments. It is less well known that Huxley has also written a utopian novel, *Island* (1962), published about 30 years after *Brave New World*. Whereas *Brave New World* vividly depicts a world in which humans have become less-than-human by means of biotechnological and socio-scientific techniques, *Island* sketches an idyllic community in which scientific knowledge is carefully employed for the enhancement of the quality of human lives. In this article I claim that these two novels can be understood as a kind of elaborate thought experiments of what the world *could* look like if certain powers and technologies became available to us. In this sense, they can be considered as heuristic 'tools' to help us think about the possible worlds that technology could bring about.

In this article I will discuss Huxley's novels from this perspective, focussing especially on the role of psychopharmacological substances in both books. Psychopharmacological substances play a significant role in both *Brave New World* and in *Island*. The discussions and reflections on soma, in *Brave New World*, and on *moksha*-medicine in *Island*, can be read as two paradigmatic ways of looking at the ethical and philosophical meaning of such substances. While the first shows all the treacherous, dangerous and scary aspects of

---

Medicine, Health Care and Philosophy, Volume 10, Number 2 (June 2007): pp. 119–128.
Copyright © 2007 Springer Publishing.

psychopharmacology, the second shows its potentially positive and enhancing effects. In *Brave New World*, soma stands for alienation, de-humanization
and superficial mind-numbing pleasure. This image is reflected in many present day ethical commentaries that fear the de-humanizing and the identity-
and authenticity-corrupting effects of psychopharmacology. In contrast, the
moksha-medicine used on the Island of Pala stands for revelation, authentic
self-experience, mind-expansion and true human flourishing.

A reading of Huxley's novels can therefore, I believe, be helpful in taking
stock of and analyzing the various arguments for and against the use of psychopharmacological substances, especially their so-called 'cosmetic' use. So,
the leading question will be: what can we learn from Huxley's novels about
psychopharmacology, and how does this relate to the discussion in the ethical
and philosophical literature on this subject?

In the first part of this paper, I will show how the use of psychopharmacological substances is depicted in *Brave New World* and *Island* respectively,
and how these images hang together with the dystopian and utopian worlds
depicted in the novels. I will argue that in the current ethical discussion the
dystopian vision on psychopharmacology is dominant, but that a comparison
between *Brave New World* and *Island* shows that a more utopian view is possible as well. Next, I will illustrate this point by discussing in depth the issue
of authenticity, which is often raised in the ethical discussion on psychopharmacology, and is also present in Huxley's novels.

In the second part of the article I will draw some further conclusions
for the ethical debate on psychopharmacology and human enhancement, by
comparing the novels not only with each other, but also with our present
reality. I will contend that the debate should not get stuck in an opposition
of dystopian and utopian views, but should address important issues that demand attention in our real world: the issues of evaluation, governance and
regulation of enhancing psychopharmacological substances in democratic,
pluralistic societies.

Brave New World and soma

Brave New World (1932) is set in a future world in the year 632 After Ford.[1]
In *Brave New World*, people are no longer born and raised the way we are
used to: they are created by way of cloning and consequently grow up in bottles in the so-called Hatchery. Here, they are bred and conditioned in such
a way that they are perfectly designed for the tasks they are meant to fulfil
in society. This society is divided in casts, from Epsilon semi-morons to
Deltas, Gammas, Betas, Alphas. The Deltas and Epsilons are designed for
mean labour; they are not very bright but physically strong and resistant to
pollution and monotonous work. Others are more intelligent and designed
for white-collar work. One of the main characters is Lenina Crowne, a

popular and perfectly adjusted alpha. She dates Bernard Marx, an alpha-plus, who tends to be a bit brooding and heavyhearted—probably because of a small mistake during his hatching. Arguably the most important character in *Brave New World* is the Savage, a 'natural born', who has grown up in a Reservation between ancient Indian tribes under very harsh and primitive conditions. It is mainly through his experiences and his discussions with World Controller Mustapha Mond, that we gain insight in the culture, habits and philosophy of the World State.

The whole society of the World State revolves around economy and amusement. People work the whole day in Ford-like production processes and in the evenings they go to the 'feelies', play electromagnetic golf or have recreational sex. People have superficial friendships, but love relationships, let alone family-relationships, are absent. The main activities besides labouring are consuming and having fun. People do not go through the process of ageing, but instead remain in perfect health until in their sixties they die in a special Hospital for the Dying, in a soma-induced ecstasy. Their remains are processed into useful materials like phosphor. Community, identity and stability are considered to be the main values in the World State and the regime has succeeded very well in realizing them. As Mustapha Mond describes its achievements:

> The world's stable now. People are happy; they get what they want, and they never want what they can't get. They're well off, they're safe; they're never ill; they're not afraid of death; they're blissfully ignorant of passion and old age; they're plagued with no mothers or fathers; they've got no wives, or children, or lovers they feel strongly about; they're so conditioned that they practically can't help behaving as they ought to behave. (Ch. 16, p. 200)[2]

What is the role of the psychotropic drug soma in this perfect world? At first sight, it fits into the utopian picture of complete happiness. Soma seems somewhat comparable to alcohol: in low dosages it induces pleasant feelings and stimulates social contact. People take soma as a kind of 'holiday' from everyday life, a trip to a temporary state of bliss. It makes them happy, relaxed and good-humoured. It soon becomes clear, however, that soma is not an innocent or ideal substance. What applies for the rest of *Brave New World*'s inventions certainly applies to soma: its dystopian face shines right through the surface of utopian happiness.

> And if ever, by some unlucky chance, anything unpleasant should somehow happen, why, there's always soma to give you a holiday from the facts. And there's always soma to calm your anger, to reconcile you to your enemies, to make you patient and long-

suffering. In the past you could only accomplish these things by
making a great effort and after years of hard moral training. Now,
you swallow two or three half-gramme tablets, and there you are.
Anybody can be virtuous now. You can carry at least half your
morality about in a bottle. Christianity without tears—that's what
soma is. (Ch. 17, p. 217)

On closer inspection, the inhabitants of *Brave New World* take soma mainly
to escape from unpleasant situations and from 'real life'; it produces only
shallow feelings of well-being and no real happiness or fulfilment; and it
distracts from any human effort or true morality. In brief, soma promotes a
superficial hedonism and causes alienation from the kind of 'real human life'
that we know. Furthermore, soma is used to keep the social order as it is.
It is used as a kind of substitute for religious feelings in Community Sings
and Solidarity Services, where the values of the World State are celebrated
and enforced. It is quite literally opium for the people. Apart from its use
in semi-religious gatherings, soma is also used to keep the Delta workforce
content by free provisions after work.

'No shoving there now!' shouted the Deputy Sub-Bursar in a
fury. He slammed down the lid of his cash-box. 'I shall stop the
distribution unless I have good behaviour.' The Deltas muttered,
jostled one another a little, and then were still. The threat had
been effective. Deprivation of soma—appalling thought!
'That's better', said the young man, and re-opened his cash-box.
(Ch. 15, p. 192)

Soma is used to keep the society stable, to keep everyone content with
their fate and turn all the inhabitants of *Brave New World* into 'shiny happy
people'. Even the lack of true human passions and feelings is made up for
by a psychopharmacological substitute: everybody gets VPS (Violent Passion Surrogate) once a month, to stimulate the adrenals. This is one of the
conditions of perfect health. As Mustapha Mond explains, it is the complete
physiological equivalent of fear and rage. Consequently, fear and rage as
subjective emotions have become superfluous.

Brave New World clearly offers a dystopian, picture of the use of psycho-
active drugs. In it, soma stands for alienation, de-humanization and superficial mind-numbing pleasure. This image of psychotropic substances, especially
mood-altering drugs, is reflected in many contemporary ethical commentaries that fear the de-humanizing and corrupting effects of such drugs. In many
serious works on enhancement or the ethics of psycho-pharmacology, *Brave
New World* figures in the bibliography and is used (often merely rhetorically)

to set the stage for the discussion on possible dangers of these developments. The President's Council on Bioethics, for instance, says: "The example of 'soma', the drug in Aldous Huxley's fictional *Brave New World*, illustrates the debased value of a spurious, drug-induced contentment. Soma—like cocaine, only without side effects or addiction—completely severs feeling from living, inner sensation from all external relations, the feeling of happiness from leading a good life." (2003, p. 294) In the Council's final over-all evaluation of mood-brightening drugs this image is clearly present.

Island and the moksha-medicine

The relatively unknown novel *Island* was written by Huxley at the end of his life, in 1962, and it depicts a world that is almost the complete opposite of *Brave New World*.[3] Pala is a small island in the Pacific, where for 120 years an ideal society has flourished. A journalist named Will Farnaby is shipwrecked there and we discover this utopia though his eyes. Farnaby is actually an underground agent for an oil-magnete who wants to strike a deal with the government of Pala because of the substantial oil reserves on the island. However, the more Farnaby learns about Palanese culture, the more sympathetic to it he becomes. The people of Pala live in small communities, with different families together in so-called mutual adoption groups. Children are raised by their natural parents but their education and development are supported by the rest of the group. The circumstances are idyllic; the Palanese produce as much food and goods as they need but not more and their lifestyle displays a perfect balance between labour and relaxation and between physical exercise and mental activity. People are generally healthy, thanks to a very well-developed and mainly preventive medicine, but death and suffering are not absent or denied. In contrast, they are accepted as an inherent aspect of human life and people are educated and supported socially and psychologically to deal with them. Children are carefully educated and conditioned and jobs are assigned according to physique and temperament. Sexuality in Pala is very free and closely connected to a spiritual view of life.

The culture of Pala—which was founded by a Buddhist king and a Scottish doctor—is a mixture of eastern religious and philosophical views, and western scientific knowledge and technologies. Science and technology, but also hypnosis, education, psychology, yoga and the so-called *moksha*-medicine are employed in the service of the realization of a good and human life for everyone. As Dr. Robert MacPhail, grandson of one of Pala's founders and one of the main characters in the book, explains the goals of his society: "Our wish is to be happy, our ambition to be fully human." (Ch. 9, p. 171)

Moksha-medicine is the psychotropic substance that plays an important role in Palanese life. Moksha literally means 'liberation' but the drug is also known as the 'reality revealer' or the 'truth-and-beauty pill'. It is used to sharpen and deepen consciousness and brings about a kind of mystical or spiritual experience. It is meant to teach people more about themselves and their place in the universe. As Dr. Robert challenges the island's crown prince Murugan (who has been educated in a Swiss boarding school and is fiercely opposed to the use of 'dope'):

> [Make] a single experiment. Take four hundred milligrams of moksha-medicine and find out for yourself what it does, what it tells you about your own nature, about this strange world you've got to live in, learn in, suffer in and finally die in. Yes, even you will have to die one day—maybe fifty years from now, maybe tomorrow. Who knows? But it is going to happen, and one's a fool if one does not prepare for it. (Ch. 9, p. 170)

> Most people in Pala take the moksha medicine only a few times a year, and its effects are compared to those of meditation—a practice which has an important place in everyday Palanese life. While meditation is like daily dinner, the moksha-medicine is compared to a banquet, which is an occasional treat. Both meditation and moksha-medicine improve social intelligence, self-knowledge and self-understanding. As one of the characters, Vijaya, explains to Farnaby, moksha-medicine helps one by "getting to know oneself to the point where one won't be compelled by one's unconscious to do all the ugly, absurd, self-stultifying things that one so often finds oneself doing." (Ch. 11, p. 225)

Moreover: "It helps one to be more intelligent [. . .] Not more intelligent in relation to science or logical argument but on the deeper level of concrete experience and personal relationships". And the kind and simple Mrs Rao adds: "[I have] no talents or cleverness. But when it comes to living, when it comes to understanding people and helping them, I feel myself growing more and more sensitive and skillful." (Ch. 11, p. 225)

It can be concluded that *Island* offers a view on psychopharmacological drugs that is very different from that of *Brave New World*. In contrast to soma, the moksha-medicine stands for revelation, greater consciousness and self-understanding, mind-expansion and human flourishing. The positive and enhancing effects of the drug are put to good use and appear to stand in the service of humanity rather than to lead to its decline. This is a kind of view that is less often called upon in the ethical discussions on psychopharmacology and human enhancement. None of the books or articles that cite *Brave New World* in order to stress the inherent dangers of (psychopharmacological) enhancement cite *Island,* or other more 'utopian' descriptions. When *Brave New World* and *Island* are understood as two opposed 'Gestalts' of psycho-pharmacological enhancement, it must be concluded that the dystopian Gestalt is dominant in the ethical debate.

Ethics and the problem of authenticity

Many of the dystopian fears elicited by *Brave New World* find their positive mirror image in *Island.* The fear that psychotropic drugs will only give us a shallow hedonistic type of happiness instead of true fulfilment and 'happy souls' (President's Council, 2003) is countered by the image of deep human experience that the moksha-medicine brings about. The fear that psychotropic drugs will be like opium for the masses and suppress real and legitimate dissatisfaction with certain ways of life (Elliott, 2000) is countered by the thoughtful ways in which moksha-medicine is employed to learn about the human condition. Likewise, the fears that psychopharma-cological substances will provide an easy way out of our problems instead of stimulating us to 'work hard on ourselves' (Fukuyama, 2002), or that they will 'dehumanize' us instead of making us better people are all perfectly illustrated by *Brave New World,* while their opposites are depicted in *Island.* So, both dystopian and more utopian perspectives on the use of 'cosmetic' psychopharmacology are possible, even if in the current ethical debate the first tends to dominate.

To underpin this claim further I will now discuss in some more detail the—arguably—most problematic and most debated problem of psycho-pharmacological enhancement, that of authenticity. The debate on authenticity has been relatively well-developed, and positive as well as negative visions have been expressed. Huxley's novels can illustrate as well as supplement the various positions in the debate.

The problem of authenticity is frequently mentioned in the ethics literature about psychopharmacology. It concerns the fear that one cannot 'live truly', or not 'really be oneself', when using psychotropic drugs. The alienation found in *Brave New World* is exemplary for this fear. While the characters in *Brave New World* hardly seem to have an authentic self anyway, due to their cloned and conditioned nature, they tend to use soma to get away from anything—any situation or experience—that might induce self-reflection or self-awareness. In a famous section in *Brave New World,* Bernard and Lenina are flying over the British Channel by night, and Lenina gets more and more upset and horrified by the silent moonlight, the cloudy sky, and the black, foamed-flecked water heaving beneath them. Lenina is appalled and frightened by the fact that they are alone, without music, lights and distraction. Bernard, however, enjoys it: "It makes me feel as though . . . [. . .] as though I were more me, if you see what I mean. More on my own, not so completely a part of something else. Not just a cell in a social body. Doesn't it make you feel like that, Lenina?" But Lenina does not understand what he means and cries out: "I don't know what you mean. I am free. Free to have the most wonderful time. Everybody's happy nowadays." And when Bernard pushes his case she adds: "'I don't understand anything. Nothing. Least of all why you don't take soma when you have these dreadful ideas of yours. You'd forget all about them. And instead of feeling miserable, you'd be jolly. So jolly." Bernard, however, feels that the use of soma to become less gloomy is inauthentic: "I'd rather be myself' he said. 'Myself and nasty. Not somebody else, however jolly."(Ch. 6, pp. 80–82)

A totally opposite view comes to the fore in *Island*, where the moksha-medicine is supposed to make people *more* themselves, instead of less. Taking the drug is intended to help them reveal their authentic being and to become who they really are. Dr. Robert explains this clearly in a speech at an initiation-ceremony for a group of adolescents, who are going to use the moksha-medicine for the first time.

> 'Liberation,' Dr. Robert began again, 'the ending of sorrow, ceasing to be what you ignorantly think you are and becoming what you are in fact. For a little while, thanks to the moksha-medicine, you will know what it's like to be what in fact you are, what in fact you always have been. What a timeless bliss! But, like everything else, this timelessness is transient. Like everything else, it will pass. And when it has passed, what will you do with this experience?' [. . .] 'Will you merely enjoy them as you would enjoy an evening at the puppet show, and then go back to business as usual. Or, having glimpsed, will you devote your lives to the business, not at all as usual, of being what you are in fact?' (Ch. 10, p. 208)

Here, the idea is that the drug can help reveal a true self and can help one to become who one really is. The effect is not alienation, but revelation. Authenticity is enhanced, not violated.

Both views on the relationship between the use of psychotropic substances and authenticity or authentic identity have been expressed in the ethical discussion on psychopharmacology, especially with regard to SSRI's such as Prozac (DeGrazia, 2000, 2005; Elliott, 1998, 2000; Kramer, 1993, 2000). The notion of 'becoming who you are in fact', which is central in Palanese culture, can be understood to refer to the self in the sense of personality or personal identity. The suggestion that the true self is somewhere to be discovered and revealed is, however, rejected by most present day philosophers; revelation is not the right term in connection to personal identity. The static notion of identity or self it presupposes has been criticised from various sides (e.g. feminist approaches to identity and autonomy, see MacKenzie and Stoljar, 2000).

The combined notions of self-discovery and self-creation are more apt in this context. The Palanese notion of 'becoming who you are in fact' can also be taken to suggest that the true self is not somewhere to be found but is something that one can become, perhaps by working on oneself (or one's self), by introspection and practice or by meditation and moksha medicine. Moksha medicine is then understood as a tool that can be put to use in a process of discovering and developing oneself (cf Elliott, 1998, p. 186). When authenticity is understood as identification with one's own characteristics and coherence between one's values and one's personality, such forms of self-development and self-creation are perfectly compatible with authenticity (DeGrazia, 2000).

Following this view on authenticity and personal identity we can also observe that the rejection of the use of soma in *Brave New World* as a paradigm case of inauthenticity is perhaps too easy. The connection between soma and (in)authenticity is more complicated than a superficial reading might suggest. While Bernard consciously decides that he does not want to be anyone else, that his bad moods belong to him and are an essential (if not the most pleasant) part of who he is, Lenina seems to identify completely with the superficial values of *Brave New World*. While on the interpretation of 'authenticity' given above it would indeed be unauthentic for Bernard to take soma, the same does not go for Lenina. She *is* completely 'herself'—though perhaps her self is not very deep or very well-developed. Authenticity understood as being oneself does not imply anything about the content of that self; it can be moody, or it can be shallow and hedonistically inclined. An authentic person is not necessarily a nice or interesting person. If authenticity is understood as invoking one's own values and critical faculties in the choices one makes about how to live one's life, the real problem in *Brave New World* is that it has created people who almost completely lack these faculties. Like Lenina, they are people who seem to lack the capacity for authenticity altogether—the mindless taking of soma is a symptom, but not the cause of this condition.

Apart from the discussion on authenticity as a characteristic of personal identity, there is also a discussion going on about authenticity as related to human nature, especially in the context of human enhancement (Parens, 2005). In *Island*, the world-view and religious or spiritual convictions of the people of Pala include that there is something like 'really being yourself' or 'being what you are in fact', which refers to one's nature as a human being, or one's place in a cosmological whole. Here, the idea of an authentic self is closely connected with authenticity as a human being and thus with human nature. Though the specific Palanese worldview is not the kind of view many people in today's Western culture would endorse, it shows similarities to other views of the 'naturally human', such as those invoked by the President's Council, or by Fukuyama. In the contemporary debate notions of the naturally human, or of natural human development, are still strongly present and are often taken to imply that drugs or other technologies are artificial and therefore 'unnatural' ways of interfering in this development. This line of argument is rather problematic since it remains unclear what this 'naturally human' is exactly, and how we can know what it is. Moreover, whatever is understood by 'naturally human' or 'natural human development', we constantly interfere with it through technology, medicine and the like. It remains unclear why certain unnatural interferences are problematic while others, apparently, are not.

A very important difference between the Palanese view on authenticity and that of the President's Council, is that the latter stresses that for authentic or natural human identity, contact with the 'real world' is essential. Being in touch with reality is what matters, and this is why the escapism of *Brave New World* is so forcefully rejected. On the same grounds, the 'trips' taken with moksha-medicine could be rejected. This is exactly what Murugan, the crown prince of Pala does—he rejects the use of moksha medicine on the grounds that the experiences it evokes are not real. They do not refer to anything in the outside world, he claims. The answer Dr. Robert gives him is philosophically interesting enough to quote. He compares the experience of moksha-medicine with listening to music—which does not refer to anything outside itself either. "So maybe the whole thing does happen inside one's skull. Maybe it *is* private and there's no unitive knowledge of anything but one's own physiology. Who cares? The fact remains that the experience can open one's eyes and make one blessed and transform one's whole life." (Ch. 9, p. 171)

So, it is claimed that one can learn and grow from experiences even if they are not 'real' in the sense of referring directly to something in the outside world. One can even become 'more truly human' by such experiences.[4] This is an observation that deserves further philosophical development in the discussion on psychopharmacology. What exactly we should take the notion of the 'truly human' to imply (or even the question whether such a thing exists and if so, in what way) I will not discuss here. However, if we do identify characteristics or actions that deserve to be called 'truly human', we should allow for the possibility that psychopharmacology can somehow enhance these instead of being intrinsically at odds with them.

The use of fiction and the real world

I have compared Huxley's two novels to show different possible views on psychopharmacology and to show how literature can vividly point out some of the moral problems of possible future developments. I do not want to argue here that either one of the views presented in the novels is 'right', or even that one of them is 'better' than the other. Both have the merit of showing us something about the form that the use of psychopharmacology could take, and about the moral issues that might be connected to certain uses of psychopharmacology. In general, however, the dystopian view tends to be dominant in the ethical debate.[5] The report of the President's Council, for example, though it offers a subtle and insightful discussion, tends to emphasise the dangers and the threats to our humanity, and to neglect the possible gains and advantages of going 'beyond therapy'. Authors such as Sandel, Kass and Fukuyama all paint rather dystopian pictures of our bio-technologically enhanced future.

Since the dystopian view tends to dominate the debate, a view like that in *Island* will probably be quickly rejected as 'utopian' in the sense of being unrealistic, overly optimistic, or simply naive. But if we reject the *Island*-view as unrealistic, why should we not reject *Brave New World* and the connected dystopian fears as well? Is that view not (also) completely unrealistic and overly pessimistic?

As far as I can see, there is one argument one could appeal to in order to support the claim that *Brave New World* is more realistic than *Island*, and that is the claim that the driving forces and the dominant social and cultural values in *Brave New World* are more like those in present day Western societies than the culture and values of the island of Pala. We recognise the economic drive, the consumerism, the commercialisation and the entertainment-culture of *Brave New World*. But then again, we do also recognize much of the concerns, the quests and the human experiences in *Island*. And while small-scale communities and Buddhist-inspired spirituality may not be viable options in our world, neither are Hatcheries and World Controllers. With *Brave New World* in mind, we can see the 'run on Ritalin' (Diller, 1996) as a sign that parents drug their children into becoming model-citizens; but we can also read reports of the subtlety and real concern with which parents deliberate about using or not using the drug in order to help their child (Singh, 2005, Slob 2004) that would remind us more of *Island*.

I believe it is hard to give a normatively neutral (that is: 'objective') answer to the question of which novel paints the most realistic image. But, more importantly, I believe it is actually the wrong question. The point of reading these novels is not that they show us how things are, but how they could be, and how we could look at them. Given the dominant position of the dystopian view, I think it would be good for the debate to pay more attention to the utopian view as well. This does not imply that we should uncritically applaud all the promises of the enhancement-industry, or that we should all become transhumanists overnight, but we should look seriously into the possible positive effects and applications of psychopharmacological enhancement. We should put dystopia and utopia on a par and look at the possible ethical benefits as well as the dangers. It is remarkable that there is no research or discussion whatsoever on enhancing human functions such as empathy, sympathy, trust or altruism.

Comparative analysis: lessons for enhancement debate

I will conclude by leaving the world of literary fiction and return to our own real world. While we can learn a lot from utopian and dystopian fictions, they also carry the danger of forcing us into dichotomous ways of thinking (good and bad; for or against) and oversimplified views of the world. Two aspects that are typical of utopias and dystopias alike, but do not correspond to the actual situation in our world, they are the existence of a totally controllable society and the presence of only one single view of the good life. In these respects both *Brave New World* and *Island* differ significantly from our Western society, which is characterized by great individual freedom and a pluralism of worldviews. Having recognized this, we can draw three more conclusions that are important for the psychopharmacology debate.

First, the effects of psychopharmacological substances depend greatly on the society in which they are embedded. Soma could not do its work without the whole constellation of a mind-numbing pleasure industry, without the lack of critical faculties or real love and without the specific social codes of the New World. Likewise, moksha-medicine would not work if it were not embedded in the social programme of education, training and practice of the Island of Pala. Without the specific religious or spiritual framework that gives meaning to the moksha-medicine experience, it may not even yield the same experience. Psychotropic substances are part of a comprehensive social order, the organization of society, its values and its institutions. So, whatever new psychopharmacological substances will come to do and mean in our world will be very much intertwined with our society as a whole. They will reflect the values we hold, they will be embedded in our social practices and institutions—and so we cannot judge their moral meaning without looking at these social structures, institutions and our cultural values. Whether or not new psychopharmacological substances will help create inauthentic and shallow people will depend for a great part on social factors, not on the drug or substance itself. Critique on psychopharmacological enhancement is therefore better understood as critique on the existing culture, trends and popular values, than as a critique on these substances 'as such'.[7]

However, secondly, unlike in *Brave New World* and *Island*, in which—as in all utopias—there is almost total control over society, we will not be able to completely control the place or function new psychotropic substances will get in our society. Nor will we be able to control the ways in which new substances will become embedded in society, or the ways in which such substances may alter society. Laws, regulations and other forms of government control can of course influence the course of events but they cannot control it completely. It would be an illusion to think that we can predict exactly what the social effects of new substances will be, how society will react and how common values and practices might be changed due to these new substances. It is even more illusionary to think that we can arrange and govern all these effects and changes. In our complex and pluriform world that is simply impossible.

It is dangerous to forget that in our world complete control is impossible, and even more dangerous to forget why we should be happy that this is so. *Brave New World* and other famous dystopian like *1984*—as well as the 'realised utopias' of Stalin and Mao—have all made it far too clear that total control comes only at the cost of individual freedom. Nevertheless, a conservative author like Kass[8] sometimes appears to regret that total control over society is not possible and that there seems to be no way to stop our slide off the slippery slope: "Just give us the technological imperative, liberal democratic society, compassionate humanitarianism, moral pluralism, and free markets, and we can take ourselves to *Brave New World* all by ourselves. If you require evidence, just look around." (Kass, 2000).

This position displays little respect for people's own views of the good life and little confidence in their critical faculties and in our democratic values. Fortunately, the President's Council has not adopted the same point of view as its chairman, but stipulates that it is *our freedom* that holds the key to a remedy, because it gives us the opportunity to understand happiness in the right way and to act upon this understanding. This formulation, however, overlooks another important characteristic of our present world, that of pluralism. The President's Council supposes that there is one right way to understand happiness and that we can use our freedom to find it, but apparently not to find other ways of understanding human happiness.

I believe, thirdly, that this value and life-style pluralism that characterize our world should be taken more seriously. As we have seen, the enhancement debate is in an important sense a debate about the good life and about human flourishing or human happiness. Underneath the discussion on authenticity lies a deeper discussion on what it is to be human. The moral evaluation of new psychopharmacological substances or mind-influencing drugs depends greatly on one's ideas in this respect. In *Brave New World* the dominant view is one that we intuitively tend to reject: a view in which safety, stability, and pleasure dominate all other values. In *Island* the dominant view of the good life is a view that is perhaps more attractive to us, with its emphasis on humanity, compassion and meaning.[9] However, both the dystopian and the utopian world are characterized by the fact that there is only one view of the good life. Pluralism is absent in both worlds. Dissidents hardly exist. In *Brave New World* those who are too self-conscious or hold different views on the good life (who, for example, value truth or beauty over happiness) are banned to remote islands. In *Island,* the main dissident is Murugan, the crown prince of Pala who eventually betrays Pala by handing it over to a rivalling neighbour Sultan who is only interested in the oil reserves. This ending of the novel may be taken to suggest that economic forces will eventually ruin any good society, but also that a peaceful pluralism is not possible.

Unlike the world of *Island* or *Brave New World,* our world *is* pluralistic, and people hold vastly different views on what a good life entails. In fact, a quick search on the Internet shows that there are numerous virtual communities that hold views much like those in *Brave New World* and *Island,* and that are in fact inspired by these novels and aim to make their utopia come true.[10] Besides such small-scale initiatives there are of course huge differences in lifestyle and worldview between different groups within the western world—not to mention those in other parts of the world. This implies that there will also be very different views on the use of psychopharmacological substances. It is a very important question how we should deal with this variety in views with regard to psychopharmacological enhancement and the good life. Should we simply allow people to make their own decisions about whether or not to use new substances? This is problematic, since a widespread use of such drugs will influence those who choose not to take them as well (think for example of cognition-enhancing drugs, that will influence competitive abilities). Should we aim to show that one view of the good life is correct and that consequently the use of such drugs should be banned or stimulated? Should we discuss and argue about our various views of the good life and the place of psychotropic drugs in the hope that we will reach a shared view?

Thinking in terms of good and bad, utopia and dystopia should not prevent us from considering two important givens of our actual situation: the existence of pluralism with regard to values and worldviews and the lack of absolute control that characterizes liberal democratic societies. Taking this into account, the interaction between new psychopharmacological substances and society should be understood as a two-way traffic. In figuring out how to deal with new psychopharmacological substances and possibilities for psychopharmacological enhancement, fiction can be very helpful. But we should not get stuck in it.

NOTES

1. Henry Ford (1863–1947), the American car magnate who introduced methods for mass-production of cars such as the assembly-line, is worshipped as a god in *Brave New World.*

2. Because there are numerous editions of *Brave New World* and *Island,* reference is made to both the chapter and page number of the quotations, in order to facilitate tracking down of quotations.

3. In his 1946 foreword to *Brave New World*, Huxley regrets that he has offered the Savage only two alternatives: that of the insane utopia of *Brave New World* and that of the primitive Indian village in the Reservation. If he were to rewrite the book, Huxley says, he would offer the Savage a third alternative. This alternative would consist of living in a community where the economics would be decentralist, the politics anarchist and co-operative and where science and technology would be used as though they had been made for man, instead of the other way around. Religion would be the conscious and intelligent pursuit of man's Final End. All this sounds remarkably like *Island*, suggesting that the opposed views the two works display, are in part representative of a shift in Huxley's own point of view.

4. This could also be compared to spiritual or mystical experiences; remember also the similarity between moksha-medicine and meditation. It seems odd not to recognize the ability to have such experiences and be somehow transformed or affected by them as a typically 'human' ability.

5. For an exception see Bostrom (2003).

6. Huxley wrote *Brave New World* in part as a satire on the global diffusion of the American way of life.

7. Carl Elliott (2003) has very cleverly described the various aspects and ambivalences of contemporary American culture and their relationship to enhancement technologies. The President's Council also locates the core of the enhancement debate in socio-cultural values and in questions about the nature of humanity, human flourishing and happiness.

8. Leon Kass, M.D. is the chairman of the President's Council for Bioethics

9. It can be argued that the underlying view of the good life (Huxley's view?) in both *Brave New World* and *Island* is actually the same. If *Island* is considered to be the blueprint for this good life, *Brave New World* is its negative.

10. See, for example www.island.org and www.huxley.net or www.bltc.com

WORKS CITED

Bostrom, N.: 2003, 'Human and Genetic Enhancements: A Transhumanist Perspective', *The Journal of Value Inquiry* 37, 493–506.

DeGrazia, D.: 2000, 'Prozac. Enhancement, and Self-Creation', *Hastings Center Report* 30(2), 34–40.

DeGrazia, D.: 2005, 'Enhancement Technologies and Human Identity', *Journal of Medicine and Philosophy* 30, 261–283.

Diller. L. H.: 1996. 'The Run on Ritalin. Attention Deficit Disorder and Stimulant Treatment in the 1990's', *Hastings Center Report* 26(2), 12–18.

Elliott, C.: 1998, 'The Tyranny of Happiness: Ethics and Cosmetic Psychopharmacology', in: E. Parens, (ed.), *Enhancing Hunan Traits: Ethical and Social Implications*. Georgetown University Press: Washington D.C. pp. 177–188.

Elliott, C.: 2000, 'Pursued by Happiness and Beaten Senseless. Prozac and the American Dream', *Hastings Center Report* 30(2), 7–12.

Elliott, C.: 2003, *Better than Well. American Medicine Meets the American Dream*. New York: W. W. Norton & Company.

Fukuyama, F.: 2002, *Our Posthuman Future. Consequences of the Biotechnology Revolution*. New York: Farrar, Straus and Giroux.

Huxley, A.: 1932/1994, *Brave New World*. London: Flamingo.

Huxley, A.: 1962/2002, *Island*. New York: HarperCollins Publishers.

Kass, L. R.: 2000, 'Aldous Huxley Brave New World', *First Things* 101, 51–52.

Kramer, P. D.: 2000, 'The Valorization of Sadness: Alienation and the Melancholic Temperament', *Hastings Center Report* 30(2), 13–18.

Kramer, P. D.: 1993, *Listening to Prozac. A Psychiatrist Explores Antidepressant Drugs and the Remaking of the Self.* New York: Penguin Publishers.

MacKenzie, C., and Stoljar, N. (eds.): (2000) *Relational Autonomy. Feminist Perspectives on Autonomy, Agency, and the Social Self.* New York. Oxford University Press.

Parens, E.: 2005, 'Authenticity and Ambivalence. Toward Understanding the Enhancement Debate', *Hastings Center Report* 35(3), 34–41.

President's Council on Bioethics, 2003, *Beyond Therapy. Biotechnology and the Pursuit of Happiness.* New York: Dana Press.

Singh, I.: 2005, 'Will the "Real Boy" Please Behave: Dosing Dilemmas for Parents of Boys With ADHD', *American Journal of Bioethics* 5(3), 34–47.

Slob, M. (ed.): (2004), *Een antler ik. Technologisch ingrijpen in de persoonlijkheid. (A Different Me. Technological Interference in Personality).* Diemen: Veen Magazines/Rathenau Institute.

ACKNOWLEDGMENT

This research was funded by the Netherlands Organization for Scientific Research as part of the programme Ethics, Research and Governance.

JOANNE WOIAK

Designing a Brave New World: Eugenics, Politics, and Fiction

Aldous Huxley, writing shortly after the 1932 publication of *Brave New World*, despaired about the real-world significance of one of his novel's principal themes:

> About 99.5% of the entire population of the planet are as stupid and philistine . . . as the great masses of the English. The important thing, it seems to me, is not to attack the 99.5% . . . but to try to see that the 0.5% survives, keeps its quality up to the highest possible level, and, if possible, dominates the rest. The imbecility of the 99.5% is appalling—but after all, what else can you expect?[1]

In this letter and in the novel, Huxley linked intelligence, eugenics, and politics. He further pondered the problem of dysgenics and democracy in several published essays dating from the late 1920s and early 1930s, with titles such as "What Is Happening to Our Population?" and "Are We Growing Stupider?"[2] He defended the eugenic policies of encouraging higher birthrates among the "intellectual classes" and sterilizing the lower-class "unfit," which he believed would improve the inherited mental abilities of future generations and lead to responsible citizenship.

The Public Historian, Volume 29, Number 3 (Summer 2007): pp. 105–129. Copyright © 2007 by the National Council on Public History. Published by the University of California Press.

163

Huxley's interest in eugenics was more than a "brief flirtation," as suggested by one recent biographer; on the contrary, his ongoing support for so-called race betterment was typical of left-leaning British intellectuals in the interwar period.[3] His writing, including his dystopian novel *Brave New World*, reflected public anxieties about the supposedly degenerating hereditary quality of the population and how this decline would affect England's economic and political future. For Huxley at this time in his life and in this social context, eugenics was not a nightmare prospect but rather the best hope for designing a better world if used in the right ways by the right people. This neglected aspect of his early scientific and political thinking must be taken into account when unpacking the multiple and perhaps conflicting meanings of *Brave New World*. It was simultaneously a satire on contemporary culture, a prediction of biological advances, a commentary on the social roles of science and scientists, and a plan for reforming society.

Ends and Means

As a successful novelist and a prolific "literary journalist," Aldous Huxley contributed extensively to popularizing and critiquing modern biological science and technology. He had been born in 1894 into a scientific family—Aldous's grandfather was T. H. Huxley ("Darwin's bulldog") and his younger brother was the evolutionary biologist Julian Huxley—and intended to become a medical researcher. However, this career path was scrapped after a serious eye infection at age sixteen left him with limited eyesight for the rest of his life.[4] Instead he embarked on a career as a writer, first of poetry, then reviews, then the "novels of ideas" that made his reputation during the 1920s as part of the Bloomsbury group and postwar nihilist generation.[5] In autumn 1931, he completed "a comic, or at least satirical, novel about the Future, showing the appallingness (at any rate by our standards) of Utopia and adumbrating the effects on thought and feeling of . . . quite possible biological inventions. . . . "[6] His title has now become an overused catch-phrase expressing society's ambivalence towards the new genetics and its effects on human life.[7]

Brave New World is remarkable for its accurate predictions about science and technology, economics and politics, and arts and leisure. It extrapolates future applications of genetics (IVF and cloning via Bokanovsky's Process), endocrinology (Malthusian belts), behaviorism (hypnopaedia), and pharmacology (soma). It depicts a World State in the year A.F. 632 (After Ford) where there is absolute social stability (and creative stagnation) made possible by government-controlled research in biology and psychology. Mass-produced bottle-babies are "predestined" to their future jobs using eugenic selection, cloning, and conditioning; after "decanting" from artificial wombs they are subjected to a lifetime of brainwashing techniques designed

by "Emotional Engineers." Society is strictly divided into five castes ranging from the Alpha Double Plus ruling and managerial elite to the laboring
Epsilon Minus semi-morons. The extreme scenario depicted in the book—
featuring totalitarianism, suppression of emotions, ignorance and apathy,
rampant consumerism, and vacuous entertainments such as promiscuous
sex and the "feelies"—has most commonly been read as a cautionary tale
about the dehumanizing effects of technology and the growing influence of
cultural trends that Huxley abhorred.

Since the mid-1990s, however, several leading Huxley scholars have
delved beyond the usual satirical readings of *Brave New World* to reveal more
ambiguous elements in the text. Emphasizing contextual readings, they explore the author's interests and possible intentions at the time he composed
it.[8] We now know that there was considerable cross-fertilization between
Huxley's fiction and nonfiction writing, the latter in the form of books of
lively essays and frequent contributions to magazines and newspapers in
England and America. This paper contributes to the revival of Huxley research led by David Bradshaw, James Sexton, and Robert Baker, who have
edited and interpreted his essays from the 1920s and 30s. They depict a
"hidden Huxley" who early in his literary career was an elitist technocrat and
eugenicist, influenced by H. L. Mencken and H. G. Wells. This contrasts
sharply with his later personae of progressive humanist, pacifist, and spiritualist. This rather unflattering reevaluation of the author of *Brave New World*
generated some initial excitement in academia and the media; subsequently,
however some scholars and biographers have tried to downplay the significance of this brief antidemocratic period in his life. Because this period coin-
cides with the composition of his most famous and enduring fictional work,
it surely deserves greater scrutiny in both academic and public discourses.

Proper attention to Huxley's nonfiction works has enriched our understanding of the progress of his thinking on many political, sociological, philosophical, and scientific issues, which he felt it was his responsibility to engage
with as a "man of letters." Huxley used literature and popular essays to edu-
cate his audiences, especially regarding science and technology, which were
impinging more and more on people's lives for better or worse.[9] He sought
to develop his own "outlook" or philosophy of life, which over the course of
his career ranged from cynical to technocratic to mystical. Through it all he
maintained the importance of art and artists for both understanding human
life and helping to improve it. "How then must we live?" was his perennial
question.[10]

During the interwar period to be discussed here, a principal aspect
of Huxley's "outlook" was his support for the science of eugenics. He believed that human life would be improved by increasing the innate intellectual abilities of the population. This paper expands on the "hidden Huxley"

scholarship by exploring in greater depth the content of and inspiration for his eugenic pronouncements. His eugenics was consistent with the predominant or "mainline" trend in both England and the United States to focus on the problem of "feeblemindedness." American rhetoric emphasized the escalating costs of custodial care, while the psychologists who pioneered mass IQ testing raised alarms that Army recruits had an average mental age of only 13 years. Given this low standard, they wondered, "is America safe for democracy?"[11] In the British case, 1913 legislation produced tens of thousands of "mentally deficient" wards of the state, who in turn became the subject of debates by middle-class eugenicists over how to prevent them from becoming paupers or criminals and how to check their fertility lest they transmit their hereditary taint.[12] Eugenicists in both countries assumed a strict division between the socioeconomic classes in terms of mental and moral qualities.[13] An exaggerated version of this class division appeared in Huxley's fictional society featuring superior Alphas and impaired Epsilons.

Huxley's notions about race betterment also conformed to what historian Daniel Kevles has labeled "reform eugenics," a moderate doctrine promoted by left-wing scientists who repudiated race-based policies but continued to advocate for the eugenic superiority of the professional middle class.[14] So for instance as early as 1934, Huxley condemned the ideology of Nordic superiority, put forward by extremist American eugenicists and Nazi race theorists, while as late as 1958, he was still claiming that the "congenitally insufficient" were breeding more quickly than "our best stock."[15] Huxley's eugenic writing provides a prominent example of how diverse and complex the early-twentieth-century eugenics movement actually was. As recent international comparative scholarship has illustrated, eugenics took on many different forms depending on what theories of heredity, "unfit" groups, and social reforms were emphasized in specific contexts. Even within any one country, several variants of eugenics usually co-existed or even competed.[16]

Today the public's historical memory of eugenics is largely limited to the atrocities committed in the name of Nazi racial hygiene; hence readers of *Brave New World* are unlikely to recognize the novel's bizarre scenario as an expression of particular Anglo-American eugenic concerns and policies. Huxley further serves as an example of how intellectuals from all points on the political spectrum—not just conservatives or fascists—were drawn to eugenics as a progressive, technocratic means of improving the health and fitness of populations. His own political leanings were decidedly leftist: he grew up in a free-thinking family, and in 1926 when interviewed about the General Strike professed his "prejudices" to be "Fabian and mildly labourite."[17] During this early period of his career, Huxley was also close to a group of prominent Cambridge scientists who were outspoken socialists and reform eugenicists:

these included the geneticist J. B. S. Haldane, physicist J. D. Bernal, chemist Joseph Needhain, and on the periphery, philosopher Bertrand Russell.[18]

Brave New World was partly shaped by the interwar preoccupations of this "scientific Left," who supported schemes for Soviet-style planning and eugenics policies in Britain. The revisionist Huxley scholarship has fully explored his involvement in the planning movement, but not given adequate attention to the influence of relevant scientific ideas and sources. In the broadest terms, *Brave New World* is about the relationship between science and society. Huxley was asking: how, can scientific knowledge and technologies be used to improve human life, and in particular to create well-ordered states out of the perceived social and economic chaos of postwar Europe? Huxley's circle of planners, eugenicists, and socialists all strongly believed in the power of science as the means to achieve social progress. The techniques of biological and psychological engineering so notoriously predicted in the novel, along with its overall theme of the uses and abuses of science, had previously been the subjects of popular books by Haldane, Russell, and Bernal. All championed the "scientific outlook," yet queried whether current political and moral systems were adequate to ensure that science would serve the well-being of the masses and not just the capitalists. In particular, Haldane's short 1923 text *Daedalus, or Science and the Future,* deserves more attention as the main inspiration and model for Huxley's fictional scientific society.[19]

Daedalus described several "perverse" but foreseeable advances in biological knowledge and its applications, including hormonal birth control, in vitro fertilization (IVF), and ectogenesis. Haldane's purpose had been to inform and amuse (or shock) his audience with these prophesies about scientifically managed human reproduction. His tone was essentially sanguine: he validated the wisdom and benevolence of future scientists who would guide society towards technological achievements, eugenic perfection, and moral revolution. A decade later *Brave New World* would address the same dilemmas: how is scientific knowledge to be used, who should control it, and do the ends always justify the means? Given the context in which it was composed, Huxley's story can be read as resolving these issues in a relatively optimistic way. Oppressive methods—such as compulsory genetic manipulation—had been necessary and tolerable in order to achieve the desired goal of social and economic stability. Rule by meritocracy—the enlightened World Controllers of A.F. 632—was the best alternative after democracy had failed. And a stratified and soulless society was a less horrifying scenario than a country exclusively composed of low-functioning Epsilons.

Brave New World is a remarkably rich text, open to many legitimate and edifying interpretations. Initial reviews were mostly negative, criticizing its weak characterization and plot, or dismissing the satire as "a thin little joke." Various readers objected to its grim rendering of human nature; tone of resignation; disgusting portrayal of sex, reproduction, and child-rearing; and devastating anti-science worldview. On the other hand, some evidently "concluded that Huxley approved of his horrible creation."[20] Among the few contemporaries who grasped the novel's complicated messages about science were members of the scientific Left. Russell read the World State as a viable alternative to mass destruction in a future world war, and was going to title his review "A Manipulator's Paradise." Needham argued that the book very accurately predicted how biology and psychology could soon alter human life, and advised that people need to decide now whether this power should be put in the hands of dictators.[21]

In America in 1934, pioneering research on assisted reproduction in rabbits was heralded in the *New York Times* as the work of a real-life Bokanovsky.[22] Yet it was not until human IVF became a reality in the 1970s that *Brave New World* gained cultural cachet as a cautionary or antiscience tale. The first generation of professional bioethicists, such as Leon Kass and Paul Ramsey, renewed interest in the novel's extreme scenario and used it to support their slippery slope argument that IVF would inevitably lead to eugenic cloning.[23] Because it now serves as a widely shared reference point (or shorthand) for bioethics discussions, there seems to be little interest in re-evaluating the novel from the perspective of its own cultural context. However, it is such a ubiquitous text that more nuanced readings in the classroom and other public forums would certainly be valuable. Fiction can help to create public memory about the popularity, diversity, and legacy of the historical eugenics movement, and it can stimulate critical thinking about the social role of science in the past, present, and future.

Planning and Meritocracy

David Bradshaw's research on the role of planning and eugenics in the brave new world has shown that while the novel may indeed function as a commentary on dictatorship and its oppressive uses of science, Huxley himself, at least for a short time around 1930, was rebuking not the dictators but rather the masses. "The legendary liberal-humanist does not emerge unscathed from these pages."[24] Huxley as a social commentator and product of the intellectual upper-middle class expressed both "contempt and compassion" for the workers and the poor during the British economic crisis of the late 1920s and early 1930s. In 1931, he went "sight-seeing in the alien Englands of manual labour and routine," namely the Durham coalfields. He witnessed the effects of high unemployment and monotonous work (including the assembly line method introduced by one of his favorite satirical targets, Henry Ford), and, like George Orwell later in *The Road to Wigan Pier*, sang the praises of the laboring man and lamented his oppression: "In our admiration for the planning mind, let us not forget the body, without whose aid none of the plans could be put into execution."[25]

Huxley despaired of the unrewarding work and low-brow entertainments to which the masses—especially in the United States—were subjected. Americans "can live out their lives," he said in 1927 after a tour of the country, "without once being solitary, without once making a serious mental effort, without once being out of sight or sound of some ready-made distraction."[26] His bitterness about popular culture—cheap, uncreative, and effortlessly available—translated into his brave new world's insistence on "no leisure from pleasure": feeling pictures, synthetic music from sexophones, and Centrifugal Bumble-puppy, among, other mindless and standardized diversions.[27] In newspaper and magazine articles intended to be read by the masses themselves, he identified universal leisure and factory drudgery as major causes of their mental deterioration.

But at the same time, Huxley voiced opinions about the supposedly widening gulf between cultured brain workers and uncultured manual workers that illustrated his affinity with hereditarian Anglo-American eugenicists. He despaired of the innate cognitive capacities and reproductive rates of the comfort-seeking masses:

> How do they expect democratic institutions to survive in a country where an increasing percentage of the population is mentally defective? Half-wits fairly ask for dictators. Improve the average intelligence of the population and self-governance will become, not only inevitable, but efficient.[28]

Such rhetoric was fueled in part by Huxley's friendship with H. L. Mencken, the American journalist and notorious misanthrope.[29] Both men skewered the incompetence of political leaders and the follies of the common people. Huxley repeatedly rejected the "Enlightenment" notion of the "congenital equality of man."[30] The allusion above to "half-wits" and dictators clearly recalls his novel published two years earlier. The fictional Epsilons represent in extreme form his fears about biological decay and the end of democracy. But on the other end of the fictional social ladder, the production of Alphas resembled the "special breeding and training of a small caste of experts" that the technocratic Huxley hoped would take power in England and implement "scientific" government. The alternative would be to let a totalitarian regime forcefully enact more extreme reforms to rescue the nation from the Depression.[31]

Huxley stated exactly this argument in "Science and Civilisation," a radio address broadcast on the BBC two weeks before the publication of *Brave New World*. The timing was clearly deliberate. Later he told a journalist that he favored neither the conditioned stability of the novel's World State nor the outsider John Savage's desire for "freedom to be unhappy." Instead there had to be a workable compromise between the two extremes, and until that was found "our efforts might have to be limited to the training of an intellectual aristocracy."[32] It seems therefore that the novel's rigid biological caste differentiation is open to conflicting interpretations. It could be parodying the eugenicists' hereditarian beliefs about a hierarchy of ability correlated with social class, or it could be a blueprint for how to build a relatively desirable society using selective breeding. As we shall see, the second reading more closely fits Huxley's own public positions on the eugenics issue.

Huxley professed that his initial motivation for composing *Brave New World* had been simply to parody H. G. Wells and the "horrors" of his utopias.[33] Huxley's specific target was the 1923 novel *Men Like Gods*, which seemed to him naively optimistic in its predictions of a "scientific state" that controlled eugenics and education. For Wells, the success of this system was due to an "unconscious cooperation by a common impulse."[34] Huxley thought this scenario was founded on flawed assumptions about human nature, and his critique of it from this 1927 essay about eugenics would carry over into *Brave New World*:

> But if, as would be the case in a perfectly eugenized state, every individual is capable of playing the superior part, who will consent or be content to do the dirty work and obey? The inhabitants of one of Mr. Wells's numerous Utopias solve the problem by ruling, and being ruled, doing high-brow and low-brow work, in turns. While Jones plays the piano, Smith spreads the manure. . . . An admirable state of affairs if it could be arranged. . . . States function as smoothly as they do because greater part of the population is not very intelligent, dreads responsibility, and desires nothing better than to be told what to do. . . . A state with a population consisting of nothing but these superior people could not hope to last a year. The best is ever the enemy of the good. If the eugenists are in too much of an enthusiastic hurry to improve the race, they will only succeed in destroying it.[35]

Likewise in the novel, the visitor from the Reservation, John Savage, is appalled by the twinned and degenerate Bokanovsky Groups he sees in London, and wonders, "why don't you make everybody an Alpha Double Plus while you're about it?"[36] In response, World Controller Mustapha Mond explains to him the "Cypus experiment" of 200 years before, in which a colony of well-bred Alpha individuals (Huxley's eugenically fit professional middle class) had slid into civil war because everyone refused to do the needed farming and factory work. According to Mond, the only workable alternative for creating a stable, utopian world is to engineer inferior castes of menial workers and slavish consumers—the eight-ninths of the metaphorical iceberg that happily lives below the water line and keeps the world running efficiently. To aim for total human perfectibility would not produce "community, stability, identity."

Wells was not amused by Huxley's dysgenic vision and accused him of "treason to science and defeatist pessimisin."[37] Yet Huxley was in other ways very sympathetic to Wells's utopian ideals. Both were enthusiastic about what Wells in 1928 labeled the "Open Conspiracy": the eventual rejection of failed democratic systems and the establishment of a world government to be managed by a scientifically trained elite.[38] *Men Like Gods* imagined a "free association of men and women, who, as a consequence of their enlightened education, voluntarily submit to the guidance of experts," while *Brave New World* presented a darker vision of citizens programmed into subservience to the Alpha Double Plus World Controllers.[39] Huxley first espoused such a Wellsian political system as a serious alternative to democracy in his 1927 article for *Harper's* called "The Outlook for American Culture":

> The ideal state is one in which there is material democracy controlled by an aristocracy of the intellect. . . . The active and intelligent oligarchies of the ideal state do not yet exist. But the Fascist party in Italy, the Communist party in Russia, the Kuomintang in China are still their inadequate precursors.[40]

Rule by meritocracy and the virtues of a scientifically planned state were major themes of several articles Huxley published during the period of the economic slump in England (around 1925–1935), which have been analyzed by Bradshaw in order to show the origins of key ideas he explored in his fiction.[41]

Reacting to the collapse of British export trade in coal and cotton, escalating unemployment, the abandonment of the gold standard, the failure of the 1929 Labour and 1931 National governments to resolve the economic crisis, and the emergence of Oswald Mosley's fascist agenda as a seemingly rational alternative, by mid-1931 Huxley had added his voice to the movement for "rationalization" of industry and government.[42] Writing in *Nash's Pall Mall Magazine,* he made the case for government by efficiency experts "capable of acting swiftly and with a well-informed and intelligent ruthlessness," who could regulate and coordinate industry, commerce, finance, and agriculture.[43] He joined the short-lived, politically diverse pressure group for Political and Economic Planning. Like many European liberals at this time, he was briefly seduced by both Stalin's Five-Year Plan and Mosley's plan for a "strong executive" and radical economic reorganization. Britain needed to impose these kinds of solutions quickly, regardless of whether they would be constitution-al.[44] By the end of the year Huxley was sounding even more desperate:

> We may either persist in our present course, which is disastrous, or we must abandon democracy and allow ourselves to be ruled dictatorially by men who will compel us to do and suffer what a rational foresight demands.[45]

This solemn prediction of the end of democracy eerily echoes the fictional World State he was inventing at that exact moment.

Huxley's favorite model of successful planning was the work of Alfred Mond, the industrialist who in 1926 had amalgamated and rationalized the major British chemical companies.[46] Not by coincidence is the benevolent scientific dictator in *Brave New World* named Mustapha Mond. As Brad-shaw notes, Mond is granted the most compelling viewpoint in the novel and thus seems to represent Huxley's genuine admiration for scientifically minded leaders who could help pull the nation out of the slump.[47] But as James Sexton demonstrates, *Brave New World* simultaneously satirizes the "rationalizing" impulses of the real world Alfred Monds and Henry Fords.[48] Did their use of science and technology truly serve the public good, or did it entail undesirable consequences? The modern production methods of the assembly line and Taylorism are mirrored in the cloned and stunted Epsilon bodies and minds: designed for maximum efficiency and minimum human-ness, they represent "the total sacrifice of individual interests to the interests of the mechanized community."[49] The planned economy of the World State had solved the problems of unemployment and overproduction in a fashion that Huxley was clearly mocking. Compulsory consumption of goods was inculcated from birth via sleep-teaching and propaganda slogans:

> In the nurseries . . . the voices were adapting future demand to future industrial supply. 'I do love flying,' they whispered, 'I do love having new clothes'. . . . 'Ending is better than mending, ending is better than mending . . .'[50]

Likewise in "Science and Civilisation" Huxley voiced dismay at the possibil-ity that "a government of industrialists and financiers" would find it in their own best interests "to train up a race, not of perfect human beings, but of perfect mass-producers and mass-consumers."[51]

Eugenics and Citizenship

For the scientists and science popularizers in the planning movement, such as H. G. Wells, Bertrand Russell, and Aldous and Julian Huxley, "biological engineering" was a crucial component of their project.[52] What were their ideas about eugenic reform? How did Aldous Huxley's beliefs relate to the rest of the British eugenics movement? And how does this complicate our understanding of *Brave New World?* Many readers of Huxley's story probably assume that he was wholly critical of eugenics, given the way he presents gamete selection, embryo cloning, and artificial wombs as techniques for eliminating individuality and meaningful personal relationships.[53] That extreme version of eugenics (and the behavioral conditioning that goes along with it) was obviously being ridiculed. But Huxley the public intellectual was a known supporter of the eugenics movement. He held hereditarian beliefs regarding the causes of social ills and especially mental abilities, and his notions about who should and should not be allowed to reproduce discriminated against disabled people and the lower social classes. His first treatment of the eugenics issue was in 1927's "Outlook for American Culture," where he attacked mechanization of work and leisure as a leading cause of increasing "imbecility" in America. This discussion led him to claim further that some percentage of the masses already had a hereditary constitution at "lower, animal levels" that made them unable to appreciate the higher arts. He predicted that a new form of democracy was on the horizon, which would reject the false belief that everyone is "equally endowed with moral worth and intellectual ability." Society would instead be based on a "more natural hierarchy" of inherited traits, with people divided up into "psychological types and givers appropriate education and jobs.[54]

Although Huxley never joined the Eugenics Society (ES), the propagandizing arm of the British eugenics movement, he became very familiar with its rhetoric and policy proposals and began incorporating these into his articles.[55] His contempt for the masses and assumption that societies will always have innately inferior and superior groups fit closely with "mainline" eugenics ideology prior to World War II.[56] He expounded standard arguments about the "differential fertility" of the professional classes *versus* the unskilled laborers and unemployed, who were said to make up the lowest 10 percent of the social ladder.[57] "A Note on Eugenics" (1927) is especially significant because it tied mainline eugenic notions to the "Wellsian paradise" that would influence *Brave New World.* The essay ended with the warning that a eugenically perfect society could never function because all the citizens would be "malcontents." But it also explored the consequences of failure to implement eugenic reforms: what would happen if the majority became Epsilons? They would quickly be conquered by rival nations.[58] Perhaps he therefore intended the *Brave New World* scenario as a middle ground: a community of contented imbeciles governed by a relatively benign aristocracy of intellect.

In three volumes of essays published between 1925 and 1929, Huxley began to struggle with the questions that would guide all of his subsequent writing and philosophizing. How should we live? How can we achieve the ideal of a "perfected humanity" given the limitations of human nature?[59] "A Note on Eugenics" entertains several policy proposals but endorses none of them, typical of his 1920s nihilist phase. As of 1931, he was still pessimistic about achieving absolute happiness and an "egalitarian world," though he did admit at least the hope that "the heritable qualities of the progressing population shall be improved . . . by deliberate breeding; and the amount of population shall be reduced."[60] As the economic slump worsened, however, Huxley's tone shifted dramatically. The 1932 Hearst newspaper article "Are We Growing Stupider?" answers that question definitively. "Moral: let us take steps to prevent our supply [of intelligent citizens] front running short."[61] Sociological studies had shown—convincingly for Huxley and his fellow eugenicists—that the socially and economically successful classes (professionals and artisans) were being "swamped" by the higher reproductive rates of the "mentally deficient." His proposed remedy was positive eugenics: government should give financial incentives to encourage the "fit" to have more children. This was a widespread and uncontroversial policy proposal in the British and American eugenics movements. Where Huxley differed from many other British eugenicists, in both the mainline and reform camps, was in his aggressive stance on sterilization, in "What Is Happening to Our Population?

This article addressed the problem of "mental deficiency," following typical eugenic rhetoric about how social reforms and welfare measures had had the unintended effect of permitting the propagation of inferior genotypes. Hence the question of national efficiency needed to be tackled more "scientifically." In a couple of hundred years "a quarter of the population of these islands will consist of half-wits. What a curiously squalid and humiliating conclusion to English history!" Positive measures were called for to foster larger families among the professional class (from which "so many outstandingly gifted individuals have sprung"), as well as negative eugenics to prevent the procreation of the unfit, who were categorized as both cognitively disabled and poor. "There is one simple, and, so far as it goes, effective way of limiting the multiplication of sub-normal stocks: certified defectives can be sterilized."[62]

The targeted group was the so-called "feebleminded." The 1913 Mental Deficiency Act had brought tens of thousands of lower-class "sub-normal" individuals under state supervision.[63] As a whole, the British eugenics movement emphasized permanent segregation as the simplest and most humane means of preventing the "social problem group" from propagating its bad heredity. Whereas compulsory sterilization laws had gone into effect in the United States as early as 1907, no such measures ever passed in Great Britain.

Depression-era anxieties about the costs of caring for nonproductive, institutionalized persons led the Americans and Germans to accelerate their sterilization programs. By contrast, the British Eugenics Society's response to the economic slump was to form committees (led by Julian Huxley among others) that investigated whether legalizing birth control and voluntary sterilization would be effective eugenic measures.[64] The ES never officially advocated *compulsory* sterilization. Aldous Huxley thought that his compatriots were being too timid about the sterilization solution (whether he was advocating voluntary or forced sterilization is unclear). He accused "mystical democrats" of opposing negative eugenics on the grounds of mistaken belief that nurture is more important than nature, and that middle-class eugenicists were just trying to "bully the poor."[65]

During the 1930s, Huxley's friend J. B. S. Haldane led a group of genetics experts in Britain and the United States who pursued "reform eugenics."[66] While still advocating "rational policies for the guidance of reproduction" in order to cleanse the gene pool, the reformers criticized the sloppy Mendelian assumptions of the previous generation of eugenicists, acknowledged the role of environment as well as heredity in forming the individual, and showed that sterilization of the "unfit" could not in fact eliminate all defective genes.[67] They downplayed negative eugenics and most opposed sterilization because it was too likely to be misapplied to the poor and powerless members of society. The group favored leftist politics, even Marxism. Eugenic improvement could only occur, they maintained, in a socialist society with no economic barriers so that the genetic cream could rise to the top. They still assumed that intelligence was mostly an inherited trait and that only high-IQ people would have social success. Finally, they sharply criticized assumptions about biological differences between racial groups, and at least claimed to reject the idea of innate class differences as well.

For instance, Haldane in 1928 explained that the science of heredity and eugenics was being "misapplied" to legitimize "the political opinions of the extreme right." Yet the rest of his analysis employed mainline, class-based eugenic notions about how "mental capacity is strongly hereditary," "the unskilled workers are breeding much faster than the skilled classes," and therefore modern civilization was in trouble "from the over-production of 'undermen'."[68] The reform eugenicists were principally concerned with breeding for intelligence, as was likewise emphasized in Huxley's fictional community. They favored positive eugenics, such as education and propaganda methods to persuade superior individuals to have larger families. A striking example of reform eugenics was the scheme proposed in 1935 by the American geneticist H. J. Muller: he wanted to collect the sperm of the most intellectually and morally accomplished men in order to artificially inseminate as many women as possible.[69] The mind was elevated in an even more extreme fashion by another member of the group of leftist scientists, J. D. Bernal. In *The World, the Flesh, and the Devil* (1929), Bernal envisioned the culmination of the eugenics ideal: the perfection of mankind as cyborg. Brains would be placed directly into machines, creating "a 'man' who is perfect because he is freed from the sensory, motor, and biological constraints of the human body." The socialist Bernal imagined that this future world would be organized by "an aristocracy of scientific intelligence," and split into castes disturbingly comparable to Alphas and Epsilons: he called them "the altered and the non-altered humanity."[70]

Social class prejudice was always the predominant factor in British eugenics, and Huxley was clearly in the mainstream. Nothing united the diverse group of early-twentieth-century British eugenicists and other social reformers more than their shared attitude that the poor were a "race apart" from themselves. They sought to delineate "normal" citizens from the "social problem group" who were not capable of responsible citizenship—the most destitute members of the working classes who were identified as hereditary paupers, criminals, alcoholics, prostitutes, and physically and mentally disabled people. The "hidden Huxley" was a product of this prejudiced mindset. Following the meritocratic ideals of the eugenics movement as a whole, which valued the qualities of intelligence and self-control, his plan was to weed out the excess of "Epsilons" who lacked the rational capacity to participate in the democratic process.[71]

Science and Society

The fantastic biotechnologies envisioned by Bernal and Haldane obviously made a strong impression on Huxley as he was composing *Brave New World*. He borrowed heavily from Haldane's 1923 *Daedalus, or Science and the Future*. In it, a student 150 years in the future sums up some of the radical advances in biology, most notably IVF "bottle babies" and artificial wombs, which came to be used as more effective methods of selective breeding:

> It was in 1951 that Dupont and Schwarz produced the first ectogenetic child. . . . We can take an ovary from a woman, and keep it growing in a suitable fluid for as long as twenty years, producing a fresh ovum each month, of which 90 per cent can be fertilized, and the embryos grown successfully for nine months, and then brought out into the air. . . . The small proportion of men and women who are selected as ancestors for the next generation are so undoubtedly superior to the average. . . . Had it not been for ectogenesis there can be little doubt that civilization would have collapsed within a measurable time owing to the greater fertility of the less desirable members of the population in almost all countries.[72]

The text of *Brave New World* is less explicit about the criteria for eugenic selection of eggs (or sperm), but the idea clearly came from Haldane. The opening scene of the novel very briefly explains that Deltas come from Delta ovaries, for example, and that "heredity" is labeled on the embryo bottles. The pre- and postnatal conditioning processes are described in much greater detail, which of course gave Huxley ample opportunities to poke fun at Freudian psychology and behaviorism. It is notable that despite his hereditarianism, Huxley gave so much weight to nurture in the techniques of social engineering: "Hasn't it occurred to you that an embryo must have an Epsilon environment as well as an Epsilon heredity?"[73] This was actually quite typical of most versions of eugenics, and especially fit the reform eugenics agenda of re-introducing a role for environment alongside heredity.

Daedalus and *Brave New World* both raise crucial questions about the social uses and control of science. Haldane celebrated the mythological Daedalus who designed the Minotaur yet was never punished by the gods. His moral was that scientific progress cannot be resisted. Huxley may have thought of his novel as a refutation of Haldane's optimism. He continually challenged the real-life Daedaluses to justify their work in terms of how it contributed to making the world a better place. For example, his clever essay "Monks Among the Test Tubes" (1932) parodied those scientists who refused to take responsibility for the social consequences of their research:

> The monks [of science] have a very enviable lot. They work for ends about whose value they feel no doubt. . . . If people beyond the convent walls choose to put the truth to stupid or destructive uses, then so much the worse for the world. It is none of the monks' business.[74]

In "Science and Civilisation," the essay closest to the themes of *Brave New World*, he explicitly addressed the questions "to what end," "by what means," and "who is to wield the power which science gives?" Given the lack of regulation of science in the past, and the harm that it has caused deliberately and inadvertently, "the only cure for science is more science, not less. We are suffering from the effects of a little science badly applied. The remedy is a lot of science, well applied."[75] The same message also appears in *Brave New World*, in the illicit history lessons delivered by Mustapha Mond near the beginning and end of the story. He explains that science had been responsible for destroying the old world through economic collapse and anthrax bombs, and afterwards an aristocracy of scientists came into power who managed to create a stable new world using the tools of genetics, psychology, and endocrinology.[76] What is the novel saying about ends and means?

Does the goal of stability and happiness justify the methods of dictatorship and dehumanization?

Mond's answer is yes. There seemed no other choice. What did Huxley believe? He recognized that throughout history, crises and anarchy have forced people to accept tyrants and subjugation in return for security.[77] Perhaps a planned tyranny of the eugenically best over the worst was a more tolerable condition than either the "humanist's' ideal of a society of "malcontented" Alphas, or the "industrialist's' ideal of all "Half-witted" Epsilons. At this point in his career Huxley could only offer a choice between evils: "any form of order is better than chaos."[78] As Bradshaw summed up the difficulties of interpreting *Brave New World*, the novel "embodies in an absurd and distorted form ideas and opinions that Huxley framed in earnest beyond the novel's satirical parameters."[79] At that moment in history, a "new caste system based on differences in natural ability" seemed relatively attractive.

Modern readers should therefore recognize *Brave New World* as more than just a straightforward denunciation or glorification of science. It offers a sophisticated critique of how scientific knowledge emerges from and in turn serves the social, political, and economic agendas of those in power. Huxley's fiction and nonfiction works exploring the relationship between science and society resemble not only the futuristic *Daedalus*, but also the pioneering Marxist texts in the history and sociology of science, including J. D. Bernal's *Social Function of Science* (1939) and Lancelot Hogben's *Science for the Citizen* (1938). Huxley's later science monographs continued to analyze the social uses of science, but reached quite different conclusions. Whereas in *Brave New World* and its associated essays he had seemed contented to permit relatively desirable ends (social stability) be achieved at high cost and by immoral means (eugenics, social control, dictatorship), in the later writings he developed a consistent theme that only the high road can lead to true happiness.[80] His analysis focused on how the capitalist powers who controlled science and technology were using them to destroy the environment, build more and more devastating weapons, and oppress the people through methods of mass production and mass persuasion. Thus the 1946 *Science, Liberty, and Peace* opened by quoting Tolstoy:

> If the arrangement of society is bad (as ours is), and a small number of people have power over the majority and oppress it, every victory over Nature will inevitably serve only to increase that power and that oppression.[81]

Evidently the solution was to decentralize power and increase "liberty," although Huxley still provided no program for political and economic change. Once skeptical of democracy, he now demanded political equality and a science for the people. In his final novel, *Island* (1962), he even chose to depict a genuine utopia founded on the principles of self-government and sustainable science. His call for public participation in science policymaking is as vital an issue today as it was in the tumultuous 1930s.

Re-reading *Brave New World* might also inspire more critical thinking about the nature of "eugenics" in the past and present day. Popular fiction exposes the general public to the history of eugenics, and thus it surely deserves richer explication. Other examples of eugenics in fiction are Bernard Shaw's *Man and Superman* (1903), Wells's *Modern Utopia* (1905), and Perkins Gilman's *Herland* (1915). Teaching about how progressive thinkers such as Huxley (known in his day as a socialist, humanist, pacifist, and eventually spiritualist), Shaw and Wells (Fabian Society supporters), and Gilman (socialist-feminist) were so supportive of policies for restricting the reproductive rights of the "socially inadequate" calls attention to the widespread popularity of the eugenics agenda across political and national boundaries.

By the late 1930s, European and American eugenicists began trying to distance themselves from the extremes of Nazi eugenic science, rhetoric, and action. On the one hand, the 1933 German sterilization law aroused envy owing to its comprehensiveness, and on the other, the Nazi racial ideology raised alarm bells. In 1936, Julian Huxley co-authored one of the first antiracist science tracts, *We Europeans,* and in 1950–1951 he was involved with composing the UNESCO statements on race that refuted fascist abuses of science but affirmed the usefulness of racial typology for scientific research.[82] In 1939, the reform eugenicists led by Haldane and Muller produced a "Geneticists' Manifesto" that repudiated the idea of biological class and race hierarchies but maintained the goal of enhancing human hereditary traits.[83] Aldous Huxley's style of eugenics is especially interesting because it encompassed elements of both the "mainline" hereditarian, pro-sterilization school and the "reform" antiracist, socialist, environmentalist school. There was no absolute delineation between the two camps, nor did the Nazi atrocities entirely discredit the goals or activities of the eugenics movement. Society's privileged groups—including scientific and medical experts—carried on with passing judgments about desirable and undesirable qualities, and targeting for eugenic elimination those "others" who were differentiated by class, disability, and sometimes still race.

In Huxley's case, his antidemocratic phase and infatuation with the planning and eugenics movements lasted only as long as the economic crisis; after 1935, there are only a few references to eugenics in his published and unpublished writing. Nonetheless, his ongoing interest in eugenics and citizenship is one thread that ties together the several phases of his career as a novelist and literary essayist. In his 1946 foreword to *Brave New World,* he noted that the prospect of a "foolproof eugenics" to engineer a standardized and contented working class might yet become a reality.[84] A long discussion lamenting the double demographic crises of overpopulation (a favored topic of eugenicists after the war) and differential class fertility appeared in 1950. He cited approvingly the work of the (now discredited) eugenicist and psychologist Cyril Burt, who calculated that by the end of the century average IQ would drop 5 points because the less-endowed lower classes were out-reproducing the fit.[85] And finally, the 1958 text *Brave New World Revisited* reiterated his interwar concerns about mental ability and democracy:

> And what about the congenitally insufficient organisms, whom our medicine and our social services now preserve so that they may propagate their kind? . . . We are on the horns of an ethical dilemma, and to find the middle way will require all our intelligence and our good will.

As of 1958 he still wondered if the "well-fed television-watchers in the world's most powerful democracy . . . perfectly content to be ruled, from above, by an oligarchy of assorted experts" had the brains and desire to shake themselves awake "in order to halt and, if possible, reverse the current drift toward totalitarian control."[86]

Revisited dates from late in Huxley's life (he died on November 22, 1963), twenty years into the "religious philosopher" phase of his career. Yet his return to the subject matter of *Brave New World* shows that he held on to some of his youthful cynicism about the fate of free civilization, and that he considered it his life-long project to champion and critique the social uses of science, including eugenics. His work and interests were always many-sided. The late 1930s—when he befriended the science writer and spiritualist Gerald Heard and subsequently moved from Europe to California—did not represent an absolute turning point in his life, as many have contended. Contemporaries complained that Hurley had abandoned his rational and worldly interests in science and social criticism in order to throw himself entirely into the realms of spiritual enlightenment, Eastern religions, and mind-altering drugs. He lost much of his old audience and gained a new following as a counter-cultural figure. However, curiosity about the unknown spiritual world and the ultimate purpose of life was a constant throughout Huxley's career. It even appeared in the scientific society of *Brave New World* via the pious character John Savage, who debates the value of religion and suffering with the World Controller.[87] On the flip side, Huxley was forever fascinated by science and its methods, which even shaped how he undertook his mystical quest. He sought rational "evidence" for a transcendent reality by systematically studying religious and philosophical texts and experimenting with LSD.[88]

In 1946, Aldous Huxley chastised his younger self as "the amused, Pyrrhonic aesthete who was the author of the fable" *Brave New World.*[89] By exaggerating the nihilistic elements of that early work, he was asserting the novelty of his more recent contributions. He felt that his writing was now directed towards constructive ends, particularly metaphysical methods and goals.[90] If he were to rewrite *Brave New World* today, he explained in the appended foreword, he would construct a utopian society based on the religious philosophy of acheiving "man's Final End," by which he meant some kind of transcendent unification. He now wished that he had given his characters a third option besides the World State and the primitive Reservation, namely to live in small, democratic, self-sustaining communities. Most significantly, he stated overtly the novel's implied critique of those in power who used science to further their own ends, rather than make the world a better place for everyone:

> Science and technology would be used as though, like the Sabbath, they had been made for man, not (as at present and still more so in the Brave New World) as though man were to be adapted and enslaved to them. [91]

By the later part of his career, Huxley had resolved that science cannot reveal ultimate reality or solve all the world's problems. Only love, mysticism, and meditation can lead the individual to fulfillment. He felt that he had effectively satisfied his life-long goal, as expressed by a character in *Point Counter Point* in 1928: "'The problem for me is to transform a detached intellectual scepticism into a way of harmonious all-round living.'"[92] As Huxley himself had explained in 1931, his job as a novelist and public intellectual was to discover his own "outlook on life," or in other words to explicate in artistic forms his solutions to pressing social, scientific, and moral problems:

> My chief motive in writing has been the desire to clarify a point of view. . . I am chiefly interested in making clear a certain outlook on life. . . . My books represent different stages in my progress towards such an outlook. Each book is an attempt to make things clear to myself so far as I had gone at the time it was written. In that sense they are all provisional.[93]

Through his art and essays, he developed provisional solutions that ranged from being cynical about mankind's prospects during the 1920s, to favoring technocratic control over reproduction and social reform in the early 1930s, to achieving contentment in a personal mystical quest after 1937. *Brave New World* can be read as the product of both his nihilistic and eugenicist tendencies: while the despotic and soulless World State is certainly a nightmare, it is also a plausible solution to Huxley's observation that "half-wits fairly ask for dictators." The text reflects the broad popularity of eugenics ideology in that period, and illustrates the variety of Anglo-American approaches to the perceived problem of "mental deficiency" and the future of democracy. Eugenicists such as Huxley saw themselves as the "intellectual aristocracy" of Alphas. They were a separate caste from the masses of Epsilons, yet ultimately responsible for both keeping them contented and judging their fitness for citizenship. Emerging from Huxley's keen awareness of the socio-political dimensions of science, his story rings a warning bell about knowledge as power that is especially relevant now that the predicted genetic revolution has arrived. Even though genetics may not be in the hands of despots, the "monks of science" still ought to set down their test tubes once in a while and make it their business to engage in public dialogue about how their research will be put to use in society.

Huxley proclaimed himself uninterested in revisiting his finished novels of ideas, and presumably uninterested in public reaction to them (except for how well they sold). He would pen a work—express his outlook at that moment—and immediately move on to his next effort to discover "how must we live." Yet in the case of *Brave New World* he felt compelled to ameliorate the flaws in his scientific society with new commentaries in 1946 (foreword) and 1958 *(Revisited)* and a fictional democratically controlled scientific utopia in 1962 *(Island)*. Even for him, the meaning of his influential dystopian scenario was always evolving.

Notes

1. Aldous Huxley to J. Glyn Roberts, July 19, 1933, L. J. Roberts and J. Glyn Roberts Papers, National Library of Wales. Quoted in David Bradshaw, "Introduction," *The Hidden Huxley: Contempt and Compassion for the Masses 1920–1936* (London: Faber and Faber, 1994), xx.

2. Aldous Huxley, "What Is Happening to Our Population?" *Nash's Pall Mall Magazine*, April 1934, reprinted in *The Hidden Huxley*, 147–158. "Are We Growing Stupider?" *Hearst*, March 30, 1932, reprinted in Aldous Huxley, *Complete Essays*, vol. 3, eds. Robert Baker and James Sexton (Chicago: Ivan R. Dee, 2001), 323–324.

3. Nicholas Murray, *Aldous Huxley, an English Intellectual* (London: Little, Brown, 2002), 200. The word "eugenics" was coined by the British polymath Francis Galton, although the eugenics movement in Great Britain was never as successful in implementing policies (or as oppressive) as it was in the United States or Germany. The literature on the history of British eugenics is extensive, but includes no investigation of Aldous Huxley's role. The most comprehensive source on Anglo-American figures and policies is Daniel Kevles, *In the Name of Eugenics: Genetics and the Uses of Human Heredity* (Berkeley: University of California Press, 1985). An excellent overview is Diane Paul, *Controlling Human Heredity, 1865 to the Present* (Atlantic Highlands, NJ: Humanities Press, 1995).

4. The standard biography is by his friend Sybil Bedford, *Aldous Huxley: A Biography*, 2 vols. (London: Chatto and Windus, 1973–1974). Dana Sawyer's *Aldous Huxley: A Biography* (New York: Crossroad Publishing Company, 2002) emphasizes his spiritual development, while Nicholas Murray's book reveals new details about his and his wife Maria's sex lives.

5. "Huxley saw the intellectual climate of the interwar period as one of indecision and complexity bordering on incoherence." Robert S. Baker, *Brave New World: History, Science, and Dystopia* (Boston: Twayne Publishers, 1990), 53. In his first three novels, Huxley caricatured the upper-middle-class lives of his friends in the Bloomsbury circle, skewered failed pre-war ideologies, and created cynical characters who served as mouthpieces for a variety of ideas. Early on he struggled to make a living as a writer and perpetually hoped to score a theatrical hit (or a Hollywood screenplay) that would free him financially from having to produce books on rigid contractual demand.

6. Aldous Huxley to Leonard Huxley, August 24, 1931, *Letters of Aldous Huxley*, ed. Grover Smith (London: Chatto and Windus, 1969), 351.

7. Techno-enthusiasts who have borrowed the ubiquitous title: Roger Gosden, *Designing Babies: The Brave New World of Reproductive Technology* (New York: W. H. Freeman and Company, 1999); Lee M. Silver, *Remaking Eden: Cloning and Beyond in a Brave New World* (New York: Avon Books, 1997). Critics of biotechnology on the right and left: Leon Kass, "Preventing a Brave New World," *Human Life Review* 27 (Summer 2001), 14–35; Bryan Appleyard, *Brave New Worlds: Staying Human in the Genetic Future* (London: HarperCollins, 1999). Another example: George W. Bush, in his August 2001 speech limiting funding for embryonic stem cell research, warned: "We have arrived at that 'Brave New World' that seemed so distant in 1932, when Aldous Huxley wrote about human beings created in test tubes." Kevin Canfield, "Is Dubya a Huckster for Huxley?" *Hartford Courant*, August 16, 2001, D1, *ProQuest*, University of Washington, August 13, 2006.

8. This paper is most heavily indebted to David Bradshaw's approach and insights, especially his "Huxley's Slump: Planning, Eugenics, and the 'Ultimate Need' of Stability," in *The Art of Literary Biography*, ed. John Batchelor (New York: Oxford University Press, 1995), 151–171, and his introductory articles in *The Hidden Huxley*. Other scholars who have re-assessed Huxley's fiction in the light of his nonfiction writing are James Sexton and Robert Baker, the editors of the six-volume *Complete Essays*. Sexton is also the editor of *Aldus Huxley's Hearst Essays* (New York: Garland Publishing, 1994), which were written for the Hearst newspaper chain in the 1920s and 30s and brought much-needed income. Bradshaw's claims that the planning and eugenics essays reveal the true nature of Huxley's interests in the period around 1930 have been criticized to some extent by reviewers, but all agree that he has pointed us to a fuller understanding of Huxley's mixed motives in *Brave New World*. See for instance Robert Baker's review of *The Hidden Huxley* in *CLIO* 25 (Spring 1996): 293, *Expanded Academic ASAP*, University of Washington, August 15, 2006. Some of the, scholarly reassessments and disagreements that have emerged since the Huxley centennial in 1994 are also addressed in David King Dunaway, *Aldous Huxley Recollected: An Oral History* (New York: Carroll and Graf, 1995).

9. "I feel strongly that the man of letters should be intensely aware of the problems which surround him, of which technological and scientific problems are the most urgent. It is his business to communicate his awareness and concern. Literature sets up a vision of man which guides people to a better understanding

of themselves and their world." *Aldous Huxley, 1894–1963: A Memorial Volume*, ed. Julian Huxley (New York: Harper and Rosy; 1965), 100. He once described his profession as "an essayist who sometimes writes novels and biographies." Murray, *Aldous Huxley*, 161.

10. Murray, *Aldous Huxley*, 169.

11. James Trent, *Inventing the Feeble Mind: A History of Mental Retardation in the United States* (Berkeley: University of California Press, 1994); Stephen Jay Gould, *The Mismeasure of Man* (New York: W. W. Norton, 1996), 252.

12. Mathew Thomson, *The Problem of Mental Deficiency: Eugenics, Democracy, and Social Policy in Britain, c. 1870–1959* (Oxford: Clarendon Press, 1998).

13. Among the more politically progressive British eugenicists was Huxley's brother Julian, who in 1931 voiced typical class-based fears about the high fertility and poor genetic quality of slum dwellers. He proposed that unemployment relief should he given only to those men who promised not to have any more offspring, because of the tendency "for the stupid to inherit the earth, and the shiftless, and the imprudent, and the dull." Quoted in Gary Werskey, *The Visible College: A Collective Biography of British Scientists and Socialists of the 1930s* (London: Allen Lane, 1978), 42.

14. Kevles, *In the Name of Eugenics*, 164–175.

15. Aldous Huxley, *Brave New World Revisited* (New York: Harper and Row, 1958), 18–21; "The Double Crisis," in *Themes and. Variations* (1950), reprinted in *Complete Essays*, vol. 5, 124–145; "Race," *The New Statesman and Nation*, May 9, 1936, *Complete Essays*, vol. 4, 131–133. Here his message about racial differences was more ambiguous: "It is obvious that there is a certain correlation between lack of success in the social struggle and lack of intelligence. The thing that immigration officers should discriminate against is not race (except in those cases where miscegenation leads to biologically undesirable results), but stupidity. A country's first need is good brains, not blue eyes." "Racial History," *Hearst*, Feb. 7, 1934, *Complete Essays*, vol. 3, 377–378.

16. Mark Adams, ed., *The Wellborn Science: Eugenics in Germany, France, Brazil, and Russia* (New York: Oxford University Press, 1990); Joanne Woiak, "Drunkenness, Degeneration, and Eugenics in Britain, 1900–1914" (Ph.D. diss. University of Toronto, 1998).

17. Murray, *Aldous Huxley*, 181.

18. This group is the subject of Werskey, *Visible College*. On their "unswerving commitment to science" and their promotion of Soviet scientific planning during the early 1930s, see especially 176–211.

19. J. B. S. Haldane, *Daedalus, or Science and the Future* (1923; New York: E. P. Dutton and Company, 1924), 63–67; Bertrand Russell, *The Scientific Outlook* (London: W. W. Norton, 1931); J. D. Bernal, *The World, the Flesh, and the Devil: An Enquiry into the Future of the Three Enemies of the Rational Soul* (New York: Kegan Paul, Trench, Trubner, 1929). On the sources of and reactions to Haldane's book, see Jon Turney, *Frankenstein's Footsteps: Science, Genetics and Popular Culture* (New Haven: Yale University Press, 1998), 91–120; Susan Merrill Squier, *Babies in Bottles: Twentieth-Century Visions of Reproductive Technology* (New Brunswick, NJ: Rutgers University Press, 1994), 63–99; and K. R. Dronamraju, ed., *Haldane's Daedalus Revisited* (New York: Oxford University Press, 1995).

20. Donald Watt, ed., *Aldous Huxley: The Critical Heritage* (Boston: Routledge and Kegan Paul, 1975), 15–18 and 197–221. Huxley s reputation was on the rise in the early 1930s, and *Brave New World* sold well.

21. *Ibid.,* 20–205 and 210–212.

22. Turney, *Frankenstein's Footsteps,* 117.

23. Robin Marantz Henig, *Pandora's Baby: How the First Test Tube Babies Sparked the Reproductive Revolution* (Boston: Houghton Mifflin, 2004), 64–77.

24. Bradshaw, "Introduction," *Hidden Huxley,* xxiii.

25. Aldous Huxley, "Sight-Seeing in Alien Englands," *Nash's Pall Mall Magazine,* June 1931, *Hidden Huxley,* 71.

26. Aldous Huxley, "The Outlook for American Culture: Some Reflections on a Machine Age," *Harpers Magazine,* August 1927, *Complete Essays,* vol. 3, 187. "All the resources of science are applied in order that imbecility may flourish and vulgarity cover the whole earth. That they are rapidly doing so must be obvious to anyone who glances at a popular picture paper, looks at a popular film, listens to popular music on the radio or phonograph" (188–189).

27. Aldous Huxley, *Brave New World* (1932; New York: Perennial Classics, 1998), 55.

28. Huxley, "What is Happening to Our Population?" 154.

29. David Bradshaw, "Chroniclers of Folly: Huxley and H. L. Mencken 1920–1926," in *Hidden Huxley,* 1–30.

30. Aldous Huxley, "The Idea of Equality," in *Proper Studies* (Garden City, NY: Doubleday, Doran and Company, 1928), 23–55. His fascination with classifying and ranking people—especially according to inborn mental abilities—shaped his skepticism about democracy. He suggested there ought to be IQ tests to determine who should run for office or even be allowed to vote, and tried to delineate the "varieties of intelligence." *Proper Studies,* 56–120 and 195–204. This tendency to categorize must also have attracted him in the 1940s to the theories of William H. Sheldon, on body types and personalities, as a new explanation of human nature. Sawyer, 102–103. He used Sheldon's scheme in "Inequality," *Ends and Means: An Inquiry into the Nature of Ideals and into the Methods Employed in Their Realization* (New York: Harper and Brothers, 1937), 185–203.

31. Aldous Huxley, "Science and Civilisation," broadcast on the BBC National Programme, January 13, 1932, published twice thereafter, and reprinted in *Hidden Huxley,* 112.

32. Interview published in Alan Campbell Johnson, *Peace Offering* (London: Methuen, 1936), 152–164, quoted in David Bradshaw, "Open Conspirators: Huxley and H. G. Wells 1927–1935," in *Hidden Huxley,* 41.

33. Murray, *Aldous Husky,* 249; Bradshaw, "Open Conspirators," 31. In his lengthy career Wells published numerous utopian and dystopian stories, beginning with *The Time Machine* in 1895.

34. Baker, *Brave New World,* 25 and 33. Huxley also borrowed ideas from Wells's 1899 dystopia *When the Sleeper Wakes.* Peter Firchow, *The End of Utopia: A Study of Aldous Huxley's Brave New World* (Lewisburg, PA: Bucknell University Press, 1984), 63–64.

35. Aldous Huxley, "A Note on Eugenics," in *Proper Studies,* 329–330.

36. Huxley, *Brave New World,* 222–224.

37. Sawyer, *Aldous Huxley,* 84; and Firchow, *End of Utopia,* 59. Similarly, "in Cannes, we saw H. G. Wells who, I fear, wasn't pleased with it. On the contrary

(surprisingly enough) Edith Wharton is enthusiastic." Huxley to Harold Raymond, 19 March 1932, *Letters*, 358–359.

38. Bradshaw, "Open Conspirators," 33. Before WWI, Wells had been briefly associated with the socialist Fabian Society, the first champions of scientific planning. He inscribed a copy of his 1928 book *The Open Conspiracy: Blue Prints for a World Revolution* to Huxley. See G. R. Searle, *The Quest for National Efficiency: A Study in British Politics and Political Thought, 1899–1914* (Berkeley: University of California Press, 1971); and Donald Mackenzie, "Eugenics in Britain," *Social Studies of Science*, 6 (1976): 499–532.

39. Baker, *Brave New World*, 34.

40. Huxley, "Outlook for American Culture," 191–192. Another optimistic technocrat who moved in the same social circles was Bertrand Russell. His 1931 *The Scientific Outlook* had much in common with Huxley's work regarding the political and ethical consequences of science, and both men thought the Soviet Union was a good prototype for the future planned state. Critics disagree as to who borrowed from whom. Baker, *Brave New World*, 63–76.

41. Bradshaw, "Huxley's Slump: Planning, Eugenics, and the 'Ultimate Need' of Stability," 155–157. A useful analysis of the "planning movement" at the time of the slump is Greta Jones, *Social Hygiene in Twentieth Century Britain* (London: Croom Helm, 1986), 113–136. On the broader European antidemocratic impulses of the interwar period, see Mark Mazower, *Dark Continent: Europe's Twentieth Century* (New York: Alfred A. Knopf, 1999).

42. On the slump, see for example Peter Clarke, *Hope, and Glory: Britain 1900–1990* (New York: Penguin, 1996), 144–181; Keith Laybourn, *Britain on the Breadline: A Social and Political History of Britain Between the Wars* (Wolfeboro Falls, NH: Alan Sutton, 1990).

43. Aldous Huxley, "The Victory of Art over Humanity," *Nash's Pall Mall Magazine*, July 1931, *Hidden Huxley*, 83.

44. Aldous Huxley, "Abroad in England," *Nash's Pall Mall Magazine*, May 1931, *Hidden Huxley*, 63. He often mentioned his reading of the proto-fascist sociologist Vilfredo Pareto, on the superiority of a governing elite willing to use force. Bradshaw, "Introduction," *Hidden Huxley*, xii and xviii. James Sexton notes that *Brave New World* is a "projection of the kind of society advocated by Mosley on the right and, to a lesser degree, by Wells . . . on the liberal side of the political spectrum." "Introduction," *Aldous Huxley's Hearst Essays*, xix. In May, 1931, Aldous and Julian intended to make a trip to the Soviet Union, but Aldous backed out because he was trying to finish his novel. Bradshaw, "Huxley's Slump," 160–161.

45. Aldous Huxley, "Forewarned is not Forearmed," *Chicago Herald and Examiner*, Nov. 18, 1931, quoted in Bradshaw, "Huxley's Slump," 163. When he joined the "Next Five Years Group" in 1936 he was still skeptical that its "noble ideal" of democratically controlled planning could work. Huxley, "A Horrible Dilemma," *Time and Tide*, March 14, 1936, *Hidden Huxley*, 210–214.

46. Mond's "great Imperial Chemical Industries factory is one of those ordered universes that exist as anomalous oases of pure logic in the midst of the larger world of planless incoherence." Huxley, "Sight-Seeing in Alien Englands," 67–68. In "Victory of Art over Humanity," he likewise championed the "efficient and progressive" coordination of the docks under the London Port Authority. See also David Bradshaw and James Sexton, "Introduction," in *Aldous Huxley, Now More Than Ever* (Austin: University of Texas Press, 2000), xxi–xxiv. *Now More Than*

Ever was a play (unpublished and unproduced at the time) written in September 1932 while Huxley was still fascinated with the planning issue. The protagonist is a financier who tragically fails to rescue the iron and steel industry from dishonest speculators.

47. Bradshaw, "Huxley's Slump," 161.

48. James Sexton, "Brave New World and the Rationalization of Industry," in *Critical Essays on Aldous Huxley*, ed. Jerome Meckier (New York: G. K. Hall, 1996), 88–102. Alfred Mond defined "rationalization" as "the application of scientific organization to industry, by the unification of the processes of production and distribution with the object of approximating supply to demand" (93).

49. Aldous Huxley, "Machinery, Psychology and Politics," *The Spectator*, Nov. 23, 1929, *Complete, Essays*, vol. 3, 219.

50. Huxley, *Brave New World*, 48–49.

51. Huxley, "Science and Civilisation," 108. He also pilloried how consumerism fostered stupidity in the hilarious "Foreheads Villainous Low," in *Music at Night* (Garden City, NY: Doubleday Doran and Company, 1931), 179–187.

52. Bradshaw, "Huxley's Slump," 163–164.

53. This is the most common message that my students seem to get out of the novel. After all, the title is meant to be ironic. In particular, the character John Savage speaks for the readers' "horror and disgust" at biotechnologies that produce dehumanization: "The nightmare of swarming indistinguishable sameness. Twins, twins. . . . Like maggots they had swarmed defilingly over the mystery of Linda's death. Maggots again, but larger, full grown, they now crawled across his grief and his repentance. . . . 'How many goodly creatures are there, here!' The singing words mocked him derisively. 'How beauteous mankind is! O brave new world. . . .'" Huxley, *Brave New World*, 209.

54. Huxley, "Outlook for American Culture," 187 and 193.

55. Bradshaw, "Huxley's Slump," 164. He could not be active in British eugenics organizations because he lived in Italy and France during most of this period, and then moved his family permanently to California in 1937. After that he became deeply involved in spiritualism (the Huxley of 1954's *Doors of Perception*), and his biographers do not mention anything about contact with eugenics groups.

56. "Mainline eugenics" is the term used by Kevles and other historians to distinguish the most common form of eugenics thinking from later "reform eugenics" and other variants such as "preventive eugenics" (which said that germ plasm had to be protected from deleterious environmental influences such as alcohol or venereal disease). In Britain, mainline eugenics was dominated by the research on hereditary causation carried out at the Galton Eugenics Laboratory, led by the statistician Karl Pearson and later the geneticist R. A. Fisher. Their work correlated "anti-social" traits and fertility rates with economic status. See Kevles, *In the Name of Eugenics*, 20–40. In my dissertation, "Drunkenness, Degeneration, and Eugenics in Britain, 1900–1914," I explored the conflict between the mainline Eugenics Lab and the "preventive" eugenics camp (led by the physician Caleb Saleeby) over the eugenic significance of alcoholism.

57. The other "mainline" eugenics group—which provided Huxley with the material for these class-biased claims—was the leadership of the Eugenics Society during the 1910s and 20s. On differential fertility Huxley also cited R. A. Fisher's research, which is analyzed by Pauline Mazumdar, *Eugenics, Human Genetics and*

Human Failings: The Eugenics Society, its Sources and its Critics in Britain (New York: Routledge, 1992), 96–145.

58. Huxley, "A Note on Eugenics."

59. *Those Barren Leaves* (1925), *Proper Studies* (1927), *Do What You Will* (1929). See Murray, *Aldous Huxley*, 169, 205, and 225.

60. Aldous Huxley, "Notes on Liberty and the Boundaries of the Promised Land," in *Music at Night*, 116. After visiting the northern coal country in 1931, he wrote to a friend: "The human race fills me with a steadily growing dismay. . . . If only one could believe that the remedies proposed for the awfulness (Communism etc.) weren't even worse than the disease. . . . The only thing to do is flee and hide." Quoted by Bradshaw, "Introduction," *Hidden Huxley*, xv.

61. Huxley, "Are We Growing Stupider?" 324.

62. Huxley, "What Is Happening to Our Population?" 150 and 152.

63. Thomson, *The Problem of Mental Deficiency*, 1–9; John Radford, "Sterilization versus Segregation: Control of the Feebleminded, 1900–1938," *Social Science and Medicine* 33 (1991): 449–458.

64. Bradshaw, "Huxley's Slump," 165–168. On the Eugenics Society in the 1930s, see Richard A. Soloway, *Demography and Degeneration: Eugenics and the Declining Birthrate in Twentieth-Century Britain* (Chapel Hill: University of North Carolina Press, 1990), 193–225.

65. Huxley, "What Is Happening to Our Population?" 154.

66. The Huxleys had been close friends at Oxford University in the 1910s with Haldane and his sister Naomi (Aldous even lived in the Haldane home for a time), and for years afterward they continued to discuss together scientific topics such as "mankind's genetic improvement." Firchow, *End of Utopia*, 40–42 and 68–69.

67. The reform eugenicists' political and scientific arguments against mainline eugenics are evaluated more fully by Mazumdar, *Eugenics, Human Genetics and Human Failings*, 146–195. Another useful overview of the ideas of this group is Diane Paul, "Eugenics and the Left," in *The Politics of Heredity: Essays on Eugenics, Bioengineering, and the Nature-Nurture Debate* (Albany: SUNY Press, 1998), 11–36. Paul places them in the broader context of "biological utopians" in "Genetic Engineering and Eugenics: The Uses of History," in *Is Human Nature Obsolete? Genetics, Bioengineering, and the Future of the Human Condition*, eds. Harold Baillie and Timothy Casey (Cambridge: MIT Press, 2005), 123–151.

68. J. B. S. Haldane, *Possible Worlds, and Other Papers* (New York: Harper and Brothers, 1928), 200–206. He also popularized his ideas about how to carry out "good eugenics" in *Heredity and Politics* (London: George Allen and Unwin, 1938), and *What Is Life?* (New York: Boni and Gaer, 1947). Also see Ronald Clark, *J. B. S: The Life and Work of J. B. S. Haldane* (New York: Oxford University Press, 1968).

69. Paul, "Eugenics and the Left," 19. Muller's scheme for "germinal choice" was endorsed by the scientists on the Left and by Aldous Huxley. Kevles, *In the Name of Eugenics*, 190–191 and 263.

70. Squier, *Babies in Bottles*, 86–89; Werskey, *Visible College*, 90–91. The full text of Bernal's book is available at http://www.cscs.umich.edu/~crshalizi/Bernal.

71. Concerns about rights and democracy in the class-centered British eugenics movement, see Thomson, *Problem of Mental Deficiency*, 198–205. A similar argument could be made about race and citizenship in the American eugenics movement. The 1924 Immigration Restriction Act was based on scientific evidence of the supposed feeblemindedness of southern and eastern European immigrants

(as well as American blacks). A broader analysis of how the category "disability" has historically been used to legitimize the exclusion of "undesirable" groups (by class, race, and gender) is provided by Douglas Baynton. "Disability and the Justification of Inequality in American History," in *The New Disability History: American Perspectives*, eds. Paul Longmore and Lauri Umansky (New York: New York University, Press, 2001), 33–57.

72. Haldane, *Daedalus*, 63–67.

73. Huxley, *Brave New World*, 9–10 and 14. The "heredity" of the castes is also mentioned in passing on 74 and 222. In *Crome Yellow* (1921) Huxley had a character explain the idea of ectogenesis (gestation outside the womb) and outline a plain for making a "Rational State" based on "Directing Intelligences" who lead the "vast mass of the Herd." Haldane had been playing with these scientific ideas since his undergraduate days. Huxley squeezed them into this early novel, but only in order to ridicule them. By contrast he was ready to take these ideas much more seriously in *Brave New World*. Firchow, *End of Utopia*, 30–31.

74. Aldous Huxley, "Monks Among the Test Tubes," *Hearst*, June 25, 1932, *Complete Essays*, vol. 3, 157–159. Julian Huxley, also a science popularizer when not researching evolutionary biology, published the short story "The Tissue-Culture King" in 1923. Its literary merits are negligible, but its message is perpetually relevant: the scientist protagonist "attained to an unsurpassed power in a number of the applications of science—but to what end did all this power serve?" Turney, *Frankenstein's Footsteps*, 102–107.

15. Huxley, "Science and Civilisation," 106–107.

76. Huxley, *Brave New World*, 47–50 and 227–228.

77. Aldous Huxley, "Aristocratic Tradition," *Hearst*, December 31, 1932, *Complete Essays*, vol. 3, 352–353; *Science, Liberty, and Peace* (New York: Harper and Brothers, 1946), 23–25.

78. Huxley, "Science and Civilisation," 111.

79. Bradshaw, "Huxley's Slump," 168.

80. In particular, Huxley, *Ends and Means* (1937). This was the first book Huxley finished after suffering some kind of breakdown and writer's block in the mid-1930s.

81. Huxley, *Science, Liberty, and Peace*, 3. Similar themes are pursued in his last book, *Literature and Science* (New York: Harper and Row, 1963).

82. Jenny Reardon, *Race to the Finish: Identity and Governance in the Age of Genomics* (Princeton: Princeton University Press, 2005), 23–31.

83. "Men and Mice at Edinburgh," *Journal of Heredity* 30 (1939): 371–374.

84. Huxley, *Brave New World*, xvi.

85. Huxley, "The Double Crisis," 129. The Burt argument was also in some letters, such as Huxley to Julian Huxley, June 3, 1948, *Letters*, 582–583.

86. Huxley, *Brave New World Revisited*, 20 and 144–146.

87. For Huxley's religious ideas, see especially Sawyer, *Aldous Huxley*. The scene between John and Mond is *Brave New World*, 230–240. In another revealing scene, Mond wistfully mentions a piece of biology research he had had to censor because it threatened his scientifically constructed status quo with a "heretical" revival of spiritual values. The biologist claimed to have discovered that happiness lay "somewhere beyond, somewhere outside the present human sphere; that the purpose of life was not the maintenance of well-being, but some intensification and refining of consciousness, some enlargement of knowledge" (177).

88. In effect, he "scientized mysticism," as mysticism seemed to him the perfect religion for a scientific age. June Deery, *Aldous Huxley and the Mysticism of Science* (New York: St. Martin's Press, 1996), 8.

89. Huxley, *Brave New World*, vii.

90. The most famous of his metaphysical texts are *The Perennial Philosophy* (1945) and *The Doors of Perception* (1956).

91. Huxley, *Brave New World*, ix.

92. Quoted in Clive James, "Out of Sight: The Curious Career of Aldous Huxley," *The New Yorker*, March 17, 2003, *ProQuest*, University of Washington, April 11, 2007.

93. From an interview quoted in Bradshaw and Sexton, "Introduction," *Now More Than Ever*, xii. "The writing of FINIS at the end of a manuscript should be the equivalent of burning it." Quoted in Murray, *Aldous Huxley*, 163.

CAREY SNYDER

"When the Indian Was in Vogue": D. H. Lawrence, Aldous Huxley, and Ethnological Tourism in the Southwest

The southwest is the great playground of the White American. The desert isn't good for anything else. But it does make a fine national playground. And the Indian, with his long hair and his bits of pottery and blankets and clumsy home-made trinkets, he's a wonderful live toy to play with.

—D. H. Lawrence, "Just Back from the Snake-Dance—Tired Out"

"I had the same idea as you," the Director was saying. "Wanted to have a look at the savages. Got a permit for New Mexico and went there for my summer holiday."

—Aldous Huxley, *Brave New World*

In her 1934 classic *Patterns of Culture*, the anthropologist Ruth Benedict asserts that no one has written a better description of "the form and spirit of Pueblo dances" than D. H. Lawrence (93). Although contemporary studies have examined the ethnocentrism of Lawrence's representations of indigenous people,[1] scholars surprisingly continue to praise Lawrence for his "extraordinary effort to *get inside* Indian culture" (Kinkead-Weekes 27) and for his "true engagement with the primitive" (Storch 50–51). Reading Lawrence in this way misses a more interesting element of his Southwest writings: they are illuminating not only because they shed light on specific

MFS: Modern Fiction Studies, Volume 53, Number 4 (Winter 2007): pp. 662–696. Copyright © 2007 Purdue Research Foundation by the Johns Hopkins University Press.

cultural practices, but because they also (at times, inadvertently) illuminate the practice of cultural observation itself—which takes this writer into terrain traversed by ethnologists and tourists alike.

As made clear in his 1929 essay entitled "New Mexico," the diverse tribes of the Southwest were remarkable for Lawrence insofar as they preserved their "tribal integrity" amidst the rush of modernization. Threatening to overwhelm this tribal integrity was the already extensive commercialization of the region, epitomized for Lawrence by the figure of "the Indian who sells you baskets on Albuquerque station or who slinks around Taos plaza"—two popular venues for sightseeing and buying souvenirs. In seeking to avoid modernized Indians and commune with "a remnant of the most deeply religious race still living," Lawrence emulates the protocol of professional anthropologists like Benedict ("New Mexico" 144).

The construction of the Southwest as a site of threatened authenticity relies on a notion of cultural purity that has been complicated in recent years by James Clifford and others.[2] Yet even within its historical and ideological context, what makes this claim of discovering an unaltered indigenous culture dubious is the picture Lawrence himself paints of the region: choked with thousands of tourists crowding its plazas and pueblos, the Southwest emerges in Lawrence's derisive description as the trendy, "picturesque reservation and playground of the eastern states" ("New Mexico" 141), and Southwest Indians as "wonderful live toy[s] to play with" (*Letters* 609). In essays like "The Hopi Snake Dance"—in which three thousand tourists amusedly regard a native ceremony as if it were a "circus performance" (138)—Lawrence elaborates the process by which tribal customs and ceremonies are converted into the stuff of ethnological spectacle.[3] With the figure of "the Indian who sells you baskets on Albuquerque Station," Lawrence suggests that the star attractions of the region, its "befeathered and bedaubed darling[s]" ("Indians and Entertainment" 101), sometimes participate in their own touristification. It is hard to imagine the ideal of unchanged tribal life coexisting with the aggressive commercialization of native culture Lawrence describes. As vividly depicted in Lawrence's essays and his novella, *St. Mawr,* the reservations and pueblos of the Southwest served in the interwar period as a kind of ethnological theme park. Adapting Langston Hughes's phrase, one could say that in the 1920s and 1930s, the Indian was in vogue.[4]

Joining Lawrence in his satirical treatment of Southwest tourism is Aldous Huxley, whose depiction of the Southwest and its inhabitants is in fact indebted to Lawrence's essays and letters, the latter of which he had just finished editing for a posthumous collection when he began writing *Brave New World* (1932).[5] Although Huxley's dystopia has not been read as a novel about tourism, *Brave New World* echoes Lawrence's critique of the hype surrounding Southwest Indians by representing a New Mexican Savage Reservation as the destination for a pair of English tourists, and, conversely, charting the trajectory of John the Savage from the Reservation to London, where he winds up being exhibited as an ethnological curiosity, evocative of the "human showcases" of World's Fairs that were widespread until the mid-1920s (Greenhalgh 82). Eventually John wearies of his celebrity status as token savage and flees the New World, only to become the ultimate tourist spectacle in the novel's climactic scene.

Beginning with James Meckier's 1969 study, critics who have considered the relationship between these two authors have tended to focus on Huxley's rejection of the Lawrencian primitive—a reading I do not dispute.[6] What has not been adequately appreciated is the shared context for these writings: namely, the interwar mania for Southwest Indians. This essay argues that Lawrence and Huxley were engaged in a parallel project of satirizing what I will call "ethnological tourism": tourism that takes travelers to sites such as the tropics, reservations, and ethnological exhibits, mimicking modern ethnology's goal of observing traditional customs and ceremonies firsthand.[7] In satirizing the way that tourism transforms the reservations and pueblos of the Southwest into ethnological spectacle, Lawrence and Huxley go beyond the modern trope of anti-tourism;[8] they explore the potentially destructive effects of cultural spectatorship on indigenous cultures, and thus implicitly critique the modes of observation and representation that characterize modern ethnography as well. Coming at the vogue of the Indian from two very different perspectives—Lawrence as a primitivist longing to reconnect with lost origins, Huxley as a satirist wishing to expose primitivism as a utopian fantasy—these writers nonetheless provide a similar critique of the way both tourism and ethnography potentially disrupt local traditions, objectifying indigenous people and commodifying their culture. In this way, they are prescient observers of issues that continue to confront indigenous groups, many of whom are reliant on tourist revenue for economic livelihood, as well as ethnographers, who are increasingly self-conscious about their positioning vis-à-vis the cultures they observe.[9] I argue that Lawrence and Huxley expose the practice of turning native cultures into objects of scientific curiosity and spectacles for touristic consumption, yet do not always consider the implications of their own ethnographic gazes.

The following section places Lawrence's essays in the overlapping contexts of pertinent ethnographies, tourist advertisements, and the display practices of the Santa Fe Railway and its affiliate, the Fred Harvey Company —the force behind much Southwest tourism in the period, including the Southwest ethnological exhibitions displayed at the 1915 World's Fairs. An examination of this material suggests that though ethnography defined itself against tourism in the interwar period—assuming a specialized and ostensibly disinterested stance in contrast to a popular and commercial one—these discourses frequently overlapped and converged in the Southwest.

"So we've saved the pueblos for Fred Harvey"

A 1928 ad in *Travel* magazine for "Harveycar Motor Cruises" in New Mexico depicts a Native American couple standing before a quiet pueblo, edged by vacant desert and hills, with the ironic caption, "Is this really the New World?" The ad appeals to, and helps construct, the virtual tourist's fantasies of engaging in quasi-ethnological discovery of a people who, according to the ad copy, continue to live as in pre-Columbian times; by visiting the Southwest, tourists are invited to step back in history via the familiar trope of spatial anachronism.[10] The citizens of Huxley's *Brave New World* are meant to ask the same question ("Is this really the New World?"), albeit with a different inflection, when they visit the New Mexican Reservation—constructed as an exotic, archaic outpost of "savagery" that is a mere rocket-ride away from London. (Huxley's more Hobbesian view of the primitive, contrasting with the Romantic primitivism of the Harvey ad, will be discussed below.)

In the contemporaneous *Patterns of Culture*, Ruth Benedict seems to co-opt the language of advertisers by characterizing the Pueblo Indians of the Southwest as "one of the most widely known primitive peoples in Western civilization, . . . in easy reach of any transcontinental traveler" (57). She beckons tourists to come see these famed Indians for themselves. Reading Benedict together with Lawrence's Southwest essays—which are teeming with tourists he tries to avoid—reminds us that the emerging norms of ethnographic writing called for significant acts of erasure, as Benedict goes on to efface from her text the numerous travelers alongside whom she conducted her fieldwork.

It was the Atchison Topeka Santa Fe Railway, together with the affiliated Fred Harvey Company, that brought Southwest Indians within (in Benedict's phrase) "easy reach" of ordinary travelers.[11] Indeed, the Fred Harvey publicity machine was likely behind Lawrence's figure of "the Indian who sells you baskets on Albuquerque station," insofar as Fred Harvey aggressively employed Native American artisans to market products on railway platforms, in front of gift shops such as "the Indian Building and Curio Shop" in Albuquerque. In 1901, Fred Harvey opened its "Indian Department" to coordinate efforts in marketing the image and artifacts of the Indian, distilling what could be perceived as a comprehensive "Southwest experience" in the hotel-restaurant-museum complexes known as Harvey Houses, at least one of which Lawrence visited (Dodge 234). The Harvey Company was "*the* major source for southwest ethnological materials" for tourists, collectors, and museums, including the Smithsonian and the Field Museum of

Natural History (Weigle and Babcock 67), selling "enough Indian curios to put a touch of Navajo or Hopi in every U.S. home," in the words of one contemporary (Hartwell 31). The head of the Indian Department, Herman Schweitzer, who became known as the principle "Harvey anthropologist," explained in a letter to collector William Randolph Hearst in 1905, that the main objective in promoting "the Indians of the Southwest and their products" was "to furnish an attraction for the Santa Fe"; in other words, Fred Harvey made ethnological tourism big business (Howard 92).

Lawrence and his protagonists repeatedly profess a desire to leave behind the commercial venues for interacting with or observing Indians—the platforms of the Santa Fe Railroad and the populated plazas of Taos—to seek a more intimate cross-cultural encounter.[12] His essays and novella, *St. Mawr*, chart the movement of a self-identified sensitive cultural observer beyond the façade of the Harvey Southwest, and the establishment of a fleeting connection with what is represented as genuine native culture. In following this trajectory, Lawrence's writings emulate the emerging goals of ethnological fieldwork, even as they denounce the mystifications of ethnographic texts.[13]

"The Hopi Snake Dance" (1924) illustrates the ethnological pretensions of Lawrence's writings. With thousands of spectators generally in attendance, The Hopi Snake Dance was the most popular tourist attraction in the Southwest; indeed, it was so popular, and tourists so disruptive that outsiders were eventually prohibited from viewing it (Dilworth 72). In his essay, Lawrence occasionally includes himself among the clamoring crowd, as when he describes being chastened by the Snake Priests' solemnity, which "conquers, for a few seconds, our white-faced flippancy" ("Hopi Snake Dance" 151). For the most part, though, he distances himself from the tourists he stigmatizes—"spectators . . . packed thick . . . greedy with curiosity," regarding the "sacred religious ceremonial" as a "circus-performance" ("Hopi Snake Dance" 145)—fashioning himself as a more culturally sensitive, informed observer, who looks beyond the semblance of crude entertainment to appreciate the indigenous meaning of the ceremony. Lawrence's satire of uncouth tourists finds its counterpart in contemporaneous ethnographic texts: in the introduction to *Argonauts of the Western Pacific*, the manifesto of modern fieldwork methods, Bronislaw Malinowski characterizes the average white resident in the Trobriand Islands as "full of the biased and pre-judged opinions . . . strongly repulsive" to the ethnographic mind (5). Unlike the casual observer, according to Malinowski, the modern fieldworker aims to get inside native culture, "to grasp the native's point of view, his relation to life, to realize *his* vision of *his* world" (25). A copious reader of anthropology, Lawrence seems to co-opt the role of the modern fieldworker by leaving the ignorant tourists behind and entering into imaginative union with the Hopis:

> [The chant] reveals how deep, how deep the men are in the mystery
> they are practicing, how sunk deep below our world, to the world
> of snakes, and dark ways in the earth, where are the roots of corn,
> and where the little rivers of unchannelled, uncreated life-passion
> run like dark, trickling lightening, to the roots of the corn and to
> the feet and loins of men, from the earth's innermost dark sun.
> They are calling in the deep, almost silent snake-language, to the
> snakes and rays of dark emission from the earth's inward 'Sun'.
> ("Hopi Snake Dance" 159)

Like a modern anthropologist, Lawrence presumes to have esoteric knowledge of the ceremony, purporting to understand the "deep, almost silent
snake-language" of the priests.

When Lawrence rebukes tourists for regarding the sacred religious ceremony of the Hopis as if it were a sensational show, he is criticizing them
for misreading the dance in the very way that both contemporary ads and
ethnological display practices encouraged. In 1926 Fred Harvey inaugurated
Harveycar Indian Detours. These automobile tours, explicated by purportedly expert guides took tourists "off the beaten track" (Harveycar's slogan)
and introduced them to "real" Pueblo Indian home life as well as to native
ceremonies like the "weird Hopi Snake Dance" ("Harveycar" 37).[14] In this
way, the Indian Detours effectively anticipated the response of ethnological
tourists like Lawrence, eager to get beyond the commercial façade of Harvey's
other Southwest, the one that greeted them on the platform at Albuquerque
station. Epitomizing Dean MacCannell's idea of the "staged authenticity" of
the guided tour (*Tourist* 98), Harveycar did not conceal the staging of the
Detours: the couriers were white women costumed in stereotypical native
garb and jewelry; the drivers were cowboys, following what was already a
cinematic cliché of the Old West.

More importantly, Harveycars promised to choreograph meetings with
Indians, entities construed as sights to be seen or as artisans who seemed to be
in the business of producing crafts exclusively for touristic consumption. This
impression is conveyed by Indian Detour ads that depict Indians with baskets,
blankets, or pots, objects that seem metonymically interchangeable with the
Indians themselves, inviting the tourist to visually consume artificer as well as
artifact. A lone carload of detourists romantically reenact the discovery of indigenous Americans in these images, in a conquest that is commercial rather
than military. Meanwhile, Indians stand amicably by in the posture of dutiful
servants, as if waiting to be animated by the touristic exchange. The iconog-
raphy and rhetoric of these ads encourages tourists to regard living people as
though they were objects in a museum, as exemplified by a 1928 brochure

for Harveycar Indian Detours that invites the tourist to visit "Indian pueblos where one may 'catch archaeology live'" ("Harveycar Motor Cruises" 5).

Echoing the format of the Harvey ads, with their encapsulation of Southwest tourism as a placid encounter with aborigines who court observation, is the cover of February 1926 *Motor Camper and Tourist,* where an Anglo American couple are depicted car camping next to a Native American couple who proffer their wares. The caption "Camping with the Original Americans" seems at first to serve as an invitation to the reader of the magazine to do just that. Yet the cozy preposition "with" belies the oppositional logic of the image, which depicts more of a cross-cultural staring contest than a slumber party. The impression that it is the tourists rather than the "Original Americans" who are on display is conveyed not only by their orientation (facing us rather than turned away), but also by the illusion that the poles supporting the tent's awning demarcate an exhibit space. In inverted fashion, the scene evokes the practice prevailing at World's Fairs of exhibiting various colonized peoples in simulated "natural habitats" for the edification and pleasure of paying visitors. Insofar as this issue of *Motor Camper and Tourist* is meant to promote tourism to the Southwest rather than to encourage tourists to be self-conscious, one can assume that this reversal is not meant to be darkly satirical; nevertheless, the image inadvertently highlights the potential invasiveness of the tourists' gaze, in a way that resonates with Huxley's and Lawrence's satire.

Vacationing in the Southwest and visiting ethnological displays at World's Fairs were not unrelated phenomenon: the elaborate "Painted Desert Exhibition" at the Panama-California Expo in San Diego was sponsored and organized by the Santa Fe Railway and Fred Harvey, and functioned both as a virtual vacation spot in itself and as an ingenuous, and highly effective advertisement for travel to the Southwest.[15] Ten acres of painstakingly simulated Southwest landscape, with imported sandstone, cactus, and sagebrush, as well as plaster and cement made to resemble clay, the Painted Desert was built and inhabited by three hundred Apache, Navajo, and Pueblo Indians. Despite the obvious stagecraft involved in constructing the exhibit, one reporter called it an "open reservation," reinforcing the implied link between the "real" and the virtual Southwest (Kropp 40). Ambiguity about whether fair-goers were to interpret ethnic others as sideshow curiosities or objects of scientific interest was introduced by the spatial logic of the fairgrounds themselves: while the grounds were conventionally divided into an amusement zone ("the Midway" or "Joy Zone") and a zone for education, science, and technology, ethnological exhibits might be placed at either end, and often appeared at both, blurring the distinction between these categories. At the Panama-California Expo, museum organizers doubly cued spectators to read the Hopi Snake Dance as performed for their entertainment, by the placement of the performance in the amusement zone and by its billing as "dramatically sensational" (Dilworth x).[16]

Curtis Hinsley argues that the overriding message of ethnological display was that ethnicity could be consumed, that other cultures, arrayed as so many commodities, were there to be economically colonized and exploited. According to Hinsley the displays transformed living individuals into so many storefront mannequins, like the Indians in the Harvey ads who seem interchangeable with their merchandise: the "observer does not stop to learn; rather, he or she strolls, window-shopping in the department store of exotic cultures" (365). Hinsley goes on to link this practice of "consuming" other cultures to tourism: "public curiosity about other peoples, mediated by the terms of the marketplace, produced an early form of touristic consumption" (363). Indeed, touring the ethnological exhibits and concession stands at World's Fairs was not unlike touring the reservations and pueblos of the Southwest: in the Joy Zone of the Panama-Pacific Expo, fairgoers were transported in little cars to view the sites associated with a replica of "The Grand Canyon of Arizona," including a simulated Indian village; on the way they could stop and purchase a Navajo blanket at a concession stand. In New Mexico or Arizona, conveyed in Harveycars, tourists could likewise watch Indians perform ceremonial dances, buy hand-crafted artifacts, and glimpse some of the quotidian strangeness of Indians constructed as exotic others. Here we have a kind of hall-of-mirrors of staged encounters: the Expo exhibit restages the Harvey Southwest experience, which, as we have seen, is itself already staged. In effect, the human showcases of the Panama-Pacific and Panama-California World's Fairs, of Indian Detours and Harvey Houses, and of myriad advertisements and ethnographic texts, were mutually supporting apparatuses for the display of native people: together, they promoted and normalized the ethnological tourist's gaze.

Lawrence seems to be describing the amusement zone of a World's Fair in "Indians and an Englishman," when he represents himself, a "bewildered straggler out of the far-flung British Empire," stumbling "like a bumpkin in a circus ring, with the horse-lady leaping over my head, the Apache war-whooping in my ear, the Mexican staggering under crosses and bumping me as he goes by, the artist whirling colours across my dazzled vision, the highbrows solemnly disclaiming at me from all the cross-roads" (92–93). The trope of theatricality—signaled by the language of audiences, circus rings, and what he calls "a masquerade of earnestness" (93)—points to the contrivance of a site where cultural others perform their otherness or are perceived as performing it by uncomprehending observers, for whom ordinary customs and dress become the stuff of exotic entertainment.

While the essay depicts Lawrence's attempt to connect with an ostensibly authentic Southwest, behind this staged, touristy façade, at the same time it reproduces key tropes of the tourism literature. Like the Harveycar ad, Lawrence seems to beckon his readers to "catch archaeology live"—to come and stare at exotic Indians before their way of life vanishes—as the essay moves from the circus of the Southwest to a secluded forest setting where the lone Englishman discovers a tribal elder preaching. Though informed that only Apaches are admitted into the circle, Lawrence boasts that he defiantly lurks on the periphery "for hours," wrapped in a Navajo blanket that simultaneously affords him the pleasure of donning an "Indian disguise" (albeit in a garment of the wrong tribe) and feeling "as good as invisible" (96). Rather than openly gawking at native rituals, as he describes the crowds observing the Hopi Snake Dance doing, Lawrence represents himself peering voyeuristically through a "leaf screen" (97)—an idiom of stealth that figures in professional anthropology as well, as evidenced by Malinowski's testosterone-driven characterization of the fieldworker as "an active huntsman" who must outfox "his quarry . . . and follow it up to its most inaccessible lairs" (8). (In *Brave New World*, Huxley seems to parody this scene, illuminating the connections between voyeurism, hunting, and cultural observation, as discussed below.) From this vantage, Lawrence describes a tribal elder as though he were a museum artifact, calling him "an old, mask-like virile figure," " a piece of living red earth," and " a figure of deep pathos" destined to perish (98)—language that resonates with the idiom of ethnographic nostalgia that characterizes the tourist literature. Despite the essay's attempt to conjure a portrait of a more intimate and spontaneous encounter with Indians than that staged for the average tourist, the Englishman of the essay's title emerges as a trespasser and a spy—more furtive than other spectators, but equally riveted by the spectacle of difference.

Spurious Indians

In the novella *St. Mawr,* the American expatriate, Lou Witt (later Lady Carrington) stands in for Lawrence as a disaffected, alienated modern individual on a spiritual quest that takes her to the Southwest. Lou and her mother Rachel Witt have come to despise the leisure class to which they marginally belong, with its superficial pursuit of vacuous amusements ("so bright and cheerful and *sporting* and brimming with *libido*" [113]). This includes Lou's bohemian husband Rico, who in her view is as superficial (and as insufficiently male) as the rest of the *beau monde*, which is represented as being in a state of "incipient decay" (94). Like Lawrence, Lou seeks a source of vitality to replenish the "rattling nullity" of her existence (87). It is the titular horse, St. Mawr, the "virgin" desert of the Southwest, and the novella's aboriginal characters that embody the vital, primal (and phallic) antidote to the moribund modern condition (78).

While the spiritual poverty of bourgeois European and American culture is certainly a target of critique here, Lawrence is equally concerned with the impoverishment of Indian culture and of once pristine landscapes brought about by processes of modernization, including the tourist industry. En route to America, all the fashionable tourist destinations repulse Lou and her mother: "that post-war Monte Carlo, the Riviera" is characterized as "still more depressing even than Paris" (126) and likewise Texas, with its "Cowboys right out of Zane Grey," disappoints (131). Even the characters' arrival in New Mexico—a site that has been imagined as a pocket of resistance in the sweep of globalization—is surrounded by a sense of anticlimax: "They found the fiesta over in Santa Fe: Indians, Mexicans, artists had finished their great effort to amuse and attract the tourists. *Welcome, Mr. Tourist*, said a great board on one side of the high road. And on the other side, a little nearer to the town: *Thank You, Mr. Tourist*" (132). Their post-fiesta arrival conveys the impression of belatedness that also characterizes Lawrence's essays, the sense that the attempt to escape modern life may be doomed, as these travelers follow the well-trod footsteps of those who have come before them. Looking to escape the contrivance and superficiality of everyday life, Lou and Rachel encounter a Southwest where, in James Buzard's apt description from another context, "all experience is predictable and repetitive, all cultures and objects mere 'touristy' self-parodies" (4). Lawrence's disapprobation of the staging of local culture for the benefit of tourists is here writ large in a comic mode.

Just as in his essays, in *St. Mawr*, Lawrence implies that one must look past the façade presented to the average tourist, past the veneer of modernization, to glimpse the elusive, endangered essence of indigenous culture. In depicting modern civilization as moribund and alienating, and indigenous cultures of the Southwest as vital, Lawrence replicates a distinction made by anthropologist Edward Sapir in *Dial* magazine in 1919, between "genuine" and "spurious" cultures. For Sapir, modern civilization epitomizes "spurious" culture insofar as it is fragmented, overly mechanized, and spiritually sterile, whereas American Indians embody "genuine" culture, which is "inherently harmonious, balanced, [and] self-satisfactory" (90). Lawrence operates within this framework up to a point, but in dwelling on the transformation of native culture into ethnological spectacle as I have been discussing, he presents the threat of a world where modernization is turning all cultures into spurious ones.[17] Unlike Sapir, Lawrence maps the genuine/spurious distinction onto Southwest Indians themselves.

The character Geronimo Trujillo, or Phoenix, functions as a key site in the novella for worrying about the distinction between "genuine" and "spurious" Indians. It is Mrs. Witt who patronizingly renames the Mexican-Indian groom "Phoenix," making the man interchangeable with a place, and reproducing the colonial dynamic of naming that would have been the common practice of Witt's ancestors in the antebellum plantation society of the South. Like the aboriginal Welshman Morgan Lewis, Phoenix is described as barbarically potent and animalistic; aligned with St. Mawr, and so with the primal, natural world, he sits "on a horse as if he grew there" (*St. Mawr* 20). Yet this character's hybridity troubles identity categories: son of a Mexican father and an Indian mother, he is also a shell-shocked veteran of WWI, and one who has cast his lot with American expatriates in Europe. Even before the war, historical circumstances conspired to alienate him from his indigenous past; he was educated in "one of the Indian high schools," such as Carlisle, whose mission was consistent with that of US government's then recent policy of assimilation (8).[18] Phoenix's modern pedigree thus renders him potentially spurious according to Lawrence's (and Lou's) schema; his education, travel, and fraternization with other expatriates, threaten to "absorb" him "into white civilization" (as Lawrence writes of the "red Indian" in "New Mexico") (144). His given name, Geronimo, invokes the career of the famous Chiricahua Apache prisoner of war who performed at the 1904 St. Louis World's Fair and in Buffalo Bill's Wild West. Geronimo's celebrity status as a Show Indian, and his participation in the ethnographically confused extravaganza, the Wild West, would presumably classify him among the Indians on the platform of the Santa Fe, whom Lawrence regards as disingenuously performing native identity for paying tourists.

Still, beyond the "curious film of civilization" (141), the narrative hints that Phoenix retains a glimmer of genuine Indianness, his eyes serving as the locus of an unchanged essence of indigenous identity: though "he might pass as a sunburnt citizen of any nation, . . . when you knew him, and looked right into his eyes, you saw that unforgettable glint of the Indian" (*St. Mawr* 7). Thus fetishized, Phoenix becomes a symbol of Indian identity that is in danger of being submerged or extinguished by encroachment of the Santa Fe Railway, Fred Harvey, and other manifestations of tourism and modernization.

As in his other Southwest and Mexican fiction, Lawrence envisions bridging what he regards as the "two ends of humanity"—"our own thin end, and the last dark strand from the previous, pre-white era" (qtd. in Rossman 183)—with a sexual union, in which a white woman prostrates herself before an "aboriginal phallic male" (*St. Mawr* 135):[19] Lou is "inclined to humble herself before the furtive assertiveness of this underground, 'knowing' savage" (Phoenix) who she at first imagines is superior to her trivial, spiritually vapid husband, Rico (136). Significantly, however, she vacillates, doubting this character's status as a *genuine Indian:* "In his rootlessness, his drifting, his real meaninglessness, was he different from Rico? And his childish, spellbound absorption in the motor-car, or in the moving pictures, or in an ice-cream soda—was it very different from Rico?" (136–137). That Phoenix would be interested in cars, movies, or ice-cream sodas is presented as a threat to cultural and racial categories—according to this logic, such tastes threaten to displace native ones, such that Phoenix risks losing his real Indian credentials.[20] In Lawrence's imaginary, as in that of many of his contemporaries, it is crucial that Indians stay genuine—that is to say uncorrupted by contact with white Americans and Europeans—because it is only thus that they can revive ailing modern civilization.

Behind this characterization of Phoenix seems to loom Tony Luhan, the Pueblo Indian at the hub of Mabel Dodge's salon, who served as guide on many of Lawrence's Southwest expeditions. Some were reputedly disappointed that Tony seemed so "modern": "knocking on his door in the hopes of receiving the age-old wisdom of the Indians, they were more likely to get an earful about the automobile he loved to drive" (Rudnick 47). Mabel Dodge was partly responsible for these frustrated expectations, for she represented her husband as "seer and sage," and implied that in marrying him, she had effectively gone native: "When I left the white people's world I *really* left it—it was not a mental attitude or superficial sensational gesture" (Smith 195). At the same time, she regretted having seduced Tony away from his "pattern of life," fearing that she had made him a "spoiled Indian" (qtd in Smith 207). The word "spoiled" simultaneously infantilizes Tony and evokes a discourse of cultural ruination, where assimilation signals the destruction of traditional societies. Privately the erstwhile Greenwich Village socialite worried that by meeting her halfway in her traditions, Tony had left his own, giving up the very thing that had initially attracted her—his "otherness" (her word, qtd in Smith 207).

Tony Luhan does not figure prominently in Lawrence's Southwest writings, perhaps because, with his expensive riding boots and Cadillac, the Tiwa tribal leader must have appeared inauthentic to Lawrence. Like Phoenix's potential namesake Geronimo, Luhan was reputed to have been a Show Indian, performing in a Wild West show on Coney Island (Rudnick 192). In becoming Americanized or cosmopolitan, Phoenix, Tony, and the Indian on the platform transgress the boundaries of what Lawrence or Mabel Dodge Luhan recognize as "Indian-ness." Whereas Lawrence imagines that he can pass between worlds, temporarily entering into Indian culture and then pulling back to describe it, oscillating between insider and outsider in ethnological fashion[21]—he implies that Luhan and other Indians jeopardize their identity by crossing over into mainstream American life. Writing her from England, Lawrence scolds Mabel Dodge for taking Tony too far from the pueblo because it "saps his vitality," commenting that "it would be cruel to bring Tony to Europe;" in another letter, he wonders paternalistically "how Tony will stand New York" (Dodge 278, 279, 311). If Lawrence's quest for a genuine alternative to spurious modernity requires Indians to stay put, like Tony, Phoenix functions as an unresolved challenge to such essentialist racial and cultural categories.[22]

By eschewing the commercial side of the tourist-Indian exchange and by distancing himself from other ethnological tourists as well as what he regarded as modernized Indians, Lawrence cast himself as a critical bystander, one who played no part in the process of transforming native cultures into tourist attractions. Not all writers in Taos so comfortably exempted themselves from the phenomenon. As Alice Corbin Henderson wryly noted of the increasing commercialism of the region, the Taos Art Colony seemed to have "saved the pueblos for Fred Harvey" (qtd in Jacobs 149). In a 1924 "Fiesta edition" of the regional little magazine, *Laughing Horse,* the American writer, Witter Bynner, implicates himself in the lamentable modernizaton of Santa Fe:

> We are all doing it. We cannot help ourselves. We are attracting people here. We are advertising. We are boosting. . . . [O]ur archaeologists, artists and merchants are busily summoning Indians to Santa Fe and to Gallup for a theatrical presentation of the dances and ceremonies which have hitherto been a communal and at their best a spiritual exercise. . . . To "attract and amuse the tourists", to make a show of our town, are we cutting down and withering its beauty? Are we killing and embalming the best qualities of Santa Fe, in order that a long line may come and look? (n.p.)

In Bynner's view, artists and archaeologists join the company of merchants as "boosters" for the region. Lawrence disavows this connection, rhetorically distancing himself from other tourists. Nonetheless, his writings fully participate in the discourse of ethnographic tourism. Even Lawrence's desire to evade other tourists is anticipated by an industry that devises Harvey-car Indian Detours, promising to take tourists "off the beaten track" and provide them "intimate glimpses of Indian life otherwise not attainable" ("Harveycar Motor Cruises" 12). Figuratively donning the persona of tour guide as well as ethnographer in his Southwest writings, Lawrence implies that he, too, can provide a privileged glimpse into native life. At the limit, Lawrence's Southwest writings even function, ironically, as ambivalent advertisements; his raillery against tourists in essays such as "New Mexico," which first appeared in the travel magazine *Survey Graphic* in 1931, is offset by exalted descriptions of the landscape and people that might persuade readers to take their own "Indian Detours," following the cue of Harvey ads that share the magazine's pages.[23]

The Past as a Compensatory Utopia

Huxley had little patience with contemporaries who sought alternatives to civilized life in what he regarded as fanciful perceptions of primitive societies. In a 1931 essay, he pokes fun at ethnological tourists, remarking that of late "the few remaining primitive peoples of the earth have achieved a prodigious popularity among those with wishes to fulfill" (*Music* 129). Implicating Lawrence's writings in particular, Huxley proclaims that "the past has become a compensatory Utopia. . . . With every advance of industrial civilization the savage past will be more and more appreciated, and the cult of D. H. Lawrence's *Dark God* may be expected to spread through an ever-widening circle of worshippers" (*Music* 128, 131). In contrast to Lawrence, Huxley envisioned primitive societies in largely Hobbesian terms, and declared unambiguously that it was futile to try to go back to what both writers imagined was a prior evolutionary stage. The two writers come at the vogue of the Indian, then, from very different angles: Lawrence, seeking to penetrate the touristy façade to connect with ancient traditions, and Huxley, rejecting the idea of establishing such a connection as mere Romantic idealism.

While debunking the construction of the Southwest as a primitive utopia, *Brave New World* simultaneously debunks a competing model of ideal society endorsed by World's Fairs, which seemed to provide "a map to future perfection" in the shape of a world made safer, easier, more efficient, and more enjoyable by technology and science (Rydell 219). Conjoining these two visions was not unique: at the 1915 Panama-California Expo, organizers situated a model farm, complete with modern farm equipment, a fruit-bearing orchard, and electricity, alongside the Painted Desert exhibit displaying Southwest Indians. The juxtaposition was intended, in the words of one of the fair organizers, to provide "a sermon" on progress: to reinforce the impression of Native Americans as "the vanished although romantic past and Anglo-America as the triumphant future" (Kropp, *Great Southwest* 38). The structure of Huxley's *Brave New World* reproduces the logic of the Panama-California Expo by juxtaposing the Savage Reservation and the Fordian new world. Rather than an idealized, pastoral representation of "vanishing America," however, the Savage Reservation is defined by its harshness, dirt, and supposedly barbaric customs; a vacation there superficially reinforces the desirability of the new world with its hygiene, efficiency, and emphasis on pleasure. If, as with the Panama-Pacific, the ideological message is that Indians are quaint but that progress and conquest are inevitable and good, the shallow character Lenina gets the message: "progress *is* lovely, isn't it?" (77). Huxley ironizes this response, subverting the rosy narrative of progress and cheery futurism of the World's Fairs, by making the hygienic, efficient, hyper-technological new world a nightmare society.

When John the Savage visits Eton on his tour of the New World, he learns that the reservation where he was raised is regarded as "a place which, owing to unfavourable climatic or geological conditions, or poverty of natural resources, has not been worth the expense of civilizing" (124). Given the harsh conditions of the environment and the "civilized" characters' derogatory view of the natives' way of life (the warden tells Lenina and Bernard that the Indians are "absolute savages" who "still preserve their repulsive habits and customs" [79]), the idea of taking a holiday on a New Mexican "Savage Reservation" is made to seem ludicrous in *Brave New World*. By representing the reservation as a popular tourist destination, Huxley mocks the contemporary craze for travel to the Southwest: Lenina eagerly accepts Bernard's invitation to New Mexico, explaining that she "always wanted to see a savage reservation," and the Director of Hatcheries and Conditioning tells Bernard, "I had the same idea as you. . . . Wanted to have a look at the savages. Got a permit for New Mexico and went there for my summer holiday" (33, 96).

Surrounded by a straight fence that is said to represent "the geometrical symbol of triumphant human purpose," the reservation is constructed as a prison or zoo (80). That the "triumphant purpose" of the fence is forcible containment is made clear by the pilot's sinister pronouncement, "There is no escape from a Savage Reservation," a warning he means to mute by adding that the savages are "perfectly tame. . . . They've got enough experience of gas bombs to know that they mustn't play any tricks" (78, 81). The fence serves not only to contain its inhabitants, but also to frame them: following Lawrence, Huxley highlights the exploitative dynamics of confining indigenous people to reservations and then exposing them to the inquisitive gaze of the dominant society. As in the Joy Zone of the World's Fair or in Harvey's Southwest, on Huxley's Savage Reservation, native life is viewed as entertainment: "Everything they do is funny," the pilot remarks pointing at "a sullen young savage" whose oppressed demeanor belies this statement (81). Huxley's characters regard the quotidian life of the "savages" as a tableau for their observation: sighting an "almost naked Indian" climbing down a ladder, Lenina grips Bernard's arm and urges him, "Look" (84)—the single word highlighting the principle activity of the ethnological tourist. Whereas the tourists in Lawrence's essays thrill to exotic otherness, Huxley's character recoils in disgust, repulsed by the man's wrinkled face and toothless mouth, an anti-image of new world youthfulness.

Yet if both writers satirize tourists who regard native life as spectacle, Huxley does not share Lawrence's faith that behind the tourist façade lurks a genuine culture worth reclaiming. For Lawrence, fencing in indigenous cultures is a metaphor for civilization's unfortunate repression of its instinctual side: "'Till now, in sheer terror of ourselves, we have turned our backs on the jungle, fenced it in with an enormous entanglement of barbed wire and declared it did not exist . . . Yet unless we proceed to connect ourselves up with our own primeval sources, we shall degenerate" ("The Novel and Feelings" 757). In theory, if not in practice, Lawrence believed that tearing down the fence to connect with indigenous cultures was the last hope for a decadent civilization. In Beyond *the Mexique Bay*, Huxley explicitly rejects Lawrence's primitivism: "When man became an intellectual and spiritual being, he paid for his new privileges with a treasure of intuitions, of emotional spontaneity, of sensuality still innocent of all self-consciousness. Lawrence [mistakenly] thought that we should abandon the new privileges in return for the old treasure" (261). In essays such as "Indians and an Englishman," Lawrence hardly seems like one ready to abandon the privileges of his subject position as an Englishman; his fantasy of connection with Indians is wholly reliant on an implied distance between Indians and Englishmen that he carefully enforces. Still, for Lawrence, a rapprochement between "civilized" and "primitive" life is at least desirable, whereas for Huxley, giving up (or fencing in) "primeval sources" is the price of civilization.

From Huxley's largely anti-primitivist and sometimes xenophobic standpoint, there's no compelling reason to want to reconnect with actual primitive cultures, though he felt that certain facets of pretechnological societies could be incorporated into modern life, as discussed further below. In his travel writing, Huxley counteracts rhetoric that idealizes the "savage past" with pejorative characterizations of indigenous people, such as his description of the Mexican village, Miauhuatlán, as "the deep-rooted weed of primitive human life" (*Beyond* 207). Huxley's attitude during this period has been described as "elitist" and "provincial," despite extensive world travel (Holmes 191); a member of the British Eugenic society, he was not particularly interested in transcending cultural barriers.

Huxley invokes and then subverts the Lawrencian idea of connecting with a primitive past ostensibly embodied in Indian cultures, by showing the convergence of the traditions of the new world and those of the Savage Reservation—hence in Huxley's economy, showing that "the civilized" behave like "savages." At the Reservation's summer festival, Lenina at first "abandon[s] herself" to the primal beat of the drums (86), which reminds her of the orgiastic chanting of the new world's Solidarity Service, a ceremony described in similar terms (65). Attraction becomes repulsion when a "ghastly troop" of Indians emerges "[h]ideously masked or painted out of all semblance of humanity," flinging snakes into the middle of the square, while the dancers circle "snakily, with a soft undulating movement" (87). While many details of this scene (and of that of the Solidarity Service) resemble Lawrence's representation of the Hopi Snake Dance, Huxley debunks Lawrencian primitivism by blending the relatively pacifist details of Lawrence's description with a rendition of a seemingly violent flagellation ritual.[24]

The Hopi Snake Dance merges with a Zuñi initiation ritual when a man in a coyote mask begins to flagellate an eighteen-year-old boy. The scene is conjured graphically from Lenina's horrified perspective:

The coyote-man raised his whip; there was a long moment of expectancy, then a swift movement, the whistle of the lash and its loud flat-sounding impact on the flesh. The boy's body quivered; but he made no sound . . . The coyote struck again, again; and at every blow at first a gasp, and then a deep groan went up from the crowd. . . . The blood was streaming. . . . Suddenly Lenina covered her face with her hands and began to sob. "Oh, stop them, stop them!" she implored. But the whip fell and fell inexorably. (88)

The sanguinary description of the whipping derives not just from Huxley's imagination, but also, in part, from the language of contemporary ethnographic accounts. In the 1929–1930 Smithsonian *Annual Report of the U. S. American Ethnology Bureau* that Huxley is likely to have read, Ruth Bunzel stresses the severity of the two-step initiation into the Zuñi Katcina Cult: "At the first ceremony they are severely whipped by the katcina priests to inspire them with awe for these creatures. There is a second more severe thrashing at the second ceremony" (518). In the same publication, Leslie White describes the priests "brandishing" whips in a "menacing" manner, as another participant exclaims, "Look at the blood, how it's running down!" (73). While these ethnographers record the intensity of the thrashing, they go on to emphasize the cultural purpose behind the practice: Bunzel explains, "The katcinas whip to install awe for the supernatural, but also to remove sickness and contamination. The whipping of katcinas is a blessing. It is administered with the formula, 'May you be blessed with seeds'" (518). If Huxley reproduces these accounts' more violent imagery, he also echoes the ethnographic impulse to offer cultural justification: as John the Savage explains, he wants to participate in the ritual for "the sake of the pueblo—to make the rain come and the corn grow" (89).

The representation of the flagellation ceremony in *Brave New World* cuts in two ways, which illustrate the complicated relationship between Huxley's and Lawrence's overlapping, yet contrasting, views of ethnological tourism. On the one hand, Huxley emulates Lawrence by juxtaposing the misguided response of ethnological tourists who regard native life as spectacular entertainment with what is posited as an insider's voice that explains the indigenous meaning of the ceremony. This point is reinforced during John's new world tour, when, visiting Eton, he stumbles on a slide show about Reservation life: to John's puzzlement and humiliation, students greet images of the flagellation ritual with laughter (124). The students' irreverent response anticipates the novel's climactic scene, where a crowd of English sightseers, carried away by the thrill of the spectacle, goad John into flagellating Lenina to death, crying "Do the whipping stunt!" (196). By showing that the flagellation ceremony has an indigenous meaning that is lost on the observers from the new world, Huxley replays Lawrence's satire of the ignorance of ethnological tourists.

On the other hand, despite the pretense of openness to the indigenous meaning of the ceremony in this scene, the novel is far from pushing the reader to the conclusion that the primitive society offers a viable alternative to the new world. In his 1946 foreword to *Brave New World*, Huxley represents the Savage's self-flagellation in the novel's final pages as a "retreat from sanity" (xiv)—implying that it is an irrational cultural practice indicating recidivism to a prior evolutionary state. In imbuing the scene with gothic overtones and turning flagellation into a narrative motif, Huxley sensationalizes the ceremony, rather than demystifying it as Lawrence does the Snake Dance. Seen in this light, the specter of the whipping ceremony contributes to Huxley's debunking of Lawrence and his followers' supposedly sentimental view of "savages." While the Reservation houses "old world" values of motherhood, monogamy, and reverence for tradition, it is also a locus of squalor, what is represented as superstition, and sanguinary customs. "Queer" is Lenina's word for it, the same word Huxley uses in the 1946 foreword, where he regrets having offered the Savage "only two alternatives, an insane life in Utopia, or the life of a primitive in an Indian village, a life more human in some respects, but in others hardly less queer and abnormal" (xiv). If the new world and the reservation are equally queer it is because they are equally untenable for Huxley: civilization has run amuck, in part, because it has degenerated into a state of savagery. This obviously puts Huxley in a very different camp from Lawrence, who thinks the way forward for civilization is through a detour to the "savage" past.

Like Lawrence, Huxley was fascinated by contemporary ethnographies, though he was less interested finally in the cultures they represented than in the mode of looking at the world that they suggested. In 1929 and 1930 Huxley read Margaret Mead and Bronislaw Malinowski respectively, both of whose texts figure significantly in *Brave New World*. With irony, he characterizes Mead's *Coming of Age in Samoa* as "an account of savages more puritanical than New England Calvinists in the seventeenth century," and jokes that Malinowski's *Sexual Life of Savages* has inspired him "to write a companion treatise on the *Sexual Life of Gentleman and Ladies*," adding, "There'd be much odder customs to record than among those extraordinarily rational Trobrianders" (*Letters* 343, 314). This insistence on the superior reason and stricter morality of "Neolithic savages" (*Letters* 326) should be read in the voice of a satirist, whose real agenda is to point up the foibles of his own culture rather than to seriously investigate the beliefs of others. In *Beyond the Mexique Bay*, Huxley reiterates the idea of turning an ethnographic eye back on his own culture: having spent numerous days (and pages) observing the curious customs of Central Americans, he imagines the humiliation of having a party of

Mexicans look "on in observant silence while I went through the curious old custom, say, of taking tea in Bloomsbury" (144). Huxley recognizes that the cultural voyeur's binoculars may be turned around, such that English cultural practices become a spectacle for foreign eyes.

In *Brave New World*, Huxley finds an opportunity to write his mock ethnography of modern society, with a particular focus on modern sex lives. The Controller Mustapha Mond contrasts the "appalling dangers of [old fashioned] family life," encompassing misery, sadism, and chastity, with the relative ease of the social structures and sexual practices of the new world. In defending new world sexuality, he cites as model societies both "the savages of Samoa," whose children played "promiscuously among the hibiscus blossoms," and the Trobriand Islanders, among whom fatherhood was supposedly unknown (28). The analogy between Samoan and Trobriand "savages" and the characters of the new world is reinforced by the description of "civilized" children, "naked in the warm June sunshine," sexually frolicking next to blooming shrubs and murmuring bees, and, a few pages later, "naked children furtive in the undergrowth" (21, 31). These passages echo Mead's description of "lusty" Samoans engaged in casual romantic "trysts" among palm fronds and hibiscus blossoms, in the opening pages of *Coming of Age in Samoa* (12–13). The tie between the "savages" studied by Mead and Malinowski and the people of the new world is also reinforced by references to climate: in the new world, embryos are "hatched" in a "tropical" environment, and soma offers an escape to what sounds like the "tropical paradise" of modern ads: "the warm, the richly coloured, the infinitely friendly world of a *soma*-holiday" (7, 60). In *Brave New World*, England has gone tropical and, paradoxically, given the reign of technology and science in the new world, England has gone native.

While the playful analogy turns the English into ethnographic others, enacting Huxley's fantasy of writing a mock ethnography of curious English customs, the point is not finally that all cultures are relative, or that we are "one family of man" with negligible differences among us. Instead, conceived in an increasingly outmoded evolutionary framework, the formulation is meant to broadcast an attitude of irony concerning the new world's dismissal of traditional family values, the abrogation of monogamy and of fatherhood marking the pathetic descent of the citizens of the new world into primitive irresponsibility. Gesturing to the children of the new world naked in the undergrowth and concluding his discourse on the cultures of Samoa and the Trobriand Islands, the Controller declares triumphantly, "Extremes . . . meet. For the good reason that they were made to meet" (28). Huxley adopts this idea of wedding the two worlds of primitive and civilized societies from Lawrence—for whom such a union is a fantasy, while for Huxley, it is a misguided quest. Extremes meet most dramatically in the characterization of John the Savage, born ignominiously to a new world mother and raised on the Reservation.

John the Savage goes to London

Replaying and in some senses ironically reversing a long tradition of native display in England, which was at the height of its popularity while Huxley was coming of age, John the Savage is brought back to London where he is exhibited as the civilized-man-brought-up-in-savagery. Proposing to bring John back to London, Bernard tells Mustapha Mond, "I ventured to think . . . that your fordship might find the matter of sufficient scientific interest" (108). As in the human showcases of the World's Fairs and of Harvey's Southwest, the aims of entertainment overwhelm those of science. John's mother Linda, in self-imposed exile for having committed the obscenity of natural childbirth, is exhibited in a parody of native display that draws attention to its dehumanizing effects: "There was a gasp, a murmur of astonishment and horror, a young woman screamed. . . . Bloated, sagging, and among those firm youthful bodies, those undistorted faces, a strange and terrifying monster of middle-agedness, Linda advanced into the room" (115). While Linda is displayed as a grotesque, John becomes a star, like Geronimo, who purportedly cashed in on his stardom by selling autographed photographs of himself to tourists. Touring the new world, visiting its institutions and inquiring about its customs, John is an ad hoc ethnographer, but soon becomes a traveling tourist site, drawing droves of unwanted observers wherever he goes.

When John becomes fed up with being the object of both popular and scientific interest ("I'm damned if I'll go on being experimented with," 186), he flees to a lighthouse in Surrey, where he briefly—and seemingly incoherently, given my reading of Huxley's view of primitivism developed thus far—returns to some of the ways of the Reservation, enjoying the simple pleasure of making bows and arrows to kill rabbits, for instance. Indeed, John seems to have traded what Sapir would label spurious culture for a way of life that is represented as potentially more genuine. His retreat to nature, prayer, and handcrafts gestures toward a way of life that is integrated and meaningful—an antidote, though an ineffectual one, to the hyper-specialization of the new world. While Huxley explicitly rejects the idea of returning to primitive origins, he allows that it may be possible "to introduce a salutary element of primitivism into our civilized and industrialized way of life"; specifically, to emulate the "wholeness" of primitive societies, while retaining "the material and intellectual advantages resulting from specialization" (*Beyond* 214, 217). Huxley's travel writings and his send-up of Mead's Samoans in *Brave New World* suggest that he wished to divorce this facet of "primitivism" from primitive cultures themselves, which he regarded according to well-worn primitivist clichés as unhygienic, childlike, superstitious, incapable of individuality, and so forth. It is significant that John does not return to the Reservation: it is the idea of a harmonious, integrated existence, not Indian society itself, that Huxley's protagonist fleetingly, and futilely, attempts to recuperate.

Again, this points to an important distinction between Lawrence and Huxley: Lawrence finds intrinsic value in Indian cultures such as the Hopi, whereas for Huxley, they have value only insofar as they can help to reveal or amend the deficiencies of modern life. Huxley explains his limited, theoretical interest in primitive cultures in this way in his travelogue *Beyond Mexique Bay:* "Most of the little we know about the anthropology of civilized peoples is the fruit of inquiries into the nature of primitive societies. Central America, being just Europe in miniature and with the lid off, is the ideal laboratory in which to study the behavior of the Great Powers" (62). Huxley actually borrows the metaphor of the primitive culture as a "laboratory" for studying "ourselves" from anthropology: Mead makes much the same point in her *Coming of Age in Samoa,* from which he repeatedly quotes in his writings of this period. But for Huxley (unlike for Lawrence or Mead), "savages" are not interesting in themselves—only as a means of shedding light on "civilized" problems.

Without any social framework to sustain him, John's attempt to salvage the "salutary elements" of Reservation life fails, and the Savage becomes the ultimate media event. Tourists arrive en masse, wielding cameras like the spectators ridiculed in Lawrence's Southwest essays; insatiable voyeurs, they pursue John like game as he retreats "in the posture of an animal at bay" (195). Huxley's violent metaphor of the hunt is sustained in the characterization of the reporter, Darwin Bonaparte—whose name fuses the persona of naturalist with that of conqueror. The "Feely Corporation's most expert big game photographer," he successfully "tracks" John, hiding in an oak tree to get clandestine footage of the savage's rituals of atonement (194). As if invoking the image of Lawrence behind the leaf-screen, Bonaparte becomes a warped version of the ethnologist, looting cultural secrets. John's appropriated image is turned into a spectacle for mass consumption when the footage is used to create a sensational, comic *feely* called *The Savage of Surrey.* The commodification of John's decontextualized image burlesques the impulse to mass produce and sell images of indigenous people, for example in picture post cards, Westerns, or the merchandise of the Harvey Company.

Much as Lenina and Bernard are encouraged to regard Indians on the reservation as inhuman, these tourists view the Savage as an animal in a zoo, "staring, laughing, clicking their cameras, throwing (as to an ape) pea-nuts" (195). Huxley pushes the "greedy curiosity" of the thousands of spectators who long to see *"live rattlesnakes"* in Lawrence's essays up a few notches, turning his sightseers into a blood-thirsty mob who cry in unison to see "the whipping stunt"—a de-sacralized ritual, turned into a tourist event. The tourists are shown to be the real savages, according to a prejudicial perspective that considers primitive cultures to be driven by instinct and mindless collectivity rather than intellect and individuality, when they descend into their own rituals, which echo those of the Indian tribe: "Then suddenly somebody started singing 'Orgy-porgy' and, in a moment, they had all caught up the refrain and, singing, had begun to dance. Orgy-porgy, round and round and round, beating one another in six-eighth time. Orgy porgy" (198). The frenzied crowd helps goad the Savage into flagellating Lenina to death, then taking his own life.

While the novel joins Lawrence in savaging ethnological tourists, it rejects Lawrencian primitivism. "The whipping stunt"—shorn of its cultural associations—signifies a descent into irrationality and barbarism, so that the novel ends with a specter of what Jenni Sharpe has called in another context "Eurosavagery," where the grossest acts of savagery are perpetrated by those who are supposedly "civilized" (6). These qualities bleed back into the original cultural practice, such that the customs of the Reservation seem deserving of their name ("savage"). Thus the novel, in a sense, is anti-modern *and* anti-primitive, at once satirizing the Kodak-wielding ethnological tourists of Huxley's and Lawrence's day by literalizing the symbolic violence of cultural voyeurism, and counteracting romantic stereotypes of primitive cultures with equally (and probably more damning) stereotypes of savagery.

Conclusion

However much the image of the modern fieldworker as lone discoverer of a pristine culture suggests that ethnology and tourism are antithetical, the texts I've discussed suggest that in the Southwest in the 1920s and 1930s, these domains were linked in significant discursive and institutional ways. The Southwest Pueblos were not only a popular tourist destination in this period, but also "the most-visited venue" for ethnographic research in America (Stocking 220). Whether directly employed by the Harvey Company or working under some other institutional or academic auspices, ethnographers must have served as another group of boosters for the region, inadvertently encouraging tourists to come and observe the local people, whose daily lives were deemed as engrossing as their colorful ceremonies. In Southwest ethnographies, as in Harvey ads and ethnological exhibits, Indians are depicted as sights to be seen, like the famed landscape of Taos or the Painted Desert. In Huxley's depiction of John the Savage as a simultaneous object of scientific and popular scrutiny, and in the melding of the personae of tour guide and ethnologist in Lawrence's essays, the lines between ethnology and tourism blur as well. Huxley and Lawrence are joined in their project of debunking ethnological tourists and, to an extent, ethnologists, but whereas Lawrence installs himself and his protagonists as sensitive observers of indigenous cultures in contrast to the entertainment-seeking tourists, Huxley insists that the motives that inform such a quest are misguided—that primitive life is not a utopian state to be recovered.

While both writers were attuned to the dynamics of cultural observation, from our later historical vantage point, it is easy to see the limitations of their perspectives as well. Lawrence could perceive that *other* tourists, brandishing cameras, might be galling to the Indians they observed, but in endeavoring to differentiate his clandestine form of looking from that of the less discrete observers, he impossibly wished away the similarities of his own position and that of the tourists he satirized.[25] Huxley makes no apology for sharing in what he identifies as the modern predilection for observing others, a relationship he characterizes as a "squint through the binoculars and then good-bye" (*Beyond* 142). However, if Huxley labored less strenuously to differentiate himself from the binocular-wielding tourists both writers mock than Lawrence did, perhaps this is because he had less at stake, for he did not seek intimate knowledge of the indigenous cultures he encountered.

As differently motivated as their criticisms of ethnological tourism were, Lawrence and Huxley shared the premise, common to their time, that indigenous cultures were vanishing before their eyes. Under the potentially intrusive gaze of outsiders, is it inevitable that local cultures will be destroyed, turned by the tourist industry into marketable simulacra of themselves? In a 1996 study of the Wild West Shows, the historian L. G. Moses counters the impression that commercializing Indian cultures in the Wild West heyday led to the erosion of traditions: given the prevailing governmental policy of assimilation, he maintains, "the performances actually helped to preserve traditional native culture, even while acquiescing in its transformation into a popularization—even parody—of itself" (qtd. in Kasson 164). In another context, Michel Picard has recently shifted the terms of the debate productively. In his study on Balinese culture, Picard's concern is not whether tourism destroys or preserves, but rather, the way it contributes to the reshaping of native culture. Picard concludes that the Balinese have been "active subjects who [creatively] construct representations of their culture to attract tourists," such that tourism in Bali has become *part of* Balinese culture, participating in "an ongoing process of cultural invention" (46, 47).

Similarly, Southwest Indians seem to have self-consciously tailored their identity in the context of tourism, as suggested by the response of a group of Pueblo Indians to a 1976 court case that ultimately hinged on the question of cultural identity. As Deirdre Evans-Pritchard explains, Indians selling their wares along the Portal of the Museum of New Mexico's Palace of Governors in Santa Fe Plaza continue to draw hundreds of thousands of tourists each year, who regard the Indian craftspeople and merchants, as in Lawrence's day, as "a world-famous landmark" (287). The court case ensued when the museum evicted white artists Paul and Sarah Livingston from the Portal, and they in turn sued the museum for discriminating against them on the basis of race (and lost, on the basis that the museum, as a preserver of culture, had the right to discriminate on a *cultural,* rather than racial, basis). To bolster the museum's case, Pueblo Indians collected tourists' signatures to vouch for their unique right to sell wares in the plaza, in a battle that they represented as one to "retain their identity" (289). What is interesting about this case for my discussion is that the basis for authentic Indian identity cited in this case was one forged in the context of touristic encounters. "The Indian who sells you baskets" whom Lawrence derided as a figure of the commercialization of indigenous culture has become, this case suggests, a new standard for what Dean McCannell would call a "recreated" ethnic identity. In this way, the Portal case suggests that cultural identities may be more responsive, adaptable, and resilient than either Huxley or Lawrence had reason to believe.

NOTES

1. For example, in "Lawrence in doubt: a theory of the 'other' and its collapse," Howard Booth argues that from 1917 to 1925 Lawrence oscillated between affirming and repudiating American Indians as a source of renewal for moribund civilization, embracing primitive cultures theoretically, but rejecting them in practice, in racist and sometimes imperialist terms. Mariana Torgovnick points out that Lawrence's definition of "the primitive" "furnishes no consistent political or anthropological thematic," but lapses into primitivist caricature in representing groups he credits, at least theoretically, with complexity and nuance (142).

2. In *Routes: Travel and Translation in the Late Twentieth Century,* James Clifford suggests that the circumscribed, pure, authentic, pristine culture that is the object of modern anthropological investigation (as evidenced in the influential ethnographies of Bronislaw Malinowski and Margaret Mead) is largely a mythical construction, obscuring the many links that connect all cultures, including modes of transportation and translation.

3. My use of the term is informed by Guy Debord's definition of the spectacle as "a social relation among people, mediated by images" (4), and in this regard, I am following Leah Dilworth who has discussed the Southwest of the 1920s, as mediated by the Fred Harvey Company, as tourist spectacle (68). I intend the term in a more general sense as well—referring to that which is put on display in a manner that heightens its strangeness. This sense captures the emphasis in both ethnology and tourism on observing the exotic.

4. I am referring to Langston Hughes's "When the Negro was in Vogue." In this well-known retrospective essay about the Harlem Renaissance, Hughes contemplates what it was like to be in the spotlight as white customers poured into places like the Cotton Club and Jungle Alley in Harlem, and "strangers were given the best ringside tables to sit and stare at the Negro customers—like amusing animals in a zoo." He makes the point that the "ordinary Negro" did not profit from the Harlem "vogue"—a point applicable to the vogue of the Southwest Indian as well (152).

5. Lawrence died in March 1930, and Huxley began collecting the letters later that year and continued the project into 1931; they would be published in September of 1932. *Brave New World* was written from May to August of 1931. In addition to Lawrence's writing, in a 1963 interview, Huxley relates, "I had no trouble finding my way around the English part of *Brave New World*, but I had to do an enormous amount of reading up on New Mexico, because I'd never been there. I read all sorts of Smithsonian Reports on the place and then did the best I could to imagine it" ("Interview" 198). Firchow observes that the "Smithsonian Reports" are the Annual Reports of the US American Ethnology Bureau to the Secretary of the Smithsonian Institute.

6. Lawrence and Huxley were close friends from 1926 until Lawrence's death in March 1930. In *Aldous Huxley: Satire and Structure*, James Meckier argues that during his "Lawrencian interlude," Huxley based a string of characters on his mentor, Lawrence, including Mark Rampion in *Point Counter Point* (1928) and John the Savage in *Brave New World*. Ultimately, Meckier argues, Huxley repudiates the Lawrencian primitive and its worship of "phallic consciousness"; for Huxley, "intellect and erudition would always take precedence over his emotions and intuition" (122). Peter Firchow argues that Huxley suggests the impossibility of Lawrence's fantasy of renewing a moribund "civilization" by tapping into "primitive" culture, through the self-immolation of the character, John the Savage, who symbolically represents the union of the two. See also David Bradshaw's introduction to the 1984 Faber and Faber edition of *Brave New World*.

7. Some explanation is required for my use of "ethnological tourism" rather than "cultural" or "ethnic tourism," both commonly employed in tourism studies. "Cultural tourism" construes culture in a broad sense, embracing travel to the Lake District to buy Beatrix Potter paraphernalia as well as travel to Waikiki to watch staged performances of fire ceremonies. (For elaboration of these terms, see Chris Rojek and John Urry.) I use "ethnological" rather than "cultural" to refer more narrowly to tourism that seeks so-called premodern or traditional cultures as its main object, following in the footsteps of modern ethnologists such as Ruth Bunzel and Margaret Mead. "Ethnic tourism"—defined by Van den Berghe and Keyes as that where "the prime attraction is the cultural exoticism of the local population and its artifacts (clothing, architecture, theater, music, dance, plastic arts)"—is closer to the meaning I intend (345). I employ "ethnological" rather than "ethnic," however, to emphasize the potential bond between the ethnologist and the tourist, figures who often work in the same settings and share some of the same objectives, most notably aiming to see "natives as they really live." A final note: Though the terms "ethnology," "ethnography," and "anthropology" acquire different connotations later in the twentieth century, I use "ethnology" to refer to studies of cultures conducted in the field, as opposed to armchair theorizing. This usage is consistent with professional nomenclature of the day, as in the US American *Ethnology* Bureau, and with Lawrence's and Huxley's respective usages of the term.

8. See Dean MacCannell and James Buzard.

9. On postmodern ethnography and self-reflexivity, see George E. Marcus and Michael M. J. Fischer, *Anthropology as Cultural Critique: An Experimental Moment in the Human Sciences*, and James Clifford, *The Predicament of Culture: Twentieth-Century Ethnography, Literature, and Art*.

10. The term "anachronistic space" is Anne McClintock's (40–42). See Dilworth's *Imagining Indians in the Southwest* for an analysis of the Columbian discovery motif in Fred Harvey advertisements (120–124).

11. The Los Angeles-Chicago line of the Atchison Topeka Santa Fe was completed in 1887, and the Santa Fe (together with Fred Harvey) began its advertising blitz around the turn of the century; tourism tapered off during the Depression (Weigle and Fiore 10). My discussion of the ATSF Railway/Fred Harvey Company is greatly indebted to a stimulating, well-researched collection of essays edited by Marta Weigle and Barbara Babcock, called *The Great Southwest of the Fred Harvey Company and the Santa Fe Railway.*

12. In "The Indian-Detour in Willa Cather's Southwestern Novels," Caroline M. Woidat similarly situates Cather's writing in relation to tourist advertisements produced by the Santa Fe Railway and the Fred Harvey Company, making a compelling case that Cather's fiction echoes the conceits of the tourist literature (and specifically, the preference for the "vanished Native Americans [of the Mesa-Verde Cliff Dwellings] to those still living"), even as Cather attempted to distance herself and her characters from tourism per se (30). Whereas Woidat focuses on the discovery motif in the ads and in Cather's fiction, which, she argues, represents Anglo-Americans enacting a pioneer fantasy in "a sanitized version of American history" (35), I focus here on the intersection of ethnographic and touristic discourses, which collaborate in the transformation of indigenous cultures into objects-to-be-observed.

13. Though Lawrence would insist that he was "no ethnologist" ("Indians and an Englishman" 95), he frequently positions himself in his Southwest essays as an authoritative observer, explicating indigenous customs and ceremonies in ethnographic fashion. Moreover, the disclaimer may imply a critique of ethnographic practice, rather than the false modesty of an amateur. In "Indians and Entertainment" (1924), Lawrence charges ethnologists such as Adolph Bandelier, author of the ethnological romance, *The Delight Makers,* of "sentimentalizing" Indians to the same extent as the general public, and calls for writers to "debunk the Indian" ("Indians and Entertainment" 103). Hence "I am no ethnologist" may imply "I am not one of that sentimentalizing crowd" rather than "I am not a qualified observer."

14. The Hopi Snake Dance frequently gets "top billing" in Harveycar and other tourism brochures for the Southwest.

15. Twenty-one million visitors attended the concurrently running Panama-California Expo in San Diego and Panama-Pacific in San Francisco. One ad for the Santa Fe Railway ran "Plan now to go and visit the *Grand Canyon of Arizona* on the way" (qtd. in Kropp 39); conjoining these destinations in this fashion makes the virtual fair locales such as *The Painted Desert* functionally indistinguishable from real Southwest locations such as The Grand Canyon. Not only did the virtual Southwest serve as an advertisement for "real" travel to New Mexico and Arizona, but World's Fairs more generally have been regarded as providing "a seminal force behind the rise of mass tourism" (Rydell and Gwin 1): Greenhalgh asserts that World's Fairs were the "largest gatherings of people—war or peace—of all time" (1).

16. The St. Louis Fair of 1904 scheduled performances of the Hopi Snake Dance in the Midway amusement zone as well, while presenting a model government-run Indian school in the education zone. In the wake of the 1887 Dawes Act, the St. Louis-Expo organizers used the structure of the fair to implicitly

endorse the official government policy of assimilation, while undermining the value and seriousness of traditional Hopi culture. See Kasson for a history of governmental policy toward Native Americans.

17. Several of Lawrence's essays discussed here, including "Indians and an Englishman" (1923), were also first published in *Dial* magazine. Whether Lawrence read Sapir or not, the genuine/spurious distinction is one that animates both his and Huxley's Southwest writings. The trivial *beau monde* of England depicted in *St. Mawr* is suggestive of *spurious culture*, whereas the Indians of Lawrence's Southwest essays and fiction, who have stubbornly maintained the ways of their ancient race, in Lawrence's eyes, exhibit the attributes of *genuine culture*.

18. According to Kasson, institutions like the Carlisle Indian Boarding School took Native Americans from their parents to Americanize them, "teaching them trades, deportment, and the English language" (164)—explicitly aiming to eradicate traditional culture. In a letter to Catherine Carswell from New Mexico (18 May, 1924), Lawrence makes his anti-assimilationist position clear: "There is something savage, unbreakable in the spirit of the place out here—the Indians drumming and yelling at our camp-fire in the evening—But they'll be wiped out, too, I expect—schools and education will finish them" (*Letters* 602).

19. In *St. Mawr,* not only does Lou Witt fantasize about a union with Phoenix to regenerate her desiccated culture, but also her mother proposes to (and is rejected by) the Welsh groom, Lewis, another "aboriginal" male in the novella. In *The Plumed Serpent*, Lawrence simultaneously weds the races and denigrates a "cocksure" modern woman by having his protagonist, the Irish woman Kate Leslie, marry a "pure [Mexican] Indian" Cipriano, who ultimately remains inscrutable to her. By marrying him, she is made to bow down before the phallic mystery of the indigenous god Quetzalcoatl with which he has associated himself, to be debased (feeling "condemned to go through these strange ordeals") and, ultimately, to be psychologically annihilated.

20. The assumption that real Indians unswervingly follow traditional customs, eschewing mainstream American professions, education, and culture, is still one being contested, as demonstrated by the campaign launched by the American Indian College Fund in March 2001 to challenge the stereotype of the static, traditional Indian. This campaign features images of American Indians engaged in study or in a range of respected professions (such as medicine or the law) with the caption "Have you Ever Seen a Real Indian?" The campaign is designed to counteract public ignorance about Indian people, who are too often regarded, according to the organization's website, as "extinct" or "museum relics," stereotypes that have their roots in the rhetoric of ethnological salvage this essay explores.

21. James Clifford describes the participant-observation method of fieldwork in these terms in *Predicament of Culture*, 34.

22. In *Our America*, Walter Benn Michaels argues that in a category of fiction he calls "nativist modernism," the refusal to procreate functions as a means of policing racial and cultural identities. However, while the aboriginal males' refusal to couple with white American females in *St. Mawr* does defend the boundary between Indians and whites (in accordance with Michaels' argument about nativist modernism), withdrawing the threat of miscegenation does not clear the muddied cultural waters in the text: because Phoenix is modernized like the Harvey Indians, he remains of dubious cultural authenticity for Lawrence.

23. Woidat has demonstrated that Cather's writings functioned in this way. She notes, "even Cather's archbishop [from *Death Comes for the Archbishop* (1927)] became a kind of advertisement: the Bishop's Lodge Hotel at Santa Fe enjoyed such rich profits from his story that the managers offered her unlimited free accommodations" (note 18, page 47).

24. In his 1946 Preface, Huxley explains that the flagellation ritual is half "fertility cult and half *Penitente* ferocity" (xiv); thus critics have understood Huxley to blend Lawrence's description of the Hopi Snake Dance and ethnographic descriptions from "the Smithsonian reports" (see note 5 above) with depictions of the flagellation rites of the Christian *Penitents* in New Mexico. Though I am indebted to Firchow for identifying Huxley's possible sources, Firchow does not specifically discuss the echoes between this passage and the reports of Ruth Bunzel and Leslie White (see *End of Utopia* 75).

25. Lawrence's desire to differentiate himself from crass observers, evident in all the essays discussed in this article, is made perhaps most overt in his essay "Taos." While the writer helps a group of unidentified Indians to raise a May Pole, a participant-observer of sorts in this borrowed custom, a tourist takes a snapshot and is promptly told to forfeit her camera. Embarrassed by what he represents as the woman's vulgarity, Lawrence boasts, "I have long since passed the stage when I want to crowd up and stare at anybody's spectacle" (102)—a dubious moral given his undeniable position as an observer of native life.

Works Cited

Benedict, Ruth. *Patterns of Culture*. 1934. Boston: Houghton, 1989.

Booth, Howard. "Lawrence in doubt: a theory of the 'other' and its collapse," in *Modernism and Empire*, eds. Howard J. Booth and Nigel Rigby. Manchester University Press, 2000.

Bradshaw, David. Introduction to *Brave New World*. London: Harper, 1994.

Bunzel, Ruth. "An Analysis of the Katcina Cult of Zūni." *47th Annual Report of the US American Ethnology Bureau to the Secretary of the Smithsonian Institute: 1929–1930*. Washington: United States Government Printing Office, 1932. 843–1087.

Buzard, James. *The Beaten Track: European Tourism, Literature, and the Ways to "Culture" 1800–1918*. Oxford: Oxford University Press, 1993.

Bynner, Witter. "A City of Change." *Laughing Horse:* 11 September 1924: n.p.

Clifford, James. *Predicament of Culture: Twentieth-Century Ethnography, Literature, and Art*. Harvard University Press, 1988.

———. *Routes: Travel and Translation in the Late Twentieth Century*. Harvard University Press, 1997.

Debord, Guy. *Society of the Spectacle*. Detroit: Black and Red, 1983.

Dilworth, Leah. *Imagining Indians in the Southwest: Persistent Visions of a Primitive Past*. Washington: Smithsonian, 1996.

Dodge Luhan, Mabel. *Lorenzo in Taos*. London: Secker, 1933.

Evans-Pritchard, Deidre. "The Portal Case: Authenticity, Tourism, Traditions, and the Law." *The Journal of American Folklore* 100.397 (1987): 287–296.

Firchow, Peter Edgerly. *The End of Utopia: a Study of Aldous Huxley's* Brave New World. London: Associated University Press, 1984.

Greenhalgh, Paul. *Ephemeral Vistas: The Expositions Universelles, Great Exhibitions and World Fairs, 1851–1939*. Manchester University Press, 1988.

Hartwell, Dickinson. "Let's Eat with the Harvey Boys." *Colliers* 9 April 1949: 30–34.

"Harveycar Motor Cruises: off the beaten path in the Great Southwest". Harveycars: 1928. New Mexico Guide Book Collection (AC 332, Box 1, Folder 13), Fray Angelico Chavez History Library, Santa Fe.

Hinsley, Curtis M. "The World as Marketplace: Commodification of the Exotic at the World's Columbian Exposition, Chicago, 1893." *Exhibiting Cultures: The Poetics and Politics of Museum Display.* Ed. Ivan Karp and Steven D. Lavine. Washington: Smithsonian, 1991.

Holmes, Charles M. "The Sinister Outer World: Aldous Huxley and International Politics." *Literary Companion to British Literature: Readings on Brave New World.* Ed. Katie de Koster. San Diego: Greenhaven, 1999.

Howard, Kathleen L. "'A most remarkable success': Herman Schweizer and the Fred Harvey Indian Department." Weigle and Babcock, 87–101.

Hughes, Langston. "When the Negro was in Vogue." 1940. *The Heath Anthology of American Literature.* Ed. Paul Smith, et.al. Lexington, Mass.: Heath, 1990.

Huxley, Aldous. *Beyond the Mexique Bay.* 1934. NY: Vintage, 1960.

———. "Interview with Aldous Huxley." *Writers at Work: The Paris Interviews, Second Series.* Ed. George Plimpton. NY: Penguin, 1977.

———. *Brave New World and Brave New World Revisited.* NY: Harper, 1965.

———. *Letters of Aldous Huxley.* Ed. Grover Smith. NY: Harper, 1969.

———. *Music at Night and Other Essays.* 1931. NY: Harper, 1970.

———. "To Julian Huxley." 13 July 1929. Letter 290 of *Letters.* 313–314.

———. "To Mrs. Kethevan Roberts." 28 November 1930. Letter 323 of Letters. 343–344.

———. "To Norman Douglas." 7 January 1930. Letter 300 of *Letters.* 326–327.

Jacobs, Margaret D. *Engendered Encounters: Feminism and Pueblo Cultures: 1879–1934.* Lincoln: University of Nebraska Press, 1999.

Kasson, Joy S. *Buffalo Bill's Wild West: Celebrity, Memory, and Popular History.* New York: Hill, 2000.

Kinkead-Weekes, Mark. "Decolonizing imagination: Lawrence in the 1920s." *The Cambridge Companion to D. H. Lawrence.* Ed. Anne Fernihough. Cambridge University Press, 2001.

Kropp, Phoebe. "'There is a little sermon in that': Constructing the Native Southwest at the San Diego Panama-California Exposition of 1915." Weigle and Babcock 36–46.

Lawrence, D. H. "Hopi Snake Dance." Lawrence, *Mornings.* 136–169.

———. "Indians and an Englishman." McDonald 91–99.

———. "Indians and Entertainment." Lawrence, *Mornings.* 100–108.

———. *Letters of D. H. Lawrence.* Ed. Aldous Huxley. London: Heinemann, 1932.

———. *Mornings in Mexico.* London: Secker, 1927.

———. *"New Mexico."* McDonald 141–145

———. "The Novel and Feelings." McDonald 756–758.

———. *St. Mawr.* 1924. NY: Random, 1953.

———. "To Catherine Carswell." 18 May 1924. *Letters.* 609–610.

———. "To J. M. Murry." 7 February 1924. *Letters.* 601–602.

MacCannell, Dean. *The Tourist: A New Theory of the Leisure Class.* NY: Schocken, 1976.

Malinowski, Bronislaw. *Argonauts of the Western Pacific.* 1922. Prospect Heights, IL: Waveland, 1984.

Marcus, George E. and Michael M. J. Fischer. *Anthropology as Cultural Critique: An Experimental Moment in the Human Sciences.* Chicago: University of Chicago Press, 1986.

McClintock, Anne. *Imperial Leather: Race, Gender and Sexuality in the Colonial Contest*. New York: Routledge, 1995.

McDonald, Edward D., ed. *Phoenix: The Posthumous Papers of D. H. Lawrence*. NY: Viking, 1936.

Mead, Margaret. *Coming of Age in Samoa*. 1928. NY: Harper, 2001.

Meckier, James. *Aldous Huxley: Satire and Structure*. London: Chatto, 1969.

Merrild, Knud. *With D. H. Lawrence in New Mexico: A Memoir of D. H. Lawrence*. New York: Barnes, 1965.

Michaels, Walter Benn. *Our America. Nativism, Modernism, and Pluralism*. Durham: Duke University Press, 1995.

Picard, Michel. "Cultural Heritage and Tourist Capital: Cultural Tourism in Bali." *International Tourism: Identity and Change*. Ed. Marie-Francoise Lanfant, John B. Allcock and Edward M. Bruner. London: Sage, 1995.

Pratt, Mary Louise. "Fieldwork in Common Places." *Writing Culture: The Poetics and Politics of Ethnography*. Berkeley: University of California Press, 1986.

Rojek, Chris and John Urry, ed. *Touring Cultures: Transformations of Travel and Theory*. London: Routledge, 1977.

Rossman, Charles. "D.H. Lawrence and New Mexico." *D. H. Lawrence: A Centenary Consideration*. Ed. Peter Balbert and Phillip L. Marcus. Ithaca: Cornell University Press, 1985.

Rudnick, Lois Palken. *Utopian Vistas: The Mabel Dodge Luhan House and the American Counterculture*. Albuquerque: University of New Mexico Press, 1996.

Rydell, Robert W. and Nancy Gwinn, eds. *Fair Representations: World's Fair and the Modern World*. Amsterdam: Vrije University Press, 1994.

Rydell, Robert W. *All the World's a Fair: Visions of Empire at American International Expositions. 1876–1916*. Chicago: University of Chicago Press, 1989.

Sapir, Edward. "Culture, Genuine and Spurious." *Culture, Language and Personality: Selected Essays*. Ed. David Mandelbaum. Berkeley: University of California Press, 1970.

Sharpe, Jenni. *Allegories of Empire: The Figure of Woman in the Colonial Text*. Minneapolis: University of Minnesota Press, 1993.

Smith, Sheri. *Reimagining Indians: Native Americans through Anglo Eyes, 1880–1940*. Oxford: Oxford University Press, 2000.

Stocking, George. "The Ethnographic Sensibility of the 1920s and the Dualism of the Anthropological Tradition." *Romantic Motives: Essays on Anthropological Sensibility*. Ed. George W. Stocking, Jr. *History of Anthropology*, Vol. 6. Madison: University of Wisconsin Press: 1989. 208–76.

Storch, Margaret. "'But Not the America of the Whites': Lawrence's Pursuit of the True Primitive." *The D. H. Lawrence Review* 25.1 (1993): 48–62.

Torgovnick, Mariana. *Gone Primitive: Savage Intellects, Modern Lives*. Chicago: University of Chicago Press, 1990.

Turner, Louis and John Ash. *The Golden Hordes: International Tourism and The Pleasure Periphery*. New York: St Martin's, 1976.

Van den Berghe, Pierre L. and Charles F. Keyes. "Introduction: Tourism and Re-Created Ethnicity." *Annals of Tourism Research* 11.3 (1984): 343–352.

Weigle, Marta and Kyle Fiore, eds. *Santa Fe and Taos: The Writer's Era 1916–1941*. Santa Fe: Ancient City, 1994.

Weigle, Marta and Barbara Babcock, eds. *The Great Southwest of the Fred Harvey Company and the Santa Fe Railway*. Phoenix: The Heard Museum, 1996.

White, Leslie. "The Acoma Indians: Ceremonies and Ceremonialism." *47th Annual Report of the US American Ethnology Bureau to the Secretary of the Smithsonian Institute: 1929–1930*. Washington: United States Government Printing Office, 1932. 63–125.

Woidat, Caroline M. "The Indian-Detour in Willa Cather's Southwestern Novels." *Twentieth-Century Literature* 48 (2002): 22–49.

ACKNOWLEDGMENT

I wish to acknowledge the valuable input of a number of people at different stages in the evolution of this project: Celia Marshik, Eric Aronoff, Matt Herman, Steven Rubenstein, Marta Weigle, Tomas Jaehn, Art Bachrach; the anonymous reviewers at *MFS;* and my colleagues at Ohio University including Joseph McLaughlin, Jeremy Webster, Johnnie Wilcox, and Andrew Escobedo. I am also grateful to the Ohio University Research Council (OURC) for awarding me a grant for archival research in New Mexico, and to the external reviewers for this grant, Melba Cuddy-Keane, Marc Manganaro, and James Buzard.

Chronology

1894	Born on July 26 in Godalming, Surrey, England, to Leonard and Julia Huxley. His grandfather, Thomas Henry Huxley, was an important scientist who developed Darwin's theories on evolution, as well as a thinker who first used the term "agnostic." He also has distant maternal relation to famed English poet Matthew Arnold.
1908	Huxley's mother dies of cancer.
1910	Eye illness renders Huxley temporarily blind, foiling plans for medical school, for which he had been preparing. Later, although his vision recovers, Huxley does not gain sufficient sight to fight in World War I.
1916	Earns B.A. from Balliol College, Oxford University. While there, Huxley makes his first literary friendships, with Lytton Strachey, Bertrand Russell, and D. H. Lawrence. Also publishes first book, a collection of poems entitled *The Burning Wheel*.
1917	Hired as schoolmaster at Eton College in Eton, England.
1919	Becomes staff member of *Athanaeum* and *Westminster Gazette*. Marries Maria Nys.
1920	Huxley's only child, Matthew, is born. In the decade following, the Huxleys travel a great deal, living in London intermittently. They visit Italy, India, and America for more extended visits.

1921	*Crome Yellow* published in London; the following year it is published in New York. It would be reprinted in both countries in the year of Huxley's death.
1923	*Antic Hay* published.
1924	As a result of early novel successes, Huxley is able to leave his editorial jobs to pursue writing full-time.
1925	*Those Barren Leaves* published. Huxleys travel around the world for most of the year.
1928	*Point Counter Point* published in the United States.
1931	During a fevered four months, Huxley writes *Brave New World*.
1937	Huxleys move permanently to the United States. By 1938 they are settled in Hollywood, and Huxley begins work as a screenwriter.
1940	Huxley writes the screenplay for the film adaptation of Jane Austen's *Pride and Prejudice*.
1946	Following World War II, Huxley pens a new introduction to *Brave New World*, recanting his stated idea of the novel, that mass social sanity was impossible in the world of his time. Huxley also publishes *The Perennial Philosophy*, Huxley's own collected writings (with others) further defining "social sanity" and musing on means of achieving it.
1954	Publishes *The Doors of Perception*, a nonfictional account of his experiences with hallucinogens and other "mind-expanding" substances, including LSD. The account provided another facet to Huxleys' fame, and the book was a counter-culture sensation in the years that followed. The rock group, The Doors, claim to have taken the inspiration for their name from this book. In all, Huxley's chemical experimentation lasted through the 1950s and into the 1960s.
1955	Maria Huxley dies.
1956	Publishes *Heaven and Hell*, another book chronicling drug experiences. He also remarries, to Laura Archera.

1958   Publishes *Brave New World Revisited*, essays which addressed problems only thematically present in the novel, as well as in a great deal of Huxley's other work.

1959   American Academy of Arts and Letters awards Huxley the Award of Merit for the Novel.

1962   Publishes *Island*, considered by some to be the utopian antidote to *Brave New World*'s dystopia.

1963   Dies November 22, 1963. His ashes were returned to England and laid to rest in his parents' grave.

2003   *Brave New World* voted "one of the BBC's all-time top 100 best-loved novels" by British readers.

Contributors

HAROLD BLOOM is Sterling Professor of the Humanities at Yale University. He is the author of 30 books, including *Shelley's Mythmaking* (1959), *The Visionary Company* (1961), *Blake's Apocalypse* (1963), *Yeats* (1970), *A Map of Misreading* (1975), *Kabbalah and Criticism* (1975), *Agon: Toward a Theory of Revisionism* (1982), *The American Religion* (1992), *The Western Canon* (1994), and *Omens of Millennium: The Gnosis of Angels, Dreams, and Resurrection* (1996). *The Anxiety of Influence* (1973) sets forth Professor Bloom's provocative theory of the literary relationships between the great writers and their predecessors. His most recent books include *Shakespeare: The Invention of the Human* (1998), a 1998 National Book Award finalist; *How to Read and Why* (2000); *Genius: A Mosaic of One Hundred Exemplary Creative Minds* (2002); *Hamlet: Poem Unlimited* (2003); *Where Shall Wisdom Be Found?* (2004); and *Jesus and Yahweh: The Names Divine* (2005). In 1999, Professor Bloom received the prestigious American Academy of Arts and Letters Gold Medal for Criticism. He has also received the International Prize of Catalonia, the Alfonso Reyes Prize of Mexico, and the Hans Christian Andersen Bicentennial Prize of Denmark.

ROBERT CECIL BALD (1901–1965) was professor in English at the University of Chicago from 1952 to 1965. He wrote *John Donne: A Life* (1970, completed after his death by Wesley Milgate).

CLYDE ENROTH (1926–2007) taught English at Sacramento State University for forty-one years.

JAMES H. QUINA JR. is assistant professor of English education in the department of language education at the University of Georgia, Athens. He wrote *Effective Secondary Teaching: Going beyond the Bell Curve* (1989).

JEROME MECKIER is professor of English at the University of Kentucky. His books include *Aldous Huxley: Satire and Structure* (1971) and *Critical Essays on Aldous Huxley* (1996), which he edited.

PIERRE VITOUX is emeritus professor of British literature and civilization at the University Paul Valery of Montpellier. His books include *History of Ideas in Great Britain* (1999), and *Amantes*, a translation of D. H. Lawrence's *Women in Love* (2000).

JANET L. GOODRICH was formerly a lecturer in romance languages and literature at the State University of New York, Binghamton.

ALEX MACDONALD is associate professor of English at Campion College at the University of Regina. He wrote *Practical Utopians: The Lives and Writings of Ed and Will Paynter, Saskatchewan Co-operative Pioneers* (2004) and *Cloud-Capped Towers: The Utopian Theme in Saskatchewan History and Culture* (2007).

BRAD BUCHANAN teaches modern British and American literature and creative writing at California State University, Sacramento.

SALLY MINOGUE is a teacher retired from the University of Kent. She edited *Problems for Feminist Criticism* (1990).

ANDREW PALMER is a senior lecturer in modern literature at Christ Church University in Canterbury. He has published on Alan Sillitoe, Bruce Chatwin, George Orwell, and Howard Jacobson.

MAARTJE N. SCHERMER is a Dutch physician and ethicist. She wrote *Different Faces of Autonomy: Patient Autonomy in Ethical Theory and Hospital Practice* (2002).

JOANNE WOIAK teaches in the disability studies program, the history department, and interdisciplinary arts and sciences at University of Washington, Bothell.

CAREY SNYDER is associate professor of English at Ohio University. She wrote *British Fiction and Cross-Cultural Encounters: Ethnographic Modernism from Wells to Woolf* (2008).

Bibliography

Aldous Huxley Annual: A Journal of Twentieth-Century Thought and Beyond Volume 4 (2004).

Aldous Huxley Annual: A Journal of Twentieth-Century Thought and Beyond Volume 5 (2005).

Aldous Huxley Annual: A Journal of Twentieth-Century Thought and Beyond Volume 6 (2006).

Aldous Huxley Annual: A Journal of Twentieth-Century Thought and Beyond Volume 7 (2007).

Aplin, John. "Aldous Huxley's Music Criticism: Some Sources for the Fiction," *English Language Notes*, Volume 21 (September 1983): pp. 58–62.

Atkins, John. *Aldous Huxley*. Columbus: Orion Press, 1968.

Baker, Robert S. "Aldous Huxley: History and Science Between the Wars," *Clio*, Volume 25 (Spring 1996): pp. 293–300.

———. Brave New World: *History, Science, and Dystopia*. Boston: Twayne, 1990.

Bedford, Sybille. *Aldous Huxley: A Biography*. New York: Knopf, 1974.

Begnoche, Suzanne R. "Aldous Huxley's Soviet Source Material: An Unpublished Letter," *English Language Notes*, Volume 34 (March 1997): pp. 51–56.

Birnbaum, Milton. *Aldous Huxley's Quest for Values*. Knoxville: University of Tennessee Press, 1971.

Bowering, Peter. *Aldous Huxley: A Study of the Major Novels*. London: Athlone Press, 1968.

Brander, Laurence. *Aldous Huxley: A Critical Study*. Cranbury: Bucknell University Press, 1970.

Brook, Jocelyn. *Aldous Huxley*. London: Longman, Green, 1954.

Clark, Ronald W. *The Huxleys*. New York: McGraw, 1968.

Dasgupta, Sanjukta. *The Novels of Huxley and Hemingway: A Study in Two Planes of Reality*. New Delhi: Prestige, 1996.

Deery, Jane. *Aldous Huxley and the Mysticism of Science*. New York: St. Martin's Press, 1996.

Donadio, Stephen. "Aldous Huxley: A Gathering of Letters, 1915–1963," *New England Review: Middlebury Series*, Volume 28, Number 4 (2007): pp. 131–157.

Dunaway, David King. *Aldous Huxley Recollected: An Oral History*. Alta Mira Press, 1998.

Filippakopoulou, Maria. "Intimacy and Recoil: Huxley Reads Poe in French," *Symbiosis: A Journal of Anglo-American Literary Relations*, Volume 8, Number 1 (April 2004): pp. 77–89.

Firchow, Peter Edgerly. "Aldous and Julian: Men of Letters, Men of Science," *Aldous Huxley Annual: A Journal of Twentieth-Century Thought and Beyond*, Volume 4 (2004): pp. 205–230.

——. *The Ends of Utopia: A Study of Aldous Huxley's 'Brave New World'* Cranbury: Bucknell University Press, 1984.

——. *Aldous Huxley: A Satirist and Novelist*. Minneapolis: University of Minnesota Press, 1972.

——, and Bernfried Nugel, eds. *Aldous Huxley: Modern Satirical Novelist of Ideas: A Collection of Essays by Jerome Meckier*. Berlin, Germany: Lit, 2006.

——, and Hermann J. Real, eds. *The Perennial Satirist: Essays in Honour of Bernfried Nugel*. Münster, Germany: Lit, 2005, pp. 245–264.

Gibson, William L. "Four Samples of Oral Biography," *The Oral History Review*, Volume 24, Number 2 (Winter 1997): pp. 101–106.

Greenblatt, Stephen J. *Three Modern Satirists: Waugh, Orwell, and Huxley*. New Haven: Yale University Press, 1965.

Harless, William. "Who's Afraid of A Brave New World," *Boulevard*, Volume 20, Number 1 [58] (Fall 2004): pp. 143–150.

Holmes, Charles M. *Aldous Huxley and the Way to Reality*. Bloomington: Indiana University Press, 1970.

Hull, James. *Aldous Huxley, Representative Man*, ed. Gerhard Wagner. Münster: Lit.; Piscataway, NJ: Transaction Publishers, 2004.

Huxley, Aldous. *Aldous Huxley: Selected Letters*, ed. and intro. James Sexton. Chicago: Ivan R. Dee, 2007.

——. *Aldous Huxley's* Brave New World, ed. and intro. Harold Bloom. Philadelphia: Chelsea House Publishers, 2004.

Huxley, Julian. *Aldous Huxley: A Memorial Volume*. New York: Harper, 1965.

Huxley, Laura Archera. *This Timeless Moment: A Personal View of Aldous Huxley.* New York: Farrar, Straus, 1968.

Izzo, David Garrett. "Aldous Huxley," *Review of Contemporary Fiction,* Volume 25, Number 3 (Fall 2005): pp. 86–136.

———. *Aldous Huxley and W. H. Auden: On Language.* Locust Hill Press, 1998.

———, and Kim Kirkpatrick, eds. *Huxley's* Brave New World: *Essays.* Jefferson, NC: McFarland, 2008, pp. 107–116.

Keulks, Gavin. "Aldous Huxley: A Centenary Bibliography (1978–1995)," *Journal of Modern Literature,* Volume 20 (Winter 1996): pp. 223–238.

Klein, Kerwin Lee. "Westward Utopia: Robert V. Hine, Aldous Huxley, and the Future of California History," *Pacific Historical Review,* Volume 70, Number 3 (August 2001): pp. 465–476.

Kuehn, Robert E., ed. *Aldous Huxley: A Collection of Critical Essays.* Englewood Cliffs: Prentice-Hall, 1974.

Leal, R. B. "Drieu La Rochelle and Huxley: Cross Channel Perspectives on Decadence," *Journal of European Studies,* Volume 15 (December 1985): pp. 247–259.

Lin, Lidan. "Aldous Huxley in the Age of Global Literary Studies," *International Fiction Review,* Volume 31, Numbers 1–2 (2004): pp. 78–87.

Mack, Robert L. "Another Thomas Gray Parody in Aldous Huxley's *Brave New World,*" *Notes and Queries,* Volume 51, Number 2 (June 2004): pp. 178–182.

Mathisen, Werner Christie. "The Underestimation of Politics in Green Utopias: The Description of Politics in Huxley's *Island,* Le Guin's *The Dispossessed,* and Callenbach's *Ecotopia,*" *Utopian Studies,* Volume 12, Number 1 (2001): pp. 56–78.

Meckier, Jerome. "On D. H. Lawrence and Death, Especially Matricide: *Sons and Lovers, Brave New World,* and Aldous Huxley's Later Novels," *Aldous Huxley Annual: A Journal of Twentieth-Century Thought and Beyond,* Volume 7 (2007): pp. 185–221.

———. "Aldous Huxley, Evelyn Waugh, and Birth Control in Black Mischief," *Journal of Modern Literature,* Volume 23, Number 2 (Winter 1999–2000): pp. 277–290.

———. "Aldous Huxley: Dystopian Essayist of the 1930s," *Utopian Studies,* Volume 7, Number 2 (1996): pp. 196–212.

———, ed. *Critical Essays on Aldous Huxley.* Boston: G. K. Hall, 1996.

———. *Aldous Huxley: Satire and Structure.* New York: Barnes & Noble, 1969.

Morissey, Thomas J. "Armageddon from Huxley to Hoban," *Extrapolation,* Volume 25 (Fall 1984): pp. 197–213.

Murray, Nicholas. *Aldous Huxley: A Biography.* New York: Thomas Dunne Books/St. Martin's Press, 2003.

Nugel, Bernfried. *Now More than Ever: Proceedings of the Aldous Huxley Centenary Symposium, Münster, 1994.* New York: Peter Lang, 1996.

————, Uwe Rasch, and Gerhard Wagner, eds. *Aldous Huxley, Man of Letters: Thinker, Critic and Artist: Proceedings of the Third International Aldous Huxley Symposium.* Riga 2004. Berlin, Germany: Lit, 2007, pp. 15–24

Pritchard, William H. "Huxley in His Letters," *Sewanee Review,* Volume 117, Number 1 (Winter 2009): pp. 121–124.

Sawyer, Dana. *Aldous Huxley: A Biography.* New York: Crossroad Publishing, 2002.

Sexton, James, ed. *Selected Letters of Aldous Huxley.* Chicago: Dee, 2007.

————. "Aldous Huxley aka Conde Nast's 'Staff of Experts' (II)," *Aldous Huxley Annual: A Journal of Twentieth-Century Thought and Beyond,* Volume 6 (2006): pp. 1–6.

————. "Aldous Huxley aka Condé Nast's 'Staff of Experts'," *Aldous Huxley Annual: A Journal of Twentieth-Century Thought and Beyond,* Volume 5 (2005): pp. 1–10.

————. "*Brave New World,* the Feelies, and Elinor Glyn," *English Language Notes,* Volume 35 (September 1997): pp. 35–38.

————. "Aldous Huxley's Bokanovsky," *Science-Fiction Studies,* Volume 16 (March 1989): pp. 85–89.

Snyder, Carey. "'When the Indian Was in Vogue': D. H. Lawrence, Aldous Huxley, and Ethnological Tourism in the Southwest," *Modern Fiction Studies,* Volume 53, Number 4 (Winter 2007): pp. 662–696.

Super, R. H. "Aldous Huxley's Art of Allusion—the Arnold Connection," *English Studies,* Volume 72 (October 1991): pp. 426–441.

Svarny, Erik. "Gender, War and Writing in Aldous Huxley's Farcical History of Richard Greenow." *Gender and Warfare in the Twentieth Century: Textual Representations.* Ed. Angela K. Smith. Manchester, England: Manchester University Press, 2004, pp. 53–75.

Thody, Peter. *Huxley: A Biographical Introduction.* New York: Scribner, 1973.

Tripathy, Akhilesh Kumar. "The Baghavad Gita in Aldous Huxley's Work," *Aldous Huxley Annual: A Journal of Twentieth-Century Thought and Beyond,* Volume 6 (2006): pp. 149–157.

Varricchio, Mario. "Power of Images/Images of Power in *Brave New World* and *Nineteen Eighty-Four,*" *Utopian Studies,* Volume 10, Number 1 (1999): pp. 98–114.

William, Donald. "Which Urges and Reasonably So The Attraction of Some for Others," *The Yale Review,* Volume 86, Number 4 (October 1998): p. 18–31.

Williams, Nicholas M. "'The Sciences of Life': Living Form in William Blake and Aldous Huxley," *Romanticism: The Journal of Romantic Culture and Criticism,* Volume 15, Number 1 (2009): pp. 41–53.

Wilson, Keith. "Aldous Huxley and Max Beerbohm's Hardy," *Notes and Queries,* Volume 31 (December 1984): p. 515.

Woodcock, George. *Dawn and the Darkest Hour: A Study of Aldous Huxley.* New York: Viking, 1972.

Acknowledgments

Robert Cecil Bald. "Aldous Huxley as a Borrower," *College English*, Volume 11, Number 4 (January 1950): pp. 183–187. Copyright © 1950 National Council of Teachers of English.

Clyde Enroth. "Mysticism in Two of Aldous Huxley's Early Novels," *Twentieth Century Literature*, Volume 6, Number 3 (October 1960): pp. 123–132. Copyright © 1960 Hofstra University. Reprinted by permission of the publisher.

James H. Quina Jr. "The Philosophical Phases of Aldous Huxley," *College English*, Volume 23, Number 8 (May 1962): pp. 636–641. Copyright © 1962 National Council of Teachers of English.

Jerome Meckier. "Aldous Huxley: Satire and Structure," *Wisconsin Studies in Contemporary Literature*, Volume 7, Number 3 (Autumn 1966): pp. 284–294. Copyright © 1966 University of Wisconsin Press. Reprinted by permission of the publisher.

Pierre Vitoux. "Structure and Meaning in Aldous Huxley's *Eyeless in Gaza*," *The Yearbook of English Studies*, Volume 2 (1972): pp. 212–224. Copyright © 1972 Maney Publishing on behalf of Modern Humanities Research Association. Reprinted by permission of the author.

Jerome Meckier. "Quarles among the Monkeys: Huxley's Zoological Novels," *The Modern Language Review*, Volume 68, Number 2 (April 1973):

pp. 268–282. Copyright © 1973 Modern Humanities Research Association. Reprinted by permission of the author.

Janet L. Goodrich. "Bringing Order out of Chaos: Huxley's *Time Must Have a Stop* and Vedanta," *Extrapolation,* Volume 40, Number 2 (Summer 1999): pp. 145–153. Copyright © 1999 Kent State University Press. Reprinted by permission of the publisher.

Alex MacDonald. "Choosing Utopia: An Existential Reading of Aldous Huxley's *Island,*" *Utopian Studies,* Volume 12, Number 2 (Spring 2001): pp. 103–115. Copyright © 2001 Society for Utopian Studies. Reprinted by permission of the author.

Brad Buchanan. "Oedipus in Dystopia: Freud and Lawrence in Aldous Huxley's *Brave New World,*" *Journal of Modern Literature,* Volume 25, Numbers 3 & 4 (Summer 2002): pp. 75–89. Copyright © 2002 Brad Buchanan. Reprinted by permission of the author.

Sally Minogue and Andrew Palmer. "Confronting the Abject: Women and Dead Babies in Modern English Fiction," *Journal of Modern Literature,* Volume 29, Number 3 (Spring 2006): pp. 103–125. Copyright © 2006 Indiana University Press. Reprinted by permission of the publisher.

Maartjen N. Schermer. "*Brave New World* versus *Island*—Utopian and Dystopian Views on Psychopharmacology," *Medicine, Health Care and Philosophy,* Volume 10, Number 2 (June 2007): pp. 119–128. Copyright © 2007 Springer Publishing. Reprinted by permission of the publisher.

Joanne Woiak. "Designing a Brave New World: Eugenics, Politics, and Fiction," *The Public Historian,* Volume 29, Number 3 (Summer 2007): pp. 105–129. Copyright © 2007 by the National Council on Public History. Published by the University of California Press. Reprinted by permission of the publisher.

Carey Snyder. "When the Indian Was in Vogue": D. H. Lawrence, Aldous Huxley, and Ethnological Tourism in the Southwest," *MFS: Modern Fiction Studies,* Volume 53, Number 4 (Winter 2007): pp. 662–696. Copyright © 2007 Purdue Research Foundation by the Johns Hopkins University Press. Reprinted by permission of the publisher.

Index